Bedford Square 8

New Writing from the
Royal Holloway Creative Writing Programme

Foreword by Andrew Motion

Ward Wood Publishing
www.wardwoodpublishing.co.uk

Published by Ward Wood Publishing
6 The Drive
Golders Green
London NW11 9SR
www.wardwoodpublishing.co.uk

Foreword © Andrew Motion 2015

Copyright of individual work remains with each author.
The moral right of authors has been asserted.
Full details of copyright holders can be found on page 234.

ISBN 978-1-908742-49-0
British Library Cataloguing in Publication Data. A CIP record for
this book can be obtained from the British Library.

Designed and typeset in Garamond and Palatino Linotype
by Ward Wood Publishing.

Cover Design by Mike Fortune-Wood

Printed and bound in Great Britain by
Imprint Digital, Seychelles Farm,
Upton Pyne, Exeter EX5 5HY.

Bedford Square 8

Contents

Foreword by Andrew Motion

Foreword

The invitation to write a foreword to this collection of work from the Creative Writing MA programme at Royal Holloway might seem to present difficulties (to do with freshness and surprise), given that it's the latest in what has become a substantial series. But such is the strength of the work included, and such is the commitment of its authors, that what might seem like a moment for repetition is in fact a chance to celebrate newness. This volume, like its predecessors, has the very distinct excitement of showing us exceptional new writers at the beginning of their writing lives. It is a great pleasure to read, and an equally great pleasure to introduce.

The course is also a great pleasure to teach. Responsibility for its several components (poetry-writing, fiction-writing, life-writing and writing under the heading of 'Place, Environment, Writing') are divided between myself, Susanna Jones, Kei Miller, Jo Shapcott and Kate Williams, as well as colleagues from the Geography Department for the PEW element of the course. Although the range of our teaching styles is inevitably wide, we share a great many common enthusiasms and commitments: to technical expertise, to imaginative ambition, to formal variety, and to the communication of adventurously strong feeling.

Over the years, a strikingly large number of our graduates have found success in their publishing careers. I hope you enjoy this chance to read the first examples of work by the next-in-line.

Andrew Motion

Mulatto

Haroon Hassan

A short story

Despite the office being small and intimate you couldn't miss the institutional gloom that hung over the place, with its metal detector and monotonous green carpets. Posters tacked to unremarkable grey walls were by turns threatening and encouraging; just inches away from a picture of a smiling woman in a graduation gown there was a second picture of a man in handcuffs, the caption promising deportation in exchange for an illegal day's work.

They weren't supposed to let his father come in with him. In the many immigration interviews Hani had endured over the years he had always been alone, and he assumed the same for this final interrogation. He tried to convince his father not to come

'Abba, they won't let you in. They only allow the candidate to come in.'

But the old man, stubborn as ever, had insisted.

'When I was your age they used to call me Mahzooz Ali. You know what that means?'

Hani knew what it meant. Every summer 'Lucky' Ali took a flight from Harare to London to spend a week with Hani, following him everywhere. He made sure he was up and about when Hani woke up, and went about his slow nocturnal routines only after Hani had gone to bed. Those visits were nothing short of torture for Hani, so much so that he was actually looking forward to the solitude implied by what he thought would be a long wait at this final interview, which, like the other long queues that wound their way through his immigrant's life, provided him with an acceptable excuse to temporarily abandon his father.

'Can you give me some idea how long this will take please?'

Hani said please to the guard, but he had long since stopped using the inflections of supplicants when talking to the first layer of officials, the guards and receptionists, who in this country at least

9

had no power. No point in wasting his supplicant's energy at the metal detector.

'I just need a rough idea, so my father knows how long I will be.'

The boy's accent was tough to place. Very la-di-da thought the guard, his gaze lingering on the old man as understanding took hold, and he connected the dots between an old Asian man and a young black fellow, whose skin, in hindsight, did not share the shiny deep black of most Africans that came through the office, but was slightly tinged with the ruddiness of a half-breed. After fifteen years working for the immigration authorities, the guard had evolved a sort of ethnographic habit, and he was annoyed at being stymied. It had happened before with these, what did they call themselves now – 'Afro Asians', easily confused with dark-skinned North Africans. He should have noticed the young man's hair, which was woolly like those Ethiopian and Somali fellows, not the close knit fur-like manes of proper blacks. But he wasn't surprised that he missed the Asian blood in this one; he was heavy after all and muscular like a West African. But even on this score, now that the young one's Indian, or was it Arab, heritage was clear the guard saw clues that he had missed. Yes he was heavy, but it was the sort of heavy you get from a gym. The boy's arms were big but they didn't have the rugged look of someone whose body has been built by honourable hard work. This guy had a bespoke build beyond what was rightfully his.

'Ah right. You two are together.' The guard was looking at the old man now, who immediately looked at his son.

Ali wasn't expecting a question. He assumed this would be the usual procession through England, with Hani constantly translating perfectly intelligible events for his benefit. But Hani's face had darkened; he was staring at the guard. Before Ali could respond Hani weighed in.

'I just said he's my father.' Hani's voice was sharp now, each word rushing from his mouth searching for its target.

'Steady there young man,' said the guard, wheezing slightly. If it wasn't for his bulbous stomach, so common in this country of pubs and ales, the red-faced little Briton would surely be rearing up to meet this aggression. His colonial epaulets and little black baton bore a close resemblance to the Rhodesian Constabulary

10

that used to roam the buses in colonial Lusaka, when Ali was a young boy there a good sixty years ago. For an instant Ali was mesmerized by his son, fearless in the face of this pudgy reddening bulldog. But the moment was quickly interrupted by a thought: When had this younger generation become so fierce? Yes, Ali had given his youth to a long war to eject colonists just like this guard, but that aggression had been tactical and would have been ill served by this sort of brazen defiance. He didn't know the answer, but he did know that this Briton held the keys. He was the gatekeeper standing between Hani and what Hani wanted. Given Hani's infinite capacity to spite his own face, this guard would surely make life difficult for the boy. Ali placed a bony hand on Hani's shoulder and stepped forward slightly.

'Sorry, sir, our accents are a complete puzzle I am sure,' said Ali. He looked at his hand on Hani's shoulder and again he was briefly mesmerized; when had Hani become so fleshy?

The guard softened instinctively when the old man tried to put his hand on his son's shoulder and the boy pulled away. The old man reminded him of Ben Kingsley in Gandhi and contrasted sharply with his heavyset yob of a son.

'Not to worry. What's your ticket number, son? They don't get called in order. They call them in batches. What's your number?' He addressed the boy's hand.

'232.'

'That's the premium batch. You should get called in about 2 hours. Won't be long. And I'll let your dad come in with you, there's space enough today.' The boy's accent made more sense now. Applicants with appointment numbers between 200 and 400 were processed quickly, the same day normally. Only the sub-200s had priority over the 200-400s. He wasn't sure what was so special about the sub-200s but they were extremely exclusive; you couldn't buy your way into that group. But the 200-400s were rich, no doubt buying their la-di-da accents at fancy British schools. This lot didn't think twice about shelling out £1000 to jump the line, instead of the rather more modest £60 that normal plus-400s paid to get their applications decided on, after what the guard thought was an eminently reasonable two week waiting period. The guard sat down in his swivelling chair next to the metal detector as father and son walked away. Arabic, not Indian;

this one was half oil-rich Arab, half black African.

Hani clearly hadn't counted on spending two hours with his father today. They hadn't spent two continuous hours together the entire week – not alone. They found seats against a grey wall with a large map of the world on it. Within the map there were magnifying circles, first blowing up Europe, then smaller and smaller areas until Croydon's industrial landscape dominated the frame. It was immediately clear that this office dealt with premium fast track applications. Everyone was well dressed, as though for church, with reams of supporting documents in tabbed coloured folders. Nonetheless, the place was full of the immigrant; various browns to black, yellows and a few whites.

Everyone was quiet and still, as though they were readying themselves for the arrival of the camp commandant who might pounce with impunity on any gratuitous talking or movement. Eighteen years of this crap, it had taken him eighteen years in various immigration offices to finally realize that none of it mattered and he could slouch in his chair and fidget with his laces. Hani felt a touch of wisdom on this note that set him apart from and above these immigrants. Here, in the West at least, it didn't matter. Everyone in that office no doubt came from some far flung place where minor officialdom had to be carefully negotiated, where guards could put you at the back of a two day queue on a whim, and certainly not where numbers were called in batches.

'You'd think he'd have run into some mulattos working in this shit-hole,' Hani said.

'That may be so, but would it hurt you to be polite? He could make life hard for you,' said Hani's father.

'Relax, I've been through these things a million times, I know what fools like that are capable of.'

'Like you knew they wouldn't let me come in with you?'

Hani didn't reply. A well-proportioned black family, obviously African, arranged itself opposite them. Unlike Hani's pointedly casual blue jeans and black sneakers, they were dressed formally.

'Well, if I hadn't shown him a little respect, you wouldn't have made it through the door, so just as well I came…'

Hani didn't let his father finish: 'I suppose I should be thankful of that light Indian skin of yours getting us in the door, then?'

The African family might have jumped right out of one of the more positive posters that hung on the walls; a perfect unit. The father wore a brown suit and a yellow tie. The wife was more traditional looking, wearing flowing colourful fabrics that were hard to follow. Her head was covered in a scarf. Two shiny children, a boy in a sad little suit of his own and a girl with a pink bow, sat obediently next to their mother. The father was hunched over some paper work. The wife whispered something in the husband's ear. Without looking up he nodded and she was quiet again. She was pretty, imprisoned as she was underneath her headscarf. Hani looked at his own father, who was looking over the top of his glasses at the family.

'Hanif, that's not what I meant,' said his father, still looking at the family.

'You're staring,' said Hani. Then he stood up and walked to the men's toilet at the back of the room. Hani's father turned to watch him walk away, his lips twisting downwards as he raised his eyebrows and assumed the gentle tortured look of a Christ nailed to a cross.

Hani bent over the sink and splashed water over his face. The toilet was clean. There was one small window about ten feet off the ground that was covered over with bars. He straightened to look at himself in a mirror that had a crack running through it. He slowly shifted from right to left so that his reflection glided from the left side of the crack to the right side, pausing briefly to let the crack split his reflection.

He didn't go straight back to his chair, but waited by the door and watched unnoticed. The wife in her colourful garb was now sitting next to Hani's father. They were talking. The husband and children were not in the room. He couldn't make out what the woman and Ali were saying, but he now imagined his father as a busy old fuddy duddy helping some poor immigrant woman with her paperwork. His father pointed to something in the woman's application while his other hand lightly touched her forearm; she ferociously corrected something on the papers in her lap.

Hani had only ever seen his mother in a photograph taken before he was born, in which she was sitting on the edge of a collection of her in-laws, holding one of his father's hands in both

13

of her own. He lost the picture his first day at boarding school in England, where he was sent to escape the war. He was twelve and Alistair Banks was at least seventeen.

'Hey mulatto, don't you have any colour photos of your family?' All his life, Hani had lots of white friends. 'Its 1972, black and white photos are for dead people. Your family dead, mulatto?' In fact, in later life he would almost marry a white girl. 'Hang on one second! I just realized this photo's in Black and Indian.' But that particular engagement was called off. And before Hani could find the courage to punch, kick or do something courageous, Banks was walking away with his mates, laughing and tearing up the photograph.

A number was called. The woman stood up and walked away, her colourful garb sashaying its way across the green-grey gloom. She turned briefly to smile and mouth 'thank you' towards Hani's father. Hani sat down, stretched out his legs and sank low in his chair. His father didn't look up.

'You manage to help that lady?' Hani asked.

'I hope so. Her brother had to leave. Those were his kids. They were late for some recital thing.'

Hani shifted towards his father. 'Where was she from?' he asked.

'Gabon. Soon as her brother left she came over. Wanted me to check her spelling and stuff.' Hani's father shifted towards his son.

'You'd think she'd ask that moron guard over there. I mean, you don't exactly look like the Queen's librarian, Sahib Master.' Hani's head bobbled around like an Indian dancer.

'She was probably more comfortable talking to a fellow African,' said his father.

'Again Sahib Master,' Hani shook his head more vigorously this time, 'you are being looking about as African as snow, you know.' His father was quick to smile at the white flag Hani had just raised. His mind drifted back to Hani's little week long vacations when he was home from boarding school. The war didn't allow many of them. The arriving, the leaving, the catching up, the fishing trips, it all had to happen in a week; the grieving, the fighting, the making up, all in a week. Hardly any time at all.

'Well genius, she must have seen us talking and figured it out,' said his dad.

The number 214 was called out.

'God, this is going to take forever. You'd think for £1000 they could get you through in under an hour,' he said looking at his father.

'It's only been 15 minutes. We'll probably be done in an hour,' said his father, looking back at Hani over the top of his glasses. Hani's lips twisted downwards as he raised his eyebrows. A massive black woman started the long process of standing up. She gripped the armrest on her chair, and reached for a plastic walking stick. The mass of clothing she was wearing shuddered as she steeled herself for the effort; two generous breaths, the second a little deeper than the first, as she built towards a heaving crescendo. The guard stepped forward and took the walking stick, genuflecting slightly so she could grip his forearm. She gratefully shifted her weight onto his, her enormous frame and his taut belly forming an improbably mass that looked somehow like toppling. Finally off the chair, the pair of them moved gingerly towards a door at the front of the room.

The Song of the Earth

Eva Chan

This is the beginning of a novel of the same name. Naomi Ito is a young violinist whose home at Matsushima was decimated on March 11 by the most powerful earthquake in Japanese history. Convinced that the musical prodigy Aoi Shibutani died protecting her, Naomi carries his violin and embarks on a journey to Italy and Russia to find a new home for her music. However, as her journey continues, Naomi begins to realise that the boundaries of her home and struggles do not lie primarily across prefectures and the world at large, but with her mother who she loves but forces herself to hate.

Symphony 1

Bless me Father, for I have sinned – this seems to be the proper way to start a confession. But I am not religious, not many Japanese are. Yet I need a confession to cleanse my sins before my life will be reborn by the grace of Aoi Shibutani. The celebrated violinist saved me, in so many ways. Perhaps I can pretend I am a composer standing on my stage, presenting my music from the first symphony to the ninth. And, my dear listeners, please observe the etiquette of a classical concert: you will not clap until the very end.

Dr Yukawa says there are always some instances in your life that redefine who you are. It does not have to be a groundbreaking event: it might even be insignificant in the eyes of others.

It was the spring after I came home from Tokyo to Matsushima. I had just turned eleven. The doctor announced that nothing could be done for my injured hand. My mother pretended nothing had happened, urging me to join the Doll Festival, the day when Japanese families pray for the growth and happiness of their daughters.

As part of the traditions, families with daughters would display a doll stand at their homes on that day. My home was a *ryokan*, a traditional family-run inn with *tatami*-matted guestrooms and an atrium where *yukata*-clad guests could socialize. All the guests had already gone out to join the street parade. In the emptied wooden atrium, I stood in front of a seven-tiered doll stand and observed the doll collection my mother had handed down to me.

On each tier, ceremonial dolls were sitting on the scarlet carpet, dressed as members of an ancient imperial court. The Emperor and Empress were on the top tier, followed by court ladies, ministers and musicians on the tiers below. I was staring at the string instrument of a musician doll when the door behind me slid open. My mother walked up to wrap me in a kimono. Her long hand trailed my body, cold and dry as a snake. From the undergarment to the robe; she finished with a knot of the sash.

We only had an event of this kind once in a year. All my classmates were so excited about it. Lines of paper lanterns in red and white hung along the two main pavements. Some hung too low and would probably crash into the brick rooftops. Shooting games. Baby castella. After a stroll around all the stalls, my best friend Rika and I ran to a stream and played in a miniature waterfall piled up with rocks. We lifted up our kimonos to our knees and kicked water at each other. The water was shallow, just below our waists. Splash. Splash. Splash.

My mother announced her presence in wooden sandals. She was holding the candy apple I had abandoned at the stall; the apple inside was too hard to chew. The red sugar coating had started to melt in her hand, all sticky and sweet, like the smile moving onto her face. I noticed, for the first time, how cloying her smile actually was.

'Naomi, be careful.'

I looked at her hands. I asked Rika to go back to her father. I walked towards my mother.

'Mama, come.' My scarred hand tightened on the sleeve of her worn-out *yukata*, the same *yukata* she wore every year.

'Naomi, where are we going?' She lowered her gaze and petted my hair with dyed hands. Her eyes narrowed.

'I will show you, come Mama.'

I dragged her along a muddy trail up a small hill. I knew this area well. Rika and I always came here, as if it was our own playground.

'Mama, go there and look.' I gestured to a narrow ledge. The spring humidity made the soil she stepped on fragile, ready to collapse. Sakura trees at the other side of the stream had blossomed in one massive wave and their petals fell, like tufts of feathers drifting directly from the sky. Countless petals floated on the stream. No one knew how deep this part of the stream actually was. What was I thinking? I just wanted to wash my mother clean, as though I was scrubbing the public bathtub in our *ryokan* with pellets.

My palm rested on a yellow stain on her cotton *yukata*. The legend of the Doll Festival says the dolls possess the power to contain bad spirits, and by sending the dolls downriver, they take bad spirits away with them. I imagined my mother's body floating downstream, her stickiness melting with the snow and velvety petals camouflaging all the stubborn stains. I pushed her to the stream bedded with pebbles.

'It is beautiful.' Before the tingling could reach my fingertips, she caught my hand and her fingers glued mine. 'Thank you for bringing me here, Naomi.' She smiled.

It was the only time I had the urge to do such a thing. My mother stays unclean.

*

Before entering the funeral atrium, I look at the photo. Aoi's hair is as I remember it from the time I saw him from afar at a concert one Saturday night; his crown of hair still sparkles dark brown, like a halo against his cheek and the bleached wall. Dense eyelashes form shadows over the dark circles under his eyes. An elegant nose and a timid smile stand on his impassive face.

Aoi Shibutani is immaculate. A contradiction to my unclean mother who is full of sins.

Mother had forsaken her father, long before I was born. Her father only came into my life when I was ten, the year my hand turned scarlet. I am now twenty-two, which means I have only known my grandfather for half my life. But it does not matter. Whenever I say 'Grandpa' I am referring to him, whose surname is Hijikata.

Hijikata is an honourable name. Hijikata Toshizo is believed to have been the last samurai of the Tokugawa period. It was an era

18

strictly defined by class, with the Shogun at the top of the social ladder. There were no outsiders in that period. Westerners could not enter our Japanese realm; and, on the penalty of death, Japanese were not allowed to leave and become *gaijin* in a foreign land. Shogun Tokugawa believed that this policy could protect the Japanese from the evil influence of the West. The policy was called *Sakoku*, the chained country. Until his blood dried up, Hijikata killed the revolutionists for Tokugawa. Some believe that he died in glory and honour. After Hijikata's death, Japan bloomed in the Meiji Revolution.

I doubt if Toshizo Hijikata is really my ancestor. This surname is not as unique as the TV dramas and comic books want us to believe. Nonetheless, Grandpa's family is a respected one in the academy. Generation after generation, the Hijikata have been scholars with significant publications. Grandpa himself is a retired professor who formerly taught at Tokyo University, and he carries himself with a posture that would be hard to find on another short man. He never looks up, only receives others' lowered gaze with his back very straight. How those proud shoulders must have slumped when Mother ran away from their home in Tokyo.

Mother is no longer a Hijikata; but ever since I was born in Matsushima, she has made this small town in Miyagi Prefecture into my chained island. In Matsushima, Mother's name is Satomi Ito and my name is Naomi Ito. The surname is inherited from her husband, although there is nothing worth mentioning about him. I guess he is a loved man as much as one can be loved in a small town. But he is never respected. He is just an owner of an *onsen ryokan*. *Onsen* – Western visitors used to see the English translation 'hot spring' and thought of a resort with swimming pools; then they arrived and had to wash themselves in a public bath shared with naked strangers, soaking their giant bodies in a shallow pond of sulphur mist.

Growing up in that egg-rotten sulphur smell, I never felt like sleeping the instant all the electric lights went out with the sunset. I found no interest daydreaming about the cute boys in our school that I might marry one day, and I could never imagine myself like my parents, inheriting their *onsen ryokan* and growing old there. The disharmony between my home and myself only amplified as I grew up.

19

'Nonsense, you belong here in Matsushima, with your father and me,' Mother said, when I mentioned this to her. She let me learn music afterwards to keep me occupied, so that she could watch me closely, every day.

Every day, that is, until the 11ᵗʰ of March when I was twenty-two years old. At forty-six minutes after two o'clock in the afternoon, the most powerful earthquake hit Japan and we were all buried. I found myself free and Aoi Shibutani trapped. The calloused hand pushed me away. That was all.

The funeral for Aoi Shibutani is held in Tokyo one month after the earthquake. I manage to stay at Grandpa's mansion. Even if there had been no place for me to stay in Tokyo, I would still have come. Funerals have become commonplace since the earthquake and tsunami. But it is Aoi's funeral.

'The name is Ito, Naomi Ito.' I smooth the wrinkles of my best kimono.

The receptionist has his back to me. He is instructing the others in how to arrange the sympathy flowers in the ceremony hall. The blossoms queue to be put on the side of the hall. How I wish to carry one of the bouquets away to the grave of Rika's father. He did not even have a proper funeral, with Rika gone mad.

'I am so sorry, Miss.' The receptionist bows and rushes to the reception desk. A long name list is placed horizontally on the table. He looks at the list for some time. I know some of the names there: the world-renowned conductor Ojawa and the composer Shigimoto, as well as some overseas musicians.

'Please forgive me, Miss. I am afraid I cannot find your name,' he says.

'Would you please let me inside? I just wish to pay my respects.'

'Miss, I am afraid this funeral is reserved for close friends and relatives.'

'I am not one of his fans if this is what you are assuming.' I put my hand on the edge of the table. 'It is not my wish to disturb Mrs Shibutani further, but would you please tell her I come on behalf of Professor Hijikata? Hijikata from Tokyo University.' I use the highest form of honourific Japanese.

'Would you please wait here for a moment, Miss?' The receptionist turns away with quick steps.

20

A woman comes to the entrance two minutes later. 'Miss Ito, I presume?' She is dressed in a black kimono. Her hair is tied into an elegant bun.

'Mrs Shibutani.' I bow. 'Please, just call me Naomi.'

'Thank you for coming, Miss Ito.' She bows back.

'I am sorry I have to disturb you like this.' I bow again.

Her eyes are rimmed in red, highlighted by a delicate stroke of eyeliner. 'I feel ashamed to have to ask this as a mother, but do you happen to be an acquaintance of Aoi?'

'I am the granddaughter of Professor Hijikata. I was with Grandfather when you invited him to a charity concert some years ago. Aoi played the violin so beautifully.'

'I see. Please send along my gratitude to Professor Hijikata.'

'My grandfather pays his respects as well. What can I do to help — '

'This is very kind of you, Miss Ito.' She bows again. 'I have some important guests to attend to. I hope you understand if I excuse myself now?'

'Perfectly,' I say, 'but there is one more thing.' I lift up the violin case that I have been holding in my hand. Its leather cover carries scratches; debris collapsed on it, at the moment the earthquake swallowed the life and music of its performer.

The graceful posture of Mrs Shibutani turns rigid.

'I thought it was buried in the earthquake.'

'I was in Sendai when the earthquake happened.' I walk closer. My scarred hand almost brushes her silky kimono. 'Aoi sheltered me when the concert hall collapsed. He saved my life. I am sorry to have come so late, but I had matters to attend to back home. I am forever indebted to him, so if there is anything I can do to help, with the musicians or anything — '

Her body is as composed as ever. Only the ruffles around her pressed collar quiver as her breath amplifies in the stillness of the funeral hall.

'My apologies, Miss Ito. I cannot bring myself to say anything sensible at this moment.' Her eyes dart across the modest crowd. The line of her mouth is rigid before she speaks again in a low voice. 'Please leave your contact details with the reception. I will talk to you soon at a more convenient time. I cannot take the violin now. Please keep it safe.'

21

I follow her gaze across to her guests. A couple of the names I recognized on the reception list have shown up. I would love to stay longer to pay my respects, would have done if not for the insistence in Mrs Shibutani's eyes. I return to Grandpa's mansion.

On the screen of my computer, Aoi's jaw is not as sculpted as it looked in his older funeral portrait, but it tilts up at the same refined angle. The Aoi I first met twelve years ago lifted the violin close to his chubby face with a firm movement. His fingers flew across the strings. The piece ended in applause, while I remained the only member in the audience with my hands resting on my laps, my fingers lingering on my new pair of stockings. Not once did he look at me. In a tailored suit still too mature for his age, he bowed with self-possession and looked up with a focus beyond us. He must have been looking at Paganini himself, requesting approval.

But as I meet his stare from the screen now, I feel as though he is asking something from me, as though we have become connected.

'Why don't you go to sleep? Naomi?'

My finger flicks the monitor switch. The door is ajar. The corridor is dark. From the bed I can see his silhouette, pinned on the wall as he stands at the doorframe.

'Grandpa, I could ask the same of you.'

'I am worried about you.' He pushes the door, his shadow comes inside. 'You have been in your room since you came back from the funeral. How did Mrs Shibutani take the news?'

'I will be fine,' I say. 'I may need to stay in Tokyo for a longer time.'

'What can you possibly do?'

'I honestly don't know, but I must stay for now. Mrs Shibutani said we would meet again soon. I don't know what to expect, but I do know that I don't deserve any kindness from her.'

'Shush. Never be sorry that you are alive.' He walks to my bed and sits next to me.

I lean towards him. My head rests on his shoulder blade at an odd angle due to our height difference.

'But you are fine with me staying here, aren't you, Grandpa?'

22

'I only wish you can find peace soon, my girl.' His fingers bury themselves in my hair. 'Now sleep.' He stands up, turns, and I find my hand catching the sleeve of his *yukata*.

'Grandpa, I am sorry. I lied,' I say. 'I am not all right. Can you stay?'

'Just like when you first came to Tokyo with all the nightmares.' He sits next to my bed, holding my hand. His palms are as I remember from the first time I came to Tokyo and met him, the winter I was ten. It was still snowing. Grandpa's large hand wrapped mine, and then he put both our hands into the pocket of his coat. Inside the soft wool, my hand was entwined with his calloused one. Hard and warm.

'Can you tell me the same bedtime story again? From that winter?' I ask.

'That's the only one I know.' Grandpa's Tokyo accent lifts up in the air, distant and almost surreal. 'There is a Japanese legend: when people die, their bodies are buried beneath Sakura trees. From these roots, the blood of the dead grows through the petals. A Sakura bloom is delicate like a newborn: the size of a baby's fist. Bud after bud, the Sakura trees blossom all at once – but when their two-week lives come to an end, the blossoms are carried with the wind and all of those fragile petals fall upon us. Each petal carries a person's story that asks to be continued by the living.'

'That way a new life flourishes upon a person's death. It is such a beautiful story, don't you think, Grandpa?'

There is a slight shift in Grandpa's shadow. Must be a nod. Consolation blankets me along with sleepiness. There is just one thing I need to ask before I let myself lapse into the world of blankness.

'Make Mother understand.' My head turns, half of my face buried into the feathers, my lips touch the softness of the pillowcase as they move. 'Please?'

My voice is absorbed by the pillow, almost inaudible. But Grandpa must have heard me somehow; he nods again in the shadow. A dreamless sleep welcomes me.

I open my eyes. Grandpa is still sitting by my bedside. He stares into space. It may have to do with the mist on my irises; he looks bent, his shoulders slump.

'Grandpa.' I blink.

He straightens. 'You are restless.'

'But I have not slept this well for weeks.' I smile. 'Thank you for staying with me last night.'

'Promise me that you will take care of yourself.'

'You know I will, Grandpa.'

He looks down as his large hands fold into fists, unfold and refold. 'Satomi,' he whispers.

'What about Mother?'

'Your grandmother passed away of cancer when Satomi was eleven. She was very upset. I wanted to comfort her, but there was nothing I could say or do. We did not talk for a long time, until I decided to bring her to the countryside for a change of scenery. There in Hakone, we prayed together for her lost mother at a shrine. It was the first time she had smiled for ages.'

'Grandpa, you know I don't really believe in this tradition. I am not as naïve as Mother.'

'Just go, Naomi.'

There had been a time I was naïve enough to believe in prayers. The last prayer I made was at a temple near my home by the coast. I was blessed by the thuds of a bronze bell, and the smell of sea salt and incense. My prayer is now buried with the temple, but despite myself, I can never deny Grandpa's wishes.

Hakone is like my home without the ruins. The wooden houses with their elegantly carved rooftops line the traditional Japanese street – the remains of the Edo period. Locals dressed in plain colours stroll along the brick road dotted with a few lamps. It is very easy to spot tourists from Tokyo who make the one-hour train ride for a weekend break. Their eyebrows are knit at an acute angle and everyone wears the same rigid smile. I tried so hard once to look akin to these Tokyo people.

There is a sulphur smell in the air. It has always hypnotized me, even when I was behind the reception desk in my family's *onsen ryokan*. Every time the door opened, the bell would ring, and the fresh air from the outside would rush in, waking me up from my Tokyo dreams.

I push the white entrance door plastered with cartoon stickers.

The shop is tiny, and stands out in a lovely shade of pale pink. My black leather boots click on the polished wooden floor.

'Welcome, Miss!' A woman with gray hair gives me a big smile, her teeth blinding white. 'Is there anything I can help you with?'

'What is this?' I point at a package in the fridge labelled Cherry Blossom Bean Curd Ice Cream.

'Oh. This is our brand new flavour. Would you like to have a try first?'

'That would be lovely. Thank you.'

The old lady opens the synthetic ice cream lid with her bony fingers. A few Sakura petals bathe in the artificial coral-coloured cream. They were cut at their full bloom. 'Miss, your accent is quite thick for someone from Tokyo.'

'Not really. I live in Tokyo now with my grandpa. I was born in Matsushima.'

'Matsushima?' Her smile freezes. She quickly lowers her head and passes me a spoonful of the ice cream. 'Please forgive this stupid old woman, asking insensitive questions like this.'

I swallow the plastic spoonful. The sweetness is thin and bland.

She continues, 'the earthquake was horrible. I saw it on the news. Horrible.'

'Yes, it was.'

'But Miss, you are very pretty, with such nice skin. And you dress so fashionably. I completely thought you were from Tokyo! I have been here since I was born, and I have seen so many tourists from all around Japan.'

'Thank you very much. But I doubt it. Every *Tokyo-jin* can spot me an oddity in a second. Clumsy and ungraceful.'

'Nonsense. You are as pretty as any Tokyo girl. So you are coming for the shrine, right?'

'I guess so.'

'Bless you Miss,' she pats on my arm. 'Bless you.'

The shrine is quiet. Next to a stone lantern is a corner dedicated to the Tohoku earthquake, decorated with strings of folded paper cranes. Two wooden poles, plain and ordinary, stand upright and one metre apart. Linking them are four separate threads hanging horizontally, from top to bottom. Millions of tiny papers are tied to these threads, millions of prayers folded into these fragments of papers. Some of them have been caught in the wind and are now knotted with one another.

I pay two hundred yen and get a tiny piece of white paper, it is smaller than my palm.

I tie my paper to the thread at the bottom this time, so that it will not be easily blown away. The moment I kneel down a couple in their sixties walk by. The woman is wearing a kimono of crimson silk with a silver lining, matching her grey hair bun. She lowers her head in a subtle smile, some wrinkles visible around her neck. I cannot see the face of her husband. Only a formal suit with black tailored blazer and a clean white shirt underneath, walking in the steady steps of a respectable man. Not standing with a straight back like a typical Japanese, he bends towards his wife's level and listens to whatever she has to say. Their grey hair almost intertwining, they must have been standing in this pattern for years, since the time when their hair was still ebony.

I try not to dwell on who they are. Perhaps they are landlords from the Tokyo countryside, perhaps they will walk the rest of their lives like that: the man always bending down half an inch, watching his wife's elegant smile. I kneel at the same spot as they walk away.

I feel a bit lightheaded when I stand up. My vision turns white. I blink and they are gone.

Aoi is there, by an old trunk of a Sakura tree at the left side of the entrance. Velvety petals scatter on his Italian leather shoes, on a mound of half exposed roots. The roots extend, entwine and mingle, as though they would never be separated again. He walks on, step by step. He stops in front of me wearing the same blazer as the day he gave his life to me.

He says something.

By The Damascus Gate

David Merron

Based on a true incident, the novel is set in an isolated kibbutz and in Jerusalem. The storyline is carried by the passionate liaison between Kate, a young Catholic from Belfast who comes to the kibbutz as a volunteer and Amos, a married, leading member of the community, and the resulting repercussions. The novel is set against the Palestinian/Israeli conflict in the wake of the Six-Day War. The title is taken from the ancient gate in the Old City walls where the two first meet alone.

Chapter One

Kate sat up and glanced through the east-facing window to the Mount of Olives. The ancient tombstones glared white in the early sun and the sky was a cloudless blue; it would soon be baking hot outside. She swung her feet onto the tiled floor and straightened out the small bed then, grabbing her wash-bag, padded barefoot along the tiled, whitewashed corridor to the bathroom.

Back in the room she picked up her hairbrush and sat down by the small table in her nightshirt, flicking the bristles and staring aimlessly at her toes. Amos wouldn't arrive until after eleven – nearly two hours yet – and it was only a few minutes' walk down to the Damascus Gate. Across the room, hanging on the wardrobe door, was a long blue dress. She had bought it on a whim in the *Souk* the day before. It was the colour – blue with a touch of iridescent green – like that of the hand-blown, Hebron glassware. It fitted neatly round her waist and had a loose flared skirt – was really cheap too. With so many tourists and Israelis flooding the Arab Old City, prices would soon rise – but that wasn't why she had bought it. Because she was meeting Amos? No, that would be presumptuous. Yet buying on impulse was so unlike her. Jill was sure to tease when she got back to the kibbutz.

'Wow! Don't get any wild ideas,' she had taunted the day before, when Kate told her it would be Amos coming up to Jerusalem. But already she had – even though she was just another volunteer worker amongst a dozen others, part of the flood of young people that had arrived in the country just before and since the Six-Day War, while Amos was a leading member of the small community and a reserves' officer, married to Miriam, with two small children.

Kate brushed and brushed her long red hair. It caught a stray sunbeam, for a moment reflecting a soft glow onto the nearby wall. She hunched forward gripping the brush in her lap, her mind wandering back to that traumatic evening and thinking yet again how Amos had been so sympathetic and helpful about the Arab boy – and how she'd felt towards him afterwards.

Was all that just two weeks ago? Kate laid the brush back on the small table, then glanced around the room again, once a nun's cell – it too plain whitewashed. It was nice and cool now but must be freezing in the Jerusalem winter. The Sisters presently occupied only one wing of this old stone building in the Arab quarter of Jerusalem. The rest had been turned into a women backpackers' hostel.

A nun, sure. Her older sister Eileen had entered cloisters three years ago. Wouldn't that have saved her, Kate, all that trouble in Belfast. Instead, she had run away to the LSE in London and when this crisis flared up in the Middle East with fellow students like Jill flying off to a kibbutz in Israel – or further on to Khatmandu – she'd joined them. And now, unwittingly, she had become involved with the two sides out here too.

An open letter from her mother lay on the table – Mam probably telling the women at the Holy Cross how Kathleen is in Jerusalem near the Holy Sepulchre and all that. About time she answered – and it would occupy her mind for a while. Taking a ballpoint and an air-letter from an embroidered shoulder-bag hanging on the chair, Kate swiveled round and bent over the table.

After writing a few sentences, she nibbled the end of the pen. What to write – and what to leave out. She stared absently out of the window again, up to the spire of the brown stone Augusta Victoria Hospital on the adjacent hill, then looked again at her watch. It was nearly ten. Amos said he would catch the early bus from the Beer Sheba. That usually arrived about eleven – then another half-hour for him to get to the Old City.

Time was dragging, but why was she so anxious – investing so much emotional energy into the meeting? Amos wasn't coming to see her – she was just the go-between to meet the Arab boy's uncle, to explain why she had had to bring Araf back so soon. After taking him to meet the old silversmith, Amos would probably have to catch the bus back to the kibbutz. End of story. Yet perhaps he would stay awhile and they could chat over a coffee as they did while working out in the fields. But the tingling in her chest told her she was hoping for more than that. But what? Something like the closeness of that traumatic evening during the boy's visit? She closed her eyes for a moment: Jerusalem; the old silversmith and the Arab boy – to how it all began...

The Six-Day War had just ended and Kate and Jill had come up with a truck-load of kibbutzniks and half-a-dozen other volunteers to see the Old City. Jumping down from the back of the truck they all clustered on the dusty, sunbaked area in front of the Jaffa Gate, gazing at the massive ancient ramparts and the slim, round Tower of David rising over arched gateway just in front of them. It was unreal. Just a month or so before, this was a no-man's land choked with barbed wire and mines, Jordanian snipers peering through the crenelations. Now cars, buses and lorries were disgorging their human loads; crowds of Israelis and foreign tourists were streaming through the gate into the holy city.

While most of the kibbutzniks and volunteers were making their way to the Wailing Wall, in her headstrong way Kate had decided to take off at a tangent with Jill.

'Can't stand crowds. Going to the Mount of Olives,' she called to the others. 'Want to look down on the Old City from "the other side" – as it used to be!'

They pushed through the gateway and joined the crush down the narrow, shaded, Street of the Chain but were both soon seduced by the twisting alleyways of the *Souk* with its myriad shops and stalls under long, arched passageways, all bright with dresses and silver jewellery, copper pots, intricate marquetry chess and backgammon boards, and blue Hebron glassware. And everywhere, the smell of spices and exotic fruits, and the aroma of cardamom-flavoured Turkish coffee from cafes in the cul-de-sacs.

By the time they'd reached St Stephen's gate, they had less than two hours before the truck was due to leave. The afternoon was scorching and, looking up at the sun-baked slope of the Mount to the offending modern colonnades of the Inter-Continental Hotel at the summit, both knew they were running out of time.

'Best make our way back,' said Jill, a social worker from Birmingham – loose blonde hair and strings of coloured glass beads around her neck. 'It'll still be here in a month's time, Kate.' Kate wrinkled her nose and nodded; her sandalled feet were feeling the pounding from the cobbled streets.

At that moment, as they'd turned to stroll back up the Via Dolorosa and towards the Jaffa Gate, an old man dressed in traditional beige *abaya* with a neat brown jacket over, and pointed black shoes, darted out from a row of shops in the wall to their left.

'Lovely silver, ladies. Best in Jerusalem.' He smiled under a thin grey moustache. 'Come ladies. You look. You my guests.'

Kate glanced around. Jill had been remarking how few tourists there were in this area; they were almost alone. The man held aside a hanger of dresses revealing a dark doorway beyond.

'Please. Come inside,' the man beckoned. 'I bring coffee.'

'Seen one. Seen them all,' Kate muttered, nodding to the dresses.

'And end up in some harem,' murmured Jill.

The shopkeeper sensed their hesitation.

'Please. Many Americans come to me, before… before. I make these myself.' He spoke clearly but with a pronounced accent as he held up another hanger dripping with silver chains and earrings. Then, turning to a small boy who was sitting on a stone step opposite, he called: 'Araf. *T'laateh. Udrup!*' Three coffees. Quick.' Wide-eyed, the boy sprang up and hurried into an alleyway. Kate and Jill looked at each other then Jill laughed.

'To hell with it! As long as it has central heating.' Then, at Kate's questioning eyebrows, added, 'The harem I mean!' Kate was more circumspect but some sixth sense told her that there was nothing to fear. The old man had soft eyes and wasn't as pushy as most of the shopkeepers in the *Souk,* and with Jill she felt safe – as if the two of them couldn't both be mistaken. Giggling, they turned to enter the low, arched doorway.

The man, who'd introduced himself as Yusuf, motioned them to sit on the floor cushions. A single bulb in a table lamp cast an uneven light around the arched, masonry walls that rose to a pointed vault in the centre. When they were settled, he showed them a letter from the table. It was from an American, thanking him for a Sufi ring.

'A lovely woman she was.' The old man waved his hand over the letter. 'A lovely woman.'

Kate was wondering what was specific about a Sufi ring, when the boy returned with the three tiny cups of Turkish coffee and three glasses of water. She was more concerned about the water and didn't drink it. Jill didn't seem to care.

The boy, whom Kate found out later was the silversmith's nephew Araf, sat cross-legged on the ground next to her, smooth black hair and large, dark, wondering eyes, smiling and shrugging whenever she returned his gaze. The old man took down some strings of necklaces and chains and handed them to Jill, draping one of the chains around her neck, his eyes discreetly trying to avoid where it disappeared into the deep cleavage.

'You won't see like these in the Souk!' he said. Kate was looking at some woven cloth – bright orange and purple wool on a black warp, reminding her of some African weavings she had seen. Jill finally bought some malachite-set silver earrings and a braided silver bangle, while she chose an orange and brown wool-weave to hang on her wall.

When the man asked where they were staying, Kate tried to explain about the kibbutz – the farm, tractors, cowshed, orchards, all way out in the desert. As Yusuf translated for Araf, the boy stared eagerly into her face, wide-eyed and enquiring – as though it was from another world. And from that moment, she had felt a strong empathy with the boy whose childhood was probably confined within these walls of the ancient city.

Turning her wrist to the light, Kate saw on her watch that they had now barely an hour before the truck left. They would have to hurry. She nodded to Jill and, as they stood up, Yusuf rose too and gave them each his card.

'You are very welcome at any time whenever you are in Jerusalem.' They all shook hands and as the two went out, Kate knew that she would soon be back.

'Sweet old man,' said Jill. 'And the boy took quite a shine to you,' she teased on the walk back. Kate didn't react at once but the more she thought about it, she felt that it was more from empathy with his family's situation – the local Arabs as 'second class' citizens to the dominant Israelis – like the Catholics to the Prods in Belfast. Whatever it was, the picture of the boy's eager face stayed with her long after they'd left the shop.

On the journey back in the high-sided truck, she turned to Jill.

'Y'know, wouldn't it be great for the lad to see the kibbutz?'

'Great idea,' Jill smiled. 'If his uncle lets him.'

In the weeks that followed, Kate and Jill had used their days off to come to Jerusalem, and on their second visit, as they were telling Yusuf more about the kibbutz, the doorway darkened and a young man came in. He was dressed in a light blue, open-necked shirt and tight, black trousers. Surprised, he stepped back and made as if to go out, but before anyone moved, the old man stretched out his arm and called over to him.

'Isten'eh shwieyeh, Shafik. Wait! These are my guests.' He turned to Kate and Jill, smiling. 'Ah. Ladies. This is my nephew, Shafik. Araf's brother.'

As the man stepped forward, Yusuf turned to the boy.

'Araf. Some coffee for Shafik.' Kate was sure he had spoken in English to reassure them.

The man nodded a greeting to each of them, then eased himself down onto a low stool in the corner, hands clasped, elbows on his knees. He had a smooth, clean-shaven face with wavy black hair and a sharp, angular nose. In the dim lighting, a gold ring glinted on one finger. As soon as he had settled, the man turned to the two women.

'You are from England? America?' he asked.

'I'm from England,' said Jill, 'but Kate's from Northern Ireland.' Kate bit her lip; Jill opening her mouth before engaging her brain. Kate always waited before telling anyone; saved untold explanations. To her dismay, the younger man's face showed that he had picked it up. He looked straight at her.

'You are a Catholic or a Protestant?' he asked, in a strongly accented but otherwise correct English.

'My family are Catholic,' said Kate, having long distanced herself personally from the sectarian divide.

32

'Ah. A friend of my cousin studied there. Belfast. Electronics,' he replied, then immediately continued, 'and how do you find Israel?'

'In what way?' asked Kate.

'Well... ' He paused, as if searching for words. 'We too have had our land taken over by colonists. Have become second class citizens.'

For a moment, the room was silent. Outside, a donkey brayed and a child shouted in the street. Yusuf rubbed his hands together, eyes half closed. Kate's mind flipped back to her year at the LSE. The heated debates, the New Left allying itself with African and Arab students and calling Zionism white colonialism like South Africa, and others equating Jewish settlement with the Protestant take-over in Ulster. But for this stranger to spring it on her like that? The cheek! Kate felt the blood rising in her face as she sought the right opening, but Jill, sensing her embarrassment, spoke first.

'Look, mate. We're not responsible for the world's problems.' She tossed back her mop of flaxen hair. 'We've just come to say hello to Yusuf and Araf. Okay?'

Shafik took the rebuke with a faint smile.

'Please. Don't be offended. You both look too intelligent to be just tourists. So I really would like to know what you think about... ' he waved his hand to one side, then back again, 'about what you have seen in the city.'

The short exchange allowed Kate to recover her composure and the sudden annoyance had subsided.

'Well. It's a different situation, y'know. Have you ever been to Ireland?' she asked, looking straight into his eyes; deep brown eyes. He shook his head.

'I don't need to,' he sighed. 'For us, this war was just another stage of Israeli colonial expansion. And... '

'Wait a minute. Just wait a minute,' snapped Jill. 'Who started it? Who blockaded the Straits of Tiran? Your friend Nasser! And who started shelling the Jewish city in Jerusalem? Your king Hussein!'

Again, Shafik took it coolly.

'He's not *our* king. He too was just an occupier and his soldiers were no friends either.' He would have continued. So would Jill.

Her blood was up and she relished nothing more than a good argument, but just then the boy returned with Shafik's coffee.

Yusuf seized the opportunity and stood up. 'Yes. Yes. All very well.' He spread his hands and looked around the room. 'But Shafik, these are my guests. Enough politics for one day,' he said, adding a few sharp words in Arabic.

Shafik sat back against the wall, took the small cup and sipped in silence. As if chastened, he took no further part in the conversation but Kate felt his eyes still questioning as they sat and talked to Yusuf for another few minutes, before Jill bought a silver ring.

Feeling the tension, Kate glanced at her watch and said they had to meet someone. They rose and said their goodbyes, but as they went out, Shafik followed them into the street.

'I apologise,' he said, looking at Kate. 'I should have been more polite. But for us, it is not just politics. It is our lives. Here. In this city, our city, which everyone else seems to want.'

'I do understand,' said Kate, then as if the words came of their own accord, added, 'Maybe we will have a chance to talk it over some time.'

The man smiled.

'I hope we shall.' Then, as they turned to go, added. 'If you come to see Yusuf again, perhaps he can let me know.'

As they walked away towards the Via Dolorosa, Jill nudged Kate's arm.

'Yes. Very dishy. But he's married.'

'How do you know?' said Kate, adding quickly, 'And so what?'

'Ring on finger. Or betrothed.' Then, grinning at Kate, she continued. 'So you are interested?'

'No, I'm not. Stirrer. Not in that way.'

Jill laughed. 'It's the only way... '

Kate thought back to her third visit when, on the way up, she had made her decision. Ever since that discussion with Jill, who hadn't been able come this time, the young boy had kept intruding into her thoughts – his wide eyes and eager face. Following the usual friendly small-talk with Yusuf, she had suggested that perhaps Araf might like to visit the kibbutz. She could pick him up later after shopping if he agreed.

Yusuf translated and the boy jumped up, clapping his hands together and smiling, repeating 'Thank you. Thank you!' some of the few English words he knew. And when Kate stood up to go, Yusuf took both her hands and shook them energetically, thanking her again and again; she could have sworn his eyes were moist, before he sent the boy out to their house nearby to collect some things for the journey.

Walking out to the *Souk* for some shopping, Kate had wondered why the idea of taking the young boy to the kibbutz had loomed so large in her mind after their first meeting. Was it from admiring Mairead's efforts with her joint Protesant/Catholic nursery in Belfast – something about children being able to bridge the divide and promising a better future – that Araf meeting with the kibbutz kids could start something similar? Maybe. Either way, after buying a few toiletries for Jill and herself she had a warm feeling about her decision.

Araf was waiting when she returned, and following a short, animated exchange with Yusuf and much hand shaking, she took the boy's bag and led him up to the main bus station.

It was late afternoon when they'd jumped off the bus opposite the kibbutz, and that evening Kate took Araf up to the dining hall. As with many younger kibbutzim, this was still a wooden structure but sturdily built with a terrazzo tiled floor. As well as the large main hall accommodating about twenty tables for four, there were modern kitchens at the rear. Weaving between the rows of tables, servers wheeled aluminium trolleys, some to give out main items of the meal, others with bowls of soup for each table. A third came round with buckets and cloths to clean up after each table had finished.

Pushing through the doors, Kate noticed that there were two places at Amos and Miriam's table and asked if she could join them. They both spoke English well and Kate had come to know Amos while working in the fields. She had also become friendly with his wife, Miriam, from occasionally working in her kindergarden. Miriam had an attractive, smooth face and alert, dark eyes, her long black hair tied back with a thin ribbon. Her English had a slight American accent. 'From my schoolteacher,' she said.

'Who's the lad?' asked Miriam, nodding at the boy after they had sat down.

'He's called Araf.' Kate grinned. 'You see, I met this silversmith in the Old City and this is his nephew, he's about ten or eleven. Well, I was telling them about the kibbutz and when his uncle translated for him he was totally spellbound. Must have sounded like a fairy tale I suppose. So,' she continued almost in the same breath, 'sure, wouldn't it be great for the lad to see a kibbutz.' She laughed and raised her hands. 'Do my bit for international peace and friendship!' And that was how it had started.

Changing States of Matter

Julie Lydall

Jo Tynan leaves London for love in Oslo, a capital city smaller than the northern town where she was born. Over time she evolves into a new striped identity, English and Norwegian. But Oslo proves surprisingly treacherous territory and someone in her inner circle is a quisling, threatening everything Jo has invested in love and her new life.

A Boiled Egg in Holy Week

Your lover boils you an egg. You demand it. There is anticipation and stress involved. The yolk must flow. The white must resist. Imperfect eggs will be rejected. You tap your egg and take the shell off piece by piece. This takes time. A translucent layer of skin lies between the shell and the albumen. It wrinkles and tears, attaching itself to your spoon. Your lover smacks her egg from the side with a knife, decapitates it in one go. Its head clinks onto the ceramic plate and tips over. Yolk is spilled. You nudge your spoon into the defiant white, puncturing it with a sigh, ease the top off. You examine the condition of this egg. It is deemed satisfactory. Your lover releases a lung-full of warm breath. Oh the rich, viscous heart of that egg in your mouth. Such pleasure in the way the teaspoon curves into the shell, scoops out the last smile of yellow and white. You turn the hollow egg upside down and fix it into its cup, ready to trick someone into smashing through its empty skull, but there is no one else here to play the joke on.

There isn't a word for women who want a lot of snow, but there should be. Snowaholics? Look at them sliding along in their natural habitat, all red-cheeked and buoyant. This landscape smells of freedom for them. But I feel how I'd feel about sand in a desert, overwhelmed and slightly panicky. Such a lot of snow, and so little of anything else. There are parallel lines, like train tracks, stretching away from me towards the horizon. Each track is a groove in the snow, the width of a ski. One pair for skiers going in one direction, one for skiers heading the other way. Then there is nothing but blue sky, a few stubbly pine trees, and in the distance Liv and Gunn Eva, both in red jackets, making their way across the white expanse. They look like toy soldiers. Beyond them more snow and more sky. No ski lifts, no glass-fronted hotels, no cafés or bars. Hardly the alpine resort of my imagination. It's called cross-country skiing because that's what it is – cutting across the country on skis.

I'm doing better than yesterday at staying upright and moving along though. There is definitely more coordination with the sliding of my skis, bending and lifting each knee, kicking back and pushing down with the poles. I don't have the same dread of accidentally doing the splits and rupturing my ladygarden. But I'm still the total runt of the group, travelling at half the speed of the others. It's Marit's turn to dawdle along beside me.

'You're getting the swing of it now, Jo.'

No sooner has she said that than I lean too far forward, falter and lose the rhythm. My body stutters along for a while before I settle again.

'You spoke too soon. Trying to do it right seems to make it go wrong.'

'Relax. Just notice your weight passing from one side of your body to the other and let it happen. Use your body's instinct.' Marit glides along, you can't even tell she is lifting her skis. 'Let it come naturally, like sex.'

Good advice, but my body moves like a wooden puppet and someone keeps pulling the wrong strings. I tell myself it's just a set of skills, same as riding a bike or driving, that after a while it won't seem so difficult. It's only my second day after all. But I want to improve before the Easter crowds arrive and five-year-old children start speeding past me. Liv warned me that fast skiers just shout '*løype!*' and you have to quickly step out of the tracks to let them by. It's enough of a challenge for me to stay in the tracks.

It's definitely better to think about other things than what my body is up to; trying to connect brain and limbs just confuses the process. Think about how lucky Liv and I are to be on a free holiday, just because Marit's friend got a chest infection and couldn't come. I love her *hytta*, it's like something from a

38

children's picture book. The dark wood of the walls, the little square windows with their red frames. I love how basic the cabin is – no internet, no washing machine or dishwasher. It's halfway to camping, but much warmer. Last night when Liv and I chatted as she washed and I dried, I remembered how washing up used to be a time to catch up with each other and share moments from the day.

That's the weird thing about it. There's absolutely no luxury element at the cabin, but it feels like a luxury to be there. Something to do with space and time to be together. The outside toilet was a bit of a shock, but once I realised it was only for 'number two' and that there was another toilet inside for 'number one' I calmed down. It felt a bit conspicuous leaving the breakfast table to go out there this morning, but, well, shit happens.

'Look!' Marit waves her ski pole towards the two red blobs in the white. 'Gunn Eva and Liv have stopped. They must be having a rest.'

'Good. You can swap places with Liv and get a good run in.'

'It's ok, Jo, we're not in a race. It's fantastic to be out in this weather. Perfect *påskevær.*' Marit sneaks another piece of Norwegian vocabulary into our conversation. She's good at that.

'*Påskevær?*'

'Yes, *påske,* that's Easter, and then *vær* – you know what that is.'

I certainly do. If anything, the Norwegians are more obsessed with the weather than we are. Maybe because it can be so extreme. It's an even more religious moment watching it on television here than it is at home.

'Do you mean you actually have a word that means Easter weather?'

'Yes. It's weather like this. Good snow for skiing, and lots of sun so it's warm.'

I am warm, probably more from the heat building up inside my ski jacket than the sun. It's light up here, a new kind of brightness, and there might be oceans of snow, but when we get back to Oslo the streets should be clear. It's a cheering thought. I keep my arms and legs moving in style all the way to Liv, who is standing at the track with her arms wide open. I ski straight into them and our jackets rustle together as she throws her arms around me.

'Go, Jo! You're doing so well.'

'Thanks. I don't think Marit Bjørgen needs to be worried anytime soon, but it's getting easier.'

Liv laughs. Marit Bjørgen is the only cross-country skier to impact on my consciousness. She's got upper arms twice as wide as mine and I guess she could throw a hefty punch. It's been comforting watching her win races on Liv's tiny television. You don't have to understand any Norwegian to grasp her elation.

As Liv helps me take my skis off I realise my legs are a bit shaky. They're not used to all this action after months of hibernation. She passes me black coffee from her thermos. I've been given a dispensation from carrying the daypack.

'Catch!'

Gunn Eva throws a small rectangular block towards me. It's green, yellow and red and on the front it says *KVIKK LUNSJ*. Quick lunch? What would that be? I tear open the plastic and break off a strip of chocolate. It's exactly the same as a Kit Kat. I'd never buy a Kit Kat, but this is good, the sweet chocolate mixing with the coffee and the wafer disintegrating in my mouth. I huddle closer to Liv on our polystyrene mat and slip my arm underneath her woollen top, resting it against the warm, damp skin of her back.

'Thanks, Gunn Eva. Do you know what Katrine is making for dinner?'

'She makes good chicken in a pan. Not for you. You have the pan and not the chicken. Only potato.' That's another thing I've discovered about being vegetarian here. You don't get an alternative option. You get the vegetables without the meat.

'I don't mind cooking my own dinner.'

'No, she make a different one for you. No problem.'

'Oh… that's really kind of her.'

They're a sweet couple. Marit told me they've been together forever but I'd never have put them together if I'd met them separately. It's a shame Marit doesn't have a girlfriend. I wonder why not. Maybe she doesn't want one, she seems pretty self-sufficient.

'How much longer do you think you can manage?' Liv whispers in my ear. It's an academic question, as I've got to go all the way back to the start at least. What would that be, an hour or two?

40

'I feel ok, but my thighs are tired. I'm not used to it like you. What time is it now?'

'*Klokka to.* Just after. We should get back by six, so we could do another three hours or so, or less… it's just the weather is so great.'

'I know, *påskevær*. Marit told me.' I smile at Marit, but she has her face tilted back towards the sun, her eyes closed. 'I think I could do two more hours anyway. I reckon my thighs can take it.'

'*Supert.* I'll massage your legs later if they're stiff.'

It's astonishing how much a word can change by just adding an unassuming little letter. I banished the word super from my vocabulary years ago. I kept hearing myself saying it in the classroom: super painting, super letters, super job. It started to take on its own righteous life. I even had an ink stamp, a purple smiley face that said 'Super!' underneath it. It ended up meaning nothing at all. Super had to go. Now it's slinking back into my life wearing that extra 't'. I like rounding the 'r' and topping it off with the unexpected puff of air from the 't'. *Supert.* It's a feisty little word, standing alone, no qualifying noun for a partner. An invisible, internal smile breaks out every time I say it. In amongst the grammar confusion and the challenges of sentence construction are words that give me hope. *Supert. Påskevær.*

Gunn Eva doesn't slide along with the same grace as Marit; she's more like an army tank, a slow and unstoppable force. It's relaxing skiing with her, steady and peaceful. As long as the ground is fairly level and I don't think too much about it I can do it. It's a bit like swimming, my body beginning to take over the movement and my mind floating around somewhere else.

Gunn Eva slows down. 'I take a smoke. You want to rest or I catch you?'

'Catch me up. I'm ok to keep going.'

The air here is twenty-four carat and my lungs are shining. There are a few more skiers appearing now, spots of colour in the distance. Katrine doesn't ski at all, which is reassuring. But Liv is fast, faster than Marit. Funny how someone as unambitious as me fell for such a competitive high achiever. It's not just sport either, it's everything. Like her multilingualism, how she can swap so effortlessly from one language to another. Make love to me in Spanish today; make love to me in German tomorrow. Such

41

different articulations of passion.

'Jo, stop. I think we turn back now.'

'Oh, ok.'

I stumble, losing momentum. Now I have to work out how to turn around. Gunn Eva just did some impossible looking manoeuvre, as if she put one leg on back to front. I think it's easiest in stages, shuffling the skis around a little at a time, like the second hand of a clock.

'You see the sky?'

I'm just seeing if I can get my skis aligned to fit them into the other *løype* when I sense what she means, before I see it. There's a shift in the air, a chill. Overhead the sky is whiting out and the sun is obscured.

'God, when did that happen?'

'It change quick on the mountain. You have gloves?'

I tug my gloves out of my pockets. My hands are warm but Gunn Eva has put hers on, so I do the same. She doesn't look worried, but she does look thoughtful. I have a suspicion she doesn't do worried, so thoughtful is probably not a good sign.

'What about Marit and Liv?'

'They will catch us.'

As we ski back along the plateau the stunted pine trees shake a little in the wind. I wouldn't know what to do if the weather turned nasty. Build an igloo and hide? There is no shelter up here, not a single hut or cabin or even a decent-sized tree to strap myself to in an emergency. I don't have my mobile, but then there's probably no signal anyway. Jo, stop worrying and ski. I put my head down into the wind, try not to think about the mechanics of skiing, only focusing on the pulse of it as I push my legs forward, stabbing the snow with my poles.

Liv and Marit catch up with us as we herringbone our way up a gentle incline. I like doing this, making a 'v' shape with my skis, stepping up the hill, leaving a neat fishbone pattern on the snow. I just need to watch that the ends of my skis don't touch each other and trip me up. But this is easier, digging in with the edges, getting a firm grip on the snow.

'Fantastic, Jo! You're doing really well.' Liv climbs the slope with me and I can nearly keep up with her. At the top we stand in a line, looking back at the view, the whirling white of snow and sky. The wind is furious now and I have to lean in to it to stay vertical. Gunn Eva plants her poles in the ground, spreads her arms wide and shouts.

'*Ta imot vinden!*'

'What does that mean?' I ask Liv.

'Like accept, no, more like receive, the wind?'

'Receive the wind? I like that.'

'Yes, like let the wind come. *Ta imot vinden!*'

I join in too and then all four of us are standing in that position shouting at the wind, even Marit. It is so good to shout. I am like that statue of Christ the Redeemer in Rio de Janeiro, on top of the world. And I know I am nearly home, one long hill down to the car park, then back to the cabin, to fire in the hearth and hot food.

It isn't until I set off down the hill snowplough style, keeping the tops of my skis pointed inwards and the ends wide apart, that I realise how very tired I am. My legs tremble as I struggle to hold the opposite 'v' shape from the herringbone. The wind blows against me in fits and starts, throwing me off balance. A light snow is falling, although falling is not the word. Fighting is more what it does, darting about, changing direction, flying into my eyes. I can't see very well. I fall.

The snow is soft and it doesn't hurt. But it takes me a while to work out how to get up, using one pole to push myself into an upright position again. It's much harder getting up again on a slope than on flat ground. Liv helped me up a lot yesterday. Now I don't know where she is.

The second time I fall over is only about a minute later. It's incredibly difficult keeping my balance in the wind, every time I turn I feel off-kilter. I daren't try skiing straight down the hill. I wouldn't know how to stop. I've only learned to snowplough so far, weaving my way down from one side of the hill to the other. So I just need to keep doing that and I'll arrive at the bottom.

As soon as I manage to stand up the wind hurls me down the opposite way. My shoulder hits the slope hard, raising a cloud of snow dust that blows straight into my face. It's like being spat at, cold and spiteful. My eyes smart. I struggle up again, using both poles to steady myself, scanning for any colour in this whitewash, any possibility of a human being. I don't know where anybody is.

I make sure I'm as balanced as I can be this time before I try to move, inching forwards, my skis sticking slightly on the new snow. It's better to take it slowly and stay upright. The third turn is unlucky. My right ski slides out too far as a squall hits me from behind. My belly flop is heavy, punching the air out of my lungs and twisting my leg awkwardly. My poles hang uselessly from their straps around my wrists, ridiculous arrows pointing down the slope.

Resting my forehead against the frozen ground for a few seconds I take in some iced gulps of air, then heave myself up onto my elbows and face into the turbulence. I swivel round onto my right hip, haul myself up into a sitting position, and drag my skis back together. Clamping my jaws tight together as I push down hard on the poles, I lever myself up off the ground and hover, taking longer to find my centre of gravity. I set off again, in even slower motion.

The next time I fall over I don't get up straight away. I curl into myself, keep my face out of the karate-kicking snow. Make a small, still cavern with my head and arms where the wind can't get in. Talk to myself. You are nearly there, you must be at least halfway down, you have done much scarier things than this, you are strong enough. But when I make it to my feet again I feel disorientated. The snow is filling up the air now and I can't see more than a few metres. I can't see their tracks on the snow. I can't see how wide this hill is.

But I do know which way is down. I screw myself tight inside to withstand the force of the wind and set off again. I can't understand where the others went to, and I'm beginning to worry that I've gone the wrong way entirely. Are there edges to this hill? My fingers are turning numb inside my gloves, cold air and snow finding its way inside. Ski and turn, ski and turn. Everything in me is stretched taut as elastic in the effort to stay on my feet and get down the hill.

'Fuck!' I shout when I fall again. 'Fuck!' I have no idea how much further it is. I contemplate taking my skis off and walking down – maybe that would be faster. But I'd have to carry the skis and I'm tired. Very tired. Warnings about people who lie down in the snow and never get up again flash into my mind. I must keep going, walk if I have to. I stab my pole into the snow, struggle to my feet. Again.

A red shape appears out of the white, envelops me where I stand.

'Jo, I was so worried.' Liv holds me, tight, tight, tighter. 'Where the fuck were you?'

'I thought you were with Gunn Eva and she thought you were with me. I'm so sorry.' I tune in to the distress in her voice. 'I waited at the car with Marit and then Gunn Eva arrived and you weren't with her... it's ok, you're going to be ok. They're waiting for us in the car, but we need to go, or they'll raise the alarm... you're cold.'

My fury vanishes. I want to rest here, pressed into Liv, my shield against the wind. My whole body is shuddering and I feel like it's only her arms keeping me upright. She holds me.

'How far is it?'

'Not far. Ten minutes. I'll help you.'

We negotiate our way down, Liv helping me up every time I fall. She doesn't fall once. My legs are as stiff as the skis themselves by the time Liv unclips them. When I slam the car door shut the hush inside is profound. Marit turns to look at me from the driver's seat.

'Thank God. You ok?'

I nod, don't trust myself to speak without crying. The wind clamours outside the car; snow spatters the windows. Liv puts her arm around me and I rest my head on her shoulder, close my eyes. Marit releases a sigh and puts the key in the ignition.

'What a weather. Let's go home.'

The Reluctant Indian

Sheila Chapman

The Reluctant Indian is a novel about Taksheel, an ambitious, high-caste Indian who leaves his family in Rajputana in 1932 for England. While living with family connections in London, he is manipulated by Celia, the disturbed daughter of an aristocratic family, into a single act of infidelity. Taksheel's wife, Jalbala, and their children are waiting to be sent for, his wider clan are fraying at the edges and Celia, spiralling into a fatal mania, refuses to give up their child. In 1952 Taksheel and Jalbala's youngest child will come to England to hold his father to account.

In his mind's eye, Taksheel saw himself performing his evening ablutions one last time: first outside beneath the stars in the tin bath with imported Palmolive and then, for powdering and moustache trimming, in the bedroom he shared with Jalbala. The day would be, ultimately, as all February days were, relentlessly hot. Water-starved ground had cracked and effloresced months before and red dust that was the remnant of solid earth clung to everything like damp turmeric. But, before the day broke into the symphony of heat that, after two months, had made everyone ill-tempered and lethargic, there would be a heavenly early morning, the meagre dew having tamped down the prickly dryness and the sun a gentle forerunner to its furious noontime self.

In the perfect leave-taking of his imagination, Taksheel would take breakfast for the final time with his immediate family. He would sit, as was their custom, flanked by his daughter, Dina, and Jalbala. The two older boys would sit facing him. He intended this seating arrangement to curb the rambunctiousness of the boys, aged six and four who, when not under his eye, were alternately pinching one another, tormenting the dogs, or taunting the servants. The youngest child, a baby boy, would rest on his wife's lap, suckling or contentedly gazing up at the faces surrounding him. Taksheel had already instructed the servants not to enter the room after laying out the food. He would let Dina and Jalbala serve him, which would be a novel and intimate way to enjoy his final breakfast.

After this scene of familial harmony, Taksheel imagined crossing his threshold wearing a pristine white shirt, western-style suit and polished leather shoes. He would stroll the short distance to the waiting Wolseley surrounded by family, acquaintances, servants, neighbours, local children and hawkers: in short, the whole Chaturvedi entourage. At the beginning of the line would be the lesser servants, the ones whose tasks were so menial Taksheel did not know their names. He would smile and raise his hand, his first and last acknowledgement of their existence. They would place palms together, index fingers on upper lips in mute reverence. Some would likely stoop to touch his feet. Next in line would be the third or fourth generation of their family to serve the Chaturvedi's: Rambuti the cook, Hari the gardener. These retainers would be favoured with a few well-chosen words of thanks, in Hindi of course, and an exhortation to continue in their duties faithfully whilst he was away. Next would be the many children of his many brothers, sisters, cousins, neighbours and associates. They would receive a ruffle of the hair, a pinch of the cheek.

Next would be neighbours and friends. The men would slap him on the back and force themselves to wish him the very best of good fortune. He would accept their insincere blessings amicably, serene in his crisp white shirt. He would smile over the shoulders of these men to the women in the second row, the wives wearing their second or third best saris, who would smile back before lowering their eyes and resuming sham conversations to ease their bashfulness.

Next would be his brothers and their wives. As the eldest son, he would hold their hands in both of his and look them square in the face. He would ask Baldev to ensure the orderly running of the household and in particular to supervise the education of his three sons until he could send for them to join him in England. He would ask his sisters-in-law to console Jalbala through the sadness his absence would cause and to assist her in being watchful over Dina who was, he knew, a strong-willed child. There was no use wasting time importuning Kailesh although he would miss his dear, useless, younger brother.

He anticipated that by this juncture the proceedings would have lasted an hour. He would almost be at the Wolseley. The driver would emerge and stand by the open rear door. His luggage had already been sent to the port to be loaded onto the boat. Now he would speak with his children. First Dina. He would instruct her to be a help and support to her mother, to be obedient to her uncles and grandfather and to love her brothers. Then the two boys. Their attention span was short and they had thus far failed to comprehend that their father was travelling on a large boat to a faraway country where they spoke a different language. The only solid fact that their skittering minds could grasp from the repeated explanations was that of the boat, and upon this they had become jointly fixated. How big would it be? What colour would it be? Would it have enormous sails like the ship trapped in the bottle in grandfather's study? Would there be pirates? Their inability to comprehend the momentousness of what was happening was irksome to Taksheel, and Jalabala had kept the boys away from their father these past few weeks in an effort to save them from his chiding. But it was important, Taksheel felt, that he leave them with some words that they would remember – some rule to live by that even their immature brains could process and make something useful of. He felt it should be something to do with duty and with discipline, for this latter they seemed to be completely without. But Taksheel had not framed the exact sentences in his mind. He decided to trust to the inspiration of the moment, hoping that when faced with these two small replicas of himself, unable to comprehend anything that was not physical and immediate, he would know, as a father, what was the right thing to say.

Next his father. It was impossible for Taksheel to script this exchange because his father and not he would be the author of it. He hoped to receive a blessing: an indication that his father had full faith in him and believed that he would be successful in his ventures. However, it was always difficult to know what the old man would say.

That would leave Jalbala and the baby, Jawahar. Jalbala and Jawahar. Jawahar and Jalbala. They always formed a single unit in Taksheel's mind. From the moment he had been born Jawahar had rarely been off his mother's hip. Jalbala seemed to have become so accustomed to this new appendage that she moved and spoke as if they were one being. Taksheel had often had it in mind to tell Jalbala to leave the baby with his *ayah* once in a while, to let the boy learn some self-sufficiency. But for some unexamined reason, whenever it was on his lips to say something of the sort, he felt the wrongness of doing so: like trying to rend apart something holy. He was not used to feeling things viscerally and it unnerved him. Doubtless if he had not been about to leave for England he would be compelled to take a firmer hand because it was not right to molly-coddle a baby in this way. She would make the boy feeble; womanish. Taksheel's sisters-in-law, who had also noted the unusual strength of this mother-child bond, had suggested that Jalbala was clinging to her baby to comfort her in the difficult days leading up to Taksheel's departure. Although he wanted to believe this was the case, Taksheel knew that it was not. It was unfair on the other children of course. The boys barely noticed; carelessly happy as long as they could bait squirrels or dress the dog up in their sister's clothes or find new and ingenious methods to separate a lizard from its tail. But Dina, intelligent and thoughtful Dina, did notice. Others in the extended family noticed too and felt sorry for Dina but, because she was intelligent and canny rather than winning and pretty, no one tried to make things up to her in any way: to take her under their wing until Jalbala's obsession with the boy waned.

What would he say to his wife of ten years as they stood beside the Wolseley? The woman to whom he had been betrothed when she was younger than Dina was now. The beautiful, red sari-clad girl of sixteen who, on their wedding day, had walked the Saptapadi with him around the sacred fire seven times, invoking the Gods together to grant them and the universe plenitude, love, unity and happiness. The same woman who had stood beside him as the pyre beneath the diminutive and lifeless body of his mother was lit and had wept as he had wept. The woman who had sacrificed the firmness of her body, the radiance of her skin and the slenderness of her ankles to give birth to his seven children and who had found it within herself to continue despite the loss of three of them.

Contemplating his imminent leave-taking these past months never failed to leave Taksheel feeling optimistic, almost heroic, until the daydream got to its final stages where he stood facing his wife and youngest child by the Wolseley. The mental image would break up like a reflection in a puddle when it starts to rain and he would be left with the sound of his own voice as a younger man reciting the mantra that he had chanted after each of the seven prayers he and Jalbala had said to one another on their wedding day,

'Now let us make a vow together. We shall share love, share the same food, share our strengths, share the same tastes. We shall be of one mind, we shall observe the vows together. I shall be the Samaveda, you the Rigveda, I shall be the Upper World, you the Earth; I shall be the Sukhilam, you the Holder – together we shall live and beget children, and other riches; come thou, O sweet-worded girl.'

*

'Who would ever have thought it could rain like this in February, *bhai-ya?*' Baldev asked Taksheel the morning of his departure. 'Your suit will get ruined, *yaar*. Better to wear a *salwar kameez* and change into your fine clothes when you are arriving into Liverpool.' Baldev failed to keep the mirth from his voice. Taksheel jerked back the grass matting, which the servants had hurriedly suspended in front of the windows in the middle of the night to prevent the unexpected flood dampening the Kashmiri rugs, and looked up at the sky.

'It is not a long way from the house to the car, Baldev, and the rain is stopping.'

'Just as you say, brother,' Baldev replied. 'Shall I go into the main house and tell everyone that you are ready to leave and that they should come and bid you a, how do you say, *fond-farewell?*'

Taksheel suppressed his irritation at his brother's aping of English small talk. It demeaned them all somehow but whenever he tried to convey this to Baldev he was met with indifferent jocularity.

'Yes, Baldev, please do that. I will be leaving in five minutes. The boys were taken ill in the night and their mother says they must stay out of the rain. I have already said goodbye to them. Jalbala will be outside with Dina and Jawahar. You and Kailesh and your families will be outside, I assume? And father?'

'Yes of course, brother. All the family will be there. The

servants too wanted to come and give their regards to the sahib but this rain has caused *so* many problems on the estate.' Baldev was helpless to prevent the tone of the cringing underling from creeping into his voice as he gave his elder brother news he knew would displease. 'All the men are busy trying to unblock the wells and tend to the fields where the vegetables are apparently being washed away.' Baldev chuckled, amused at the thought of *dhoti*-clad gardeners chasing after the *muli, bhindi* and *corilla* that were taking advantage of the flood to make their escape from the vegetable plots.

'The women are mainly clearing up in the big house and Kailesh's house. Dirty water has flooded very many rooms there,' Baldev said, wobbling his head from side to side (a habitual gesture of his that Taksheel had told him made him look like a cooli).

'Are we expecting anyone else?' Taksheel asked.

'Well, *bhai-ya*, of course the Misras would have come and the Colonel and his children and for absolutely certain Dr Sarathwathi and his wife would not have missed it for all the tea in China, but the rain has washed away the road. It is verily im-passable so I do not think we should wait for them. They have all sent their servants to pass on their best wishes. Some even sent *burfis* and some lovely mangoes but I do not think many will brave this rain. Also, it is very early and you know how lazy these Indians are, *yaar.*' Baldev laughed like a naughty child at his own remark and Taksheel was too agitated to point out the irony.

Baldev's wife, a smudgy-featured woman, whose years of child bearing had made no appreciable difference to her face or her figure, both having been mediocre even at the height of her bloom, entered the main room of Taksheel's house.

'Well, brother, I cannot find that naughty Dina girl,' she announced in her busy voice. 'No one has seen the little *memsahib* since the sun rose this morning and no one has time for these naughty-girl hide and seek games on such an auspicious day.' She turned to smile at her brother-in-law in what was intended to be a coquettish way. Taksheel regarded both his sisters-in-law as unattractive, female versions of their foolish husbands, and did not bother to acknowledge her statement.

'Brother, we will go and gather Kailesh and Father and we will

51

be outside in approximately two minutes.' Baldev steered his wife out of his brother's quarters as Taksheel wondered how it was that everything he said managed to be so exquisitely ridiculous.

Taksheel had his tickets in his briefcase along with his passport, bank books, and letters of introduction from his father. His tie had been tied, loosened, tied again, straightened and re-straightened. His shoes were so shiny he was afraid to let the servants at them any more in case they rubbed a hole in the leather. He stood for a moment alone in the middle of the main room of his house, listening to the rain that was, in fact, showing no signs of ceasing. He should be elated to leave this country full of imbeciles and laggards. A people so stupidly lazy that they had ceded control of themselves and all their resources to a tiny island miles away. He did not expect to miss his two younger brothers or any of the indistinguishable and undistinguished members of their respective broods with the exception, perhaps, of Kailesh. He was bored of The Gymkhana Club and bridge nights and the horse races and the weddings and funerals that went on for weeks, bored of the fasting and the hypocrisy. He had been anaesthetised by this communal, ritualised living for too many years and before he went under completely, he had to break free. He could not stand the thought of turning into one of the whiskey swilling, know-it-all anglophiles that he called his friends or to become like his own father, an erudite and thoughtful man who had had the misfortune to live long enough to be disappointed by each of his children.

Jalbala emerged from their sleeping quarters. For once, the baby was not attached to her. She was bedecked in her wedding jewellery and chimed as she walked across the rug-covered stone floor to where her husband stood. He caught her eye but quickly looked away to straighten his tie again.

'I fear it is almost time for you to leave,' she spoke softly in Hindi and moved toward him. He had always admired the quiet way she had not adopted English as the language of conversation. She spoke to him in the same language and with the same voice that she used with the children, with her sisters, with the servants. It was honest and he regretted he had never commended her for it.

'You know that I will send for you and the children as soon as I have made my way in England?' he said. 'I cannot know how long that will be but Baldev and Kailesh and my father will make sure that you are taken care of and I will send money of course as soon as that is… ' he trailed off, the right word eluding him somehow, 'feasible.'

'I know that, Taksheel,' and she reached up and placed a folded silk handkerchief into his breast pocket. It was a cornflower yellow and the finest silk. He realised she had cut it from the lengths of material that made up the sari she was wearing.

'Look at all this rain.' He shrugged resignedly and started for the doorway, adding under his breath, 'What to do?' He could see his brothers heading out into the courtyard with their children. They were not forming an aisle as in his imagination but were clumped together near the main house in an effort to shield themselves from the rain which had reached monsoon proportions. He could hear the mothers hushing their complaining children. There were no neighbours or friends amongst the group. He stepped to the threshold of his home and looked up, disbelieving, at the rain. He feared for his suit and, more than anything, for his shoes. They had not been made to withstand this weather or the pernicious red sludge that was the ground between the house and the Wolseley.

Whilst Taksheel was eyeing the rain, Jalbala had been back to their bedroom to retrieve the sleeping baby and without waking him had fastened him around her middle with a sling of cotton. She walked to her husband, ankle chains rattling and the voluminous sari sweeping the floor in her wake. She quietly bent down in front of him, loosened his shoelaces and pulled the tongues of each shoe gently forward being careful not to crease the soft leather. She then held each shoe in place one at a time so that he could step out of them which he did, wordlessly. Her hennaed hands removed the argyle wool socks one at a time. She stuffed each sock in its corresponding shoe and held them both in one hand. With the other she held the handle of an umbrella that, like an illusionist, she seemed to have produced from nowhere.

'I think it is time to walk to the car, husband,' she said quietly.

'Yes.' He took the first step outside and his toes recoiled as cold stone became warm muddy paste. He adjusted his stride to match the short steps that Jalbala's sari forced her to take and they walked in time toward the car. She held the umbrella aloft and to one side of her like a tightrope walker, arm extended fully to accommodate the difference in their height. Her gold bangles slid down her arm and stuck fast round the soft flesh just above her elbow. The rain fell on her and on her baby.

He was not after all required to speak wise words to his children and a few minutes after leaving his house, without spectacle or fanfare, he found himself standing before his father. A tall man with skin the colour and texture of aged parchment, Taksheel's father wore a white *kurta* spotted with rain and, refusing to make any concession to the weather, stood, sandaled on the mud, hair plastered to his patrician skull.

Taksheel unbuttoned his jacket and bent at the waist and knees simultaneously, giving the impression he was toppling over under the weight of his suit. Jalbala moved the umbrella to shield her husband's head. He reached down to touch his father's feet. His feet and those of his father squared off, each daubed in the same mud, each with the same bone structure, elongated second toe and high arches.

'Goodbye, my eldest son,' Taksheel's father said to him in Hindi. 'Make your way as best you can. We will be praying for your success while you are away. Look straight in front of you as you move forward through the world, son, but never forget what you have left behind you.'

'Thank you, father. I will do my best to honour you.'

The two men looked one another in the eye each trying to recognise himself in the man who stood before him. Taksheel's father swiftly turned on his heels like a General inspecting his troops and finding them wanting and set back toward the main house. The rest of the family, damp and uninterested, took this as their cue to leave, and filed away with a few carelessly shouted farewells.

Unexpectedly, there were just the three of them. The baby was awake, confused but not displeased by the drops of rain falling on his face and tickling his cheeks. Taksheel put his hand inside the makeshift cocoon in which his son lay and splayed his fingers wide over the baby's face as if trying to measure it. His fingertips felt his son's skull through downy black hair and his thumb tip nestled between the creases of the boy's several chins. The three of them stood connected like this in the rain. Taksheel closed his eyes as if this were an act of consecration. At last, the baby reached his own tiny fist up and towards his father's hand, breaking the spell. He gripped Taksheel's little finger in the surprisingly firm way of very young babies yet to be fully convinced they will not be dropped.

'Look. He does not want me to go.'

'He is not alone,' Jalbala said, looking directly up at Taksheel, as she continued to shield him from the driving rain leaving herself unprotected. This was a step in their lives, intertwined from such an early age, without precedent; there was no mandated ritual. She started to weep.

'Why do you cry, Jalbala?' Taksheel asked.

'Because I am nothing here without you.' He was surprised by the vehemence in her voice as she stood squarely in front of him, one arm raised to hold the umbrella and one hand still clasping his shoes, rain-diluted tears running down her cheeks. He did not know how to respond to the accusation in her voice.

'Wherever I am, you are my wife,' he said in what he hoped was a reassuring way and, with his little finger still held firm by their son, he spread his fingers wider still, reached his thumb up to Jalbala's forehead and placed it on the bindi, painted there with care early that morning; now just a smear.

'I have not understood why it is that you must leave us,' Jalbala said.

He sighed, remembering that evening a month ago when he had told her of his plans. He had tried to explain then. He would try again now. 'I think I can make a life that is more my own away from this place. I am sick and tired of the squalor and the filth.' He cast his arm about as if to indicate the horror and poverty just beyond the walls of Sanik Farms. 'There is something wrong with the mentality of Indian people – it is in my brothers just as it is in the lowliest *chaprassi*. I do not know what it is but I cannot change it and I can no longer tolerate it. But most of all, Jalbala, I am not like it and I do not want to become like it.'

'I do not understand, Taksheel. But I am not an educated woman.' Jalbala closed her eyes and leant forward so that Taksheel's thumb, which he had not moved during their exchange, pressed hard into her forehead.

'There are other reasons, Jalbala. The life we are all enjoying here – it cannot be sustained. You see how my brothers live, how their wives spend and there are so many children between us all. My father is an old man. Not all of our investments have been... have been... as... as... successful as we might have hoped. I must secure all of our futures. Things are changing in India, Jalbala, and we cannot go on living like heedless children.' There was no time to explain further. He had to leave now.

'England is a tiny, small island country where it rains all the time. That is why the British come here.'

Taksheel smiled weakly, saddened rather than amused that she would fall upon child-like arguments. He knew that what he was saying to her now, in one of the few unobserved, unscripted conversations that had ever taken place between them, was ultimately confusing to her. He pitied her that she had no grasp of politics and that the only argument she could marshal was to criticise the geography and climate of his destination. Almost better to be a *dhobi walla* and a man than to be a woman in this topsy-turvy country, Taksheel thought. He looked at her from head to toe and, more than her tear and rain-streaked face and more than the beaten slope to her shoulders and the too-tight wedding bangles cuffing her forearms, it was the sight of her yellow sari sullied and heavy with mud that made him want to beat his fist to his breast like a Shia devotee to make himself feel something there. The sari clung like a wet shroud around her legs giving her the appearance of a deplumed bird.

The baby's lower jaw was starting to shudder with the cold. He must get in the car and leave. If he stayed to talk to her much longer he would not be able to do it and if he did not do it today he likely never would and if that happened he would be a joke to all who knew him for the rest of his life and that would break him.

He trawled his thoughts for something to say to his wife that would be a comfort to her in the long, solitary hours she would spend in his family's compound. Solitary because she did not fit in with the women of the house now that his mother was dead and the tone of female relations was set by his sisters-in-law who formed a cabal that Jalbala had neither the desire nor the ambition to be admitted to. Conscious of the preciousness of this, their first exchange, not as equals but at least without the pretence with

56

which his other familial exchanges were doused, he did not want to hold out any false promises. He was disappointed that all he could manage was,

'Well, if I am wrong about England then I can buy another ticket, get back on the boat and come back here can I not?' He forced a smile and with his free hand gently prised open his son's reluctant fingers.

There was nothing else to say and the baby was shivering. She handed him his shoes and socks. He leant over and put his lips to his son's damp forehead and lingered there a while. For a moment, he could understand why Jalbala cleaved to him, the most placid and amenable of their four living children.

'Goodbye my son. When we meet again, you will not recognise me. But I will always know you.' Taksheel was gratified by the contented gurgling sounds the baby made in response to his caresses.

He bent down and folded his long limbs into the back of the Wolseley. The springs beneath the leather bench seat caused him to bounce up and down involuntarily like a holiday maker excited to be going on a jaunt. He placed his clean shoes beside him on the shiny leather and wound the window down.

The baby had started to cry and Jalbala swung her body gently from side to side to comfort them both. She held the umbrella up over the empty space beside her.

The engine jolted to life with a rheumatic splutter and the car started to roll forward, struggling for purchase on the slippery earth. Taksheel poked his head out of the window as if he had forgotten something. Jalbala stepped forward expectantly.

'I shall be the Samaveda, you the Rigveda?' The Sanskrit prayer issuing from his mouth was a surprise to him for he had not formed the words first in his mind before uttering them as was his habit. Although he intended it as a statement, it had come out as a question. The words hung in the moisture-laden air like fragile raindrops. She stepped forward and put her palm against the half-open window of the Wolseley, her fingers curling over the top of the window as if to prise it open. His eyes took in the manic swirls of brown hieroglyphs on her palms: another small way she had honoured him that day. The baby's cries had grown loud and so she had to raise her voice to answer,

'I shall be the Upper World, you the Earth.'

He leant forward and clumsily kissed her fingertips succeeding only in part, the rest of his kiss bestowed on the glass. He felt his lower abdomen tighten; threatening to unleash sobs. Afraid he might start to weep in front of his wife and son, Taksheel reached forward and gave the back of the driver's car an imperative thump. The wheels of the Wolseley spun in the mud. He kept his eyes averted from her face and his lips against her fingertips. As the car pulled away he called,

'I shall be the Sukhilam, you the Holder – together we shall live and beget children.'

Kali

Ariadne van de Ven

Chapter 5 from The Eyes of the Street Look Back, *a book about walking around Kolkata with camera around my neck.*

Street

(Kolkata, Tuesday 16 November 2004)

'Photo.'

I stop dead in my tracks. She's not been as absorbed in her beedi-rolling as I thought; and has waited till I'd almost walked past before making contact. She probably saw me coming, picking my way on the crowded pavement, and a minute ago almost colliding with a porter with a wide basket on his head on which a mass of bulging objects was held together by a sheet of woven plastic and a piece of rope. This is Mahatma Gandhi Road, one of the clogged-up arteries of the city, which here cuts through the commercial district. The traffic squeezes eight lanes out of four: battered light-blue state buses and dark-red private buses; trams advertising Officer's Choice whiskey or, in indecipherable Bengali, a biscuit that pretends to be wholesome; lorries with strings of chillies and limes tied to the grilles for protection from demons; pick-up trucks with young men perched on top of the cargo looking as if they own the world; cars with dark shadows for passengers; yellow Ambassador taxis with thick metal guards around the brake lights; tuk-tuk goods carriages with eyes painted next to the headlamps; bicycle carts and push carts piled high with brown boxes or jute bags; motorbikes with female side riders, incongruous helmets topping graceful saris; and assorted pedestrians taking our lives in our hands. Every vehicle that has a horn emits a blast of decibels. This is the Kolkata of TV travel documentaries and newspaper articles about global overpopulation.

Every time the lights go red, the whole crazy metal dragon comes to an abrupt halt without, miraculously, crashing into itself.

The beast switches all its engines off while it waits the three minutes for the lights to turn green again. In one beat, the roaring and the honking stops; it's as if someone has turned the sound of the world off. A hundred yards of road or more empty out while the dragons charging east and west are being held at the crossing further along and the ones on CR Avenue get the green light to roar and honk their way north and south.

High brown tenement blocks rise on each side: shops on the ground floor, then four or five floors of offices, sweatshops no doubt, flats, squats, lines full of washing on the galleries, saris lazily hanging down to dry from the flat roofs. Twenty metres ago, I photographed a ten-foot high once-white vest advertising COZI underwear on a once-pink banner strung across the higher floors of a building. Along this stretch the first floor overhangs the pavement, creating a narrow walkway underneath where the sun never penetrates. The floors above are held up by iron pillars that look too slender to bear the weight of all that unseen human activity. But like so many other things in this city, for all its overcrowding and its traffic jams and its crumbling infrastructure, it works. The building doesn't come crashing down, the lorry doesn't crush the pushcart; and nobody bumps into me as I manoeuvre the narrow pavements – not, that is, unless I'm the one being clumsy. According to all my European ideas about the world, there should be a disaster a minute. But there isn't. Somehow it works.

'Photo.'

I swing around and grin at her. She is sitting with her back to the temporarily silent, eerily empty street, on a table that will soon be transformed into a kerbside market stall, covered with books or second-hand spectacles or metal locks. She has pulled her thin knees up into her chest in a not very lady-like posture, her cotton kurta is creased. Her large, unblinking eyes are on a level with mine; she repeats her demand, daring me. I can't tell how serious she is. I lift the camera; the film is very nearly full. Please, two frames is all I need. Next to her, half a dozen brown beedis lie on the table: they are so strong that one puff causes instant and incurable smoker's cough. I remember. Is that what she is selling this morning? Will that be her income of the day?

The sun-bleached MG Road is behind her, which will confuse

60

the light meter – I need to think about this. Her hair has been thoughtlessly gathered together in a bun at the nape of her neck, a few wayward grey strands try to escape. As I spend at least a few moments every day envying Indian women's smooth, glossy, well-behaved hair, I fall in love with her unruly hairdo. Her stuck-on square bindi, which I use to focus the lens, has also slipped slightly from its dead-central position between her perfect eyebrows. I'm so close to her on the narrow pavement that it will have to be a close-up of her face, with her knees under her chin. Focus done. She is stunningly beautiful in a couldn't-care-less way – I've got to get this exposure right. My age, probably: fine wrinkles radiating from the corners of her eyes. A small nose-stud catches the light, a silver flower gleams in each ear. OK, I need a lot of light here: exposure as long as I dare, lens open so focus is critical. From my left, traffic noise approaches like an unstoppable wave of lava, heavy and dark and ruthless; the lights must have changed. But here on the pavement, her seriousness cracks open, revealing pink gums and confident, paan-stained teeth. Look at her, she's enjoying this. This'll have to be it: press the shutter release. Oh! She squeezes her eyes tight shut and sticks a very red tongue out; her timing is spot-on. Kali! I lower the camera, we look at each other and laugh. Perhaps she'd been daring herself as much as she was challenging me. As fast as I can, I transport the film and snatch a second photograph as she shakes her head in mirth. The tourist has managed it at last, she can't quite believe it.

I don't mind walking for miles, for hours, filling several rolls of film for just one exchange like that one. I don't even mind if the photos haven't worked. Or not much. But now I'm hot, tired, dusty. Film full. Black pollution in nostrils. Suddenly, my energy drains away through the soles of my sandals. It's no use trying to walk on, trying to photograph more. Time for a break. I decide to drag myself to *The Indian Coffee House* around the corner in College Street.

The mad junction of MG Road and College Street is one of the spots in the city where one can sense its layers, its traditions, and its significances. Like the nine cities of Troy, like every great city, Kolkata has layer upon layer of history. They break through each other, these layers, with new structures leaning against old buildings and memories mingling. I always try to stop here for a few minutes, behind a lamp post so that I'm not in anybody's way, to breathe it all in. Between two railway stations, this is a historical location for the Bengal Famine of 1943, the Naxalite movement of the 60s and the Bangladeshi refugees of 1971; it is a bottleneck for the bored bus conductor who hangs out of the door flicking his tickets to attract passengers; and it is the place of work for three green coconut sellers who outshout each other for customers – they will shout at me, too, but I already belong to the small, elderly man, blind in one eye and his dashing son. Loyalties are important. And now, for me, it will always be the place close to where the beedi seller demanded I make her photo. I run across College Street, dodging the dragon that comes charging up.

The entrance of *The Indian Coffee House* is almost hidden between the booksellers on both sides: only an open door and a stone staircase. Open windows throw splashes of sunlight onto the walls, papered with political posters in English and Bengali about rallies, student demos and bandhs – strikes. I slip past the telephone-and-tobacco kiosk on the ground floor and climb the stairs towards the din of voices. There's a table under a fan that is already whirring; its soft breeze cools my skin. It'll take me a lifetime to thaw the surly waiter, but the ladies' hole-in-the-ground toilet is just about clean enough and no one cares that I'm on my own. The high, shoebox-shaped hall has tobacco-yellow walls; one lonely portrait of Tagore by way of decoration; a first-floor gallery where young couples, foreheads almost touching, whisper for hours; and a battery of ceiling fans that hang, regimented, from wall-to-wall iron poles.

The Indian Coffee House doesn't need atmosphere, it has history instead. For decades, this is where the intellectual rebels have gathered to finalise their plans for changing the world. By the looks on their faces, they're still at it. The tables are small and slightly sticky and whenever one of the old wooden chairs finally collapses under the weight of the arguments, it is replaced with an ugly plastic garden chair that no one wants to sit in. There is only one kind of coffee on the menu, with too much milk and too much sugar already added. Consumer choice has not yet been invented. Sometimes, students ask if they may join me to practise their English, but today they are busy with their studies and each other and don't even throw a curious glance in my direction. It's not full yet, I can have a table to myself for now.

It's a luxury to be able to change the film sitting down, at a table even, rather than standing on a street corner with a crowd of curious people peering down into the camera and at my sweaty fingers. I slot in a new, empty film, ready to be filled with fleeting encounters. In a month's time, back in Richmond with a bagful of films, I won't remember exactly which photograph I made where and when. That I learnt the hard way. So, in my tiny photo-admin notebook, I jot down what photographs I made, on which day, at what time, on which streets. 16 November, 9.30–11am, Rabindra Sarani, MG Road, Cozi, beedi woman (10.45). And I think about her, sticking her slender tongue out at me. Kolkata is full of goddesses with their red tongues sticking out: it is the defining characteristic of the city's goddess.

The terrifying Kali is the black-skinned, red-tongued, red-lipped deity, with four arms, a mass of long black hair, and a long garland of dead men's heads. And one foot planted on a prone male. This is the pose in which she is portrayed all over the city. There must be thousands, tens of thousands of Kalis: in effigies in roadside shrines and in large temples, in small idols for the puja rooms in people's homes, on kitsch calendars, in framed drawings and on wall-mounted tiles. She can be huge and she can be tiny, sometimes she is blue but more often she is black, she smiles sweetly or frowns ferociously. At Kalighat, her main temple in South Kolkata, she is worshipped in a pared-down shape of three almond-shaped red eyes on a black background above a river-sized golden tongue. This surreal object is almost buried in a mountain of fresh flowers. This working temple is also one of the few 'attractions' Kolkata boasts of in its tourist leaflets. I've been there, done that, paid the priest (but not what he demanded), refused the red thread around my wrist because it has no significance for me and am glad I don't have to go back.

I scribble what I remember in my notebook and resolve to read up on Kali's story when I get home. I've made this resolution before. She is important to Kolkata's image of itself, although the historians say it's an urban myth that the city is named after her. Did the beedi woman deliberately imitate the goddess? Was it as unmistakable a gesture as bringing one's hands together in prayer would be anywhere in Europe? And if so, was it in jest or in

63

earnest? Could it also have been the boo-to-you of my childhood? Does it mean only one thing or can it be ambiguous? Did she expect me to stop or did I take her by surprise, too? 'Photo' was all she said. There are times that I wish I had instant, fluent Bengali

– but that might have complicated the sheer fun of the encounter. I try to catch the uncatchable eye of the waiter in charge of this corner. Look this way look this way. Ah. He sticks an unsmiling finger in the air. I nod. Another hot coffee. Perhaps my utter cluelessness as a tourist gave her the freedom to be playful for a moment or two and not to be judged by fellow Kolkatans on the basis of her appearance or her beedis or her regional background or her caste, which is probably obvious to them, or her poverty. If I'd been able to speak Bengali or Hindi, she would not have had that freedom; she would have suspected that I knew enough to judge her. She was poor. Perhaps very poor. Beedis cost next to nothing; selling half a dozen would barely make her enough 'profit' for one meal. I should've bought a couple, at tourist prices. Too late now. It would be so fascinating, though, to have climbed onto the table next to her and to have chatted.

I look up to thank the waiter for the cup on its flooded saucer. They must line them up on a table or on the floor in the kitchen, and move a huge kettle of pre-milked coffee from one cup to the next in one long industrial movement. If I spoke the language, I could have found out about her life. Rethink the language issue (again). Her unkempt hair may not have been tomboyism, it too may have been poverty. I've no idea. But she did insist that I make her photograph, and she enjoyed it. It was all entirely up to her. Perhaps that's all that matters: just the moment. Also, she'll be among my photographs and perhaps I'll be among her stories.

Darkroom

Saturday is darkroom day. On a gloomy Saturday morning in January I descend into the basement, walk to the door tucked between the bookshelves and the record shelves, close it behind me, string the black-out cloth across it and exclude the world. I turn on the electric heater and the radio, where a calm Radio 3 voice compares performances of a Great Work on CD. Not one of them is ever deemed perfect, a musical medicine for darkroom perfectionism. Let's try to make a negative sing. The films have been developed, they have had their six hours of drying over the bath; the contact sheets have been printed and I have peered at them with a magnifying glass, frame by frame, street by street, walk by walk. Now it's time for the 8x10" work prints, which will reveal the lucky moments and the many misses: out of focus, over-exposed, under-exposed, compositions refusing to come together, individuals stepping into the frame. Some Saturdays I tear my hair out, others I punch the air and execute a few dance steps to Ravel or Beethoven.

The routine is slow and deliberate. Under the red light, I slide a strip of negatives into the enlarger and send light through it onto a sheet of sensitive paper. Then the paper goes into the developing bath for one minute, into the stop bath for 30 seconds, into the fixer bath for two minutes – red light off, normal light on, moment of truth – then into running water to wash off the chemicals and finally I peg it on the washing line that stretches from bookshelf to record shelf across the basement. I rock the trays gently to make small waves wash over the paper. My breathing slows down; a minute is surprisingly long, two minutes take forever. My father used to follow this procedure in the blacked-out bathroom when we kids were very small. War photographers used to improvise in battlefield tents, guessing temperatures and times. The tradition stretches back a century while time moves in slow seconds under my hands. Under the red light, the image materialises on the paper. Magic. There is nothing else to do but think.

I wonder, sometimes, if I should 'go digital'. Friends make the most breath-taking images with pixels; although I envy them sometimes, I am hooked on film. An encounter on a particular spot at a particular time becomes a tiny thing that I can hold in my hands. Time and place are transformed into matter. There is a satisfying simplicity to it, too: aperture, exposure and focus and that's it – no menus, no complicated settings. And the images will remain locked away until the developed strip of thirty-six negatives hangs over the bath. I like the craft of printing, with its objects, its rhythms, and its sequences of white light and red light. It mirrors the making of the photograph: a short burst of light wakes up the ghost in the negative and gives it a new existence. It is easy to imagine that I am still writing with light.

On this cold, grey Saturday, it is the end of film number 81, frames 34 and 35: the woman on the MG Road. 'My' Kali. I have to make myself breathe as, out of the first frame, her face forms itself under the clear liquid. I have not messed up: this Kolkata moment has not got away. There she is, sticking her tongue out. Her face is framed by the street behind her, empty, silent and white-hot. It's as if, in a metropolis of 14 million, there were only the two of us.

I still can't read her mind of course. What on earth was she expressing? Did she just make it up on the spur of the moment? Or did she have a routine for the occasional stray tourist? It did not feel like a well-rehearsed game – although who knows. It's such a weird thing to be doing: making a photograph of a total stranger, merely because we happen to meet in the street and she happens to take a fancy to having her portrait taken. I am as perplexed as I had been that Tuesday morning in the MG Road, 8000 kilometres from here.

Kali. I have been to the library, found books, looked at stories and pictures. The ferocious Kali, destroyer and protector and mother. This is a tough one for us Europeans, used to one or the other: Mary or Medusa, goodies or baddies. My mother the tigress would understand, I think. The myth is that the gods, when losing a battle against the demons, call on the beautiful ten-armed goddess Durga. She becomes black with anger, and out of her fury springs the black goddess Kali, who destroys the demon army in a frenzied attack. She gets so carried away by her own power that she won't stop and the universe is in danger. In order to rescue the world, the gods ask her consort Shiva to lie down in front of her. She blindly steps on him and when she realises this, she comes to a sudden halt and sticks her tongue out in shame. The Bengalis love and revere her: she protects them.

It is no longer the woman who is expressing anything: it's the photograph, now with a life of its own. In this darkroom, I am the only one looking at the print and even for me its meanings have been shifting in the few minutes that I cradle it, then move it, gingerly, from tray to tray. Between developer and stop, she tells me her life story in a language I don't understand. Between stop and fixer, she reproaches me for not speaking Bengali – or Hindi, or Oriya; I have no idea which community she belongs to. It is frustrating. I often wish I could wake up with fluent Bengali. And I'm no closer to making up my mind about whether to learn Bengali or not. Because the lack of shared words also opens up a space for gestures and expressions in mouth and eyes and hands. Look at her: it is an unexpectedly eloquent space, playful, ambiguous, fascinating. As I ease the photograph out of the fixer and hold it up for the liquid to drip off for a few seconds, the silence of this photograph about words also begins to hint at the West's deafness to the voices of the East. My Kali looks back at me and makes me think about the stories we listen to – and those we do not hear.

I move the strip of film in the enlarger and print number 35. The second portrait shows her big smile. It is out of focus, because she was rocking her knees with laughter in the long exposure. 'Here's looking at you, girl,' she says, from half an inch under the developing solution in the tray.

Death in a Northern Town

Peter Higgins

*It's 1979. We're in West Yorkshire. And there's this kid: Martin Keane.
He's arrogant, pretentious and… well, you'll see. Oh, and he hates PE.
Luckily, the school's not what you'd call strict – he doesn't have to do PE if
he doesn't want to. Until this new PE teacher shows up: Mister Connolly.
'You should be out there playing rugger, not sitting in here reading.' How long
is Martin going to have to put up with this torture?*

*Meanwhile, fear stalks the land: everyone is obsessed with the Yorkshire
Ripper. Who is he? Where does he live? What does he look like? Does he
have a wife? Children? A job? Will he be caught before he can kill again?*

*And then – incredible news – the police announce that the Ripper has sent
them a tape. Listen to this: 'I'm Jack…' And the thing is, it sounds exactly
like that new PE teacher. So Martin has an idea. Working with Vincent
(his only friend) he begins to spread a terrible rumour…*

Chapter One

They took Mister Block away just before Christmas, the poor
bastard. We all agreed that he must have had a nervous
breakdown. None of my contemporaries seemed entirely sure
what a nervous breakdown actually involved. Imagine, therefore,
how impressed they were by my detailed descriptions of Mister
Block's new circumstances: the loony bin, the padded cell, the
concrete floor, the strait-jacket; his head shaved, his mouth all
slack and dribbling. No visitors. No sharp objects.

I stood in the playground, my audience surrounding me,
hanging on my every word. Vincent, at my right hand, said,
'That's dead true, that is.' Everyone nodded. I allowed myself a
small smile.

'Bollocks.'

I stretched my neck and stood on tip-toe, my right hand on
Vincent's left shoulder, trying to see over the heads of the
assembled throng, to find out who had dared to challenge me.

Bobby Snelling. Of course. I might have guessed.

Malnourished, educationally subnormal, permanently ill Bobby Snelling, with his ear-medicine and his *hair* and his unintentionally hilarious determination to always give the wrong answer in class.

I allowed the hubbub caused by his interjection to subside a little before I said, 'Excuse me?'

Snelling said, 'Total bollocks. He's not in a loony bin. My dad knows him. He just got married to some bird and they moved to Manchester.'

'Your father?' I said. 'Your father got married to "some bird" and moved to Manchester?'

Vincent laughed. I had him well trained. But I needed to get the rest of my public back on side, too. I was about to say something, but Snelling, his face now a deep crimson, persevered.

'You know what I mean,' he said. 'Mister Block. He hasn't had a nervous breakdown. That's bollocks.' (This met with murmurs of agreement from some of the less intellectually impressive boys.)

'Well,' I said, 'you can believe the official version if you want. The cover story. No, Bobby, Robert, let me finish. Thank you. If people want to believe the official version, that's fine. Go ahead. But take it from me. All of you, take it from me. Old Mister Block, old Block-Head himself, is up there, up Garston way right now, up in the Garston loony bin, even as we speak, sitting on that concrete floor, rocking back and forth, strapped into his strait jacket. That's what they do to you when you have a nervous breakdown.'

Someone piped up with, 'So, who's the new PE teacher gonna be?'

Although I had no idea who the new PE teacher was going to be, I was quite prepared to talk with impressive vagueness on the subject for the next few minutes, but Bobby Snelling beat me to it, somehow.

Shifting his weight from one foot to the other, a bundle of over-excitement, he told us he'd actually *seen* the new man *talking* to the head*master* (a watery-eyed relic with trembling hands and a much-mocked habit of getting everybody's name wrong, including, on one historic occasion, his own). Not only that, Snelling continued, the headmaster had actually intro*duced* the new PE teacher to *him*.

'I were just off home through the car park and he says, "Now

69

then, young Nellist" – you know what he's like – he says, "Meet the new PE teacher, mister... ""

'Well,' I said, interrupting Snelling's breathless reverie. 'What difference does it make what his name is? Let me rephrase that. It may make a difference to you. It makes no difference to me. After all, I don't *do* PE, do I?'

Vincent said, 'That's dead true, that is.'

Which was why that first Wednesday afternoon of that typically glum January found me sitting, as usual, in the agreeably cosy sixth-form common-room, reading (or at least attempting to read) *Northanger Abbey*. Incidentally, *Northanger Abbey* is by Jane Austen. It's not as long as the same author's *Mansfield Park* and not as famous as the same author's *Pride and Prejudice*.

My preferred spot in the common-room (upstairs, window-seat, far corner, southern aspect) afforded me an excellent view of the car park, and, beyond it, the school's playing fields, and, beyond them, the building site that was slowly but steadily being transformed into a new, much larger, school. Thin cranes swung slowly about, while, in clouds of pale dust, lorries came and went, full of rubble or bricks or whatever lorries on building sites might be full of. And, of course, when that work was done, other work would begin: the demolition of the school in which I sat.

The rugby pitch looked especially uninviting that afternoon, with its frozen mud, its iced puddles, its pathetic patches of half-hearted grass. Boys in black shorts and blue shirts were engaged in some species of warm-up exercises, while no doubt being incoherently yelled-at by the new PE teacher who was, I assumed, out there with them, somewhere.

On my desk, alongside the aforementioned paperback (and a Cadbury's Flake that I was saving for later) there lay a newspaper. Its sober front page headline and grainy black-and-white photograph told me nothing I didn't know already: *... tarpaulin ... 22 years old ... undiscovered for three weeks ... claw-hammer.*

Yawn, yawn, yawn. There was no new news. The papers were just full of the same stuff, regurgitated for our amusement and disgust, until something actually happened. Until he struck again. Thank God this was only The Guardian, always a model of polite restraint, even in those feverish days, when everything and

70

everyone had gone completely insane. Had it been a tabloid newspaper, who knows what lurid nonsense might have assaulted me.

I saw these papers, sometimes, fat little pillars of them in newsagents, or lone copies on buses or in libraries. Their blood-curdling mixture of revulsion and titillation never failed to appal. Yes, thank God this was only The Guardian ... *last seen in the Chapeltown area of Leeds at roughly 2am* ...

I picked up *Northanger Abbey*. I scratched my cheek. I chewed the end of my pen. I stared at the book. I stared out of the window. I stared at the newspaper. *Continued on page 5*...

I gritted my teeth and did my best to not turn to page five. I read yet again the graffiti etched into the desk's wooden surface – the wit and wisdom of previous generations: Cleckheaton Aggro. R luvs L. Baz phucks bumS.

Perhaps I would be able to concentrate more successfully on my studies later this evening, in the Public Library. I would go there tonight, straight after school. In that relatively rarefied atmosphere I would continue my work while doing my best to avoid Joanne Jennings, the dark-haired, long-lashed, slim-limbed library assistant who, despite (or perhaps because of) my paying her absolutely no attention whatsoever, seemed to have developed some kind of mild obsession with yours truly.

Time for a Flake. You weren't supposed to eat in here. A sign said so. You weren't supposed to do anything in here, except work. I began, carefully and quietly, to unwrap the chocolate.

Footsteps. I shrank a little into my seat, hid the chocolate under the newspaper and picked up the book. I made sure to hold my chin in my hand in order to complete the picture of studious concentration.

The footsteps did not sound like those of a sixth-former or a teacher: they sounded tentative but frenzied, the footsteps of someone who had never been in here before, and didn't like it, and wanted to get out again as soon as possible.

They got louder. They stopped behind me. I closed the book and laid it down on top of the folded newspaper. I twisted around in my chair. A large boy was looking at me. He was fully decked-out in PE kit and looked very hot. He seemed totally overawed, bless him, by the gentrified, gentlemen's club atmosphere in which he found himself.

'Vincent,' I said. 'What are you doing here?' He grinned – all overlapping teeth and Wotsits debris (he loved Wotsits). With his big eyes and floppy blond hair he struck me as even more crazed and ramshackle than usual.

When he'd got his breath back he said, 'Mister Connolly's after you.'

I sighed, and said, 'Can't you see I'm trying to *work*?'

'Yeah, but Mister *Conn*olly's after you.'

'Who?'

'What? Come on, Martin. It's PE. You're not meant to be in here.'

I closed my eyes for a moment. It was all tremendously tiresome. Perhaps, when I opened my eyes, Vincent would be gone. I opened my eyes. He was still there. He grabbed my sleeve and said, 'Come on, mate. Come *on.*'

Where was I supposed to be going? Not out there, surely? Anywhere but out there. I tried in vain to convince myself this was all just a terrible mistake. It *was* all a terrible mistake.

Vincent continued in a by now familiar strain: 'You're gonna get bollocked,' he said. 'He's gonna kill you. Come *on.* You don't wanna get bollocked.'

Three desks away from this little scene, a sixth-former, his face a fancy-dress mask of pimples and sideburns, leaned back in his chair to observe. Languidly he informed Vincent that he was not allowed up here. Up here was only for sixth-formers. Vincent pointed at me, and said, 'Neither is he. He's not in the sixth-form, neither.'

'Thanks, Vincent,' I said. 'I knew I could count on you.'

He at least had the decency to look sheepish, before saying, 'Sorry, mate.'

Through the vaguely smeared and warped glass, the sports field looked colder than ever. Above it, vast grey clouds loitered, looking bored, waiting for someone to snow on.

'Mister Connolly's in a right state,' said Vincent.

The languid sixth-former, who *was* supposed to be in here, frowned slowly and said, 'Connolly? Connolly. Yeah. The new bod. Heard he's a bit of a nutcase.' Then he looked at me and said, 'You're not meant to be in here. Go on. Piss off.'

I breathed in while a drop of sweat that felt simultaneously hot and cold travelled briskly down from my right armpit to my waist.

'Well,' I said, breathing out. 'If I *must*.' Trying to maintain some dignity, I began ramming my belongings into my satchel.

To Vincent I said, 'I do think it's a tad disloyal of *you* to come and fetch me. I rather thought I could at least count on *you* for some sort of...'

'I told him you had asthma and you weren't to do PE cos you had asthma and that, but he didn't believe me.'

'Yes, all right, Vincent.'

'He said I had to come and get you anyway, even when I told him you had that asthma, and that.'

'Yes, all *right*.'

'Don't think he believed me.'

'No. I don't suppose he did.'

I had not been in the changing rooms for quite some time. They had not, for want of a better word, changed much in the intervening years. They still stank of boys and towels and they still had that hollow ceramic sound and those dripping taps and they were still cold and threatening.

Of course it went without saying that I had neglected to bring my 'kit'. I hadn't needed my kit. After all, I wasn't supposed to be doing PE, was I? I sat down on a wooden bench. The terracotta floor was wet with chunks of mud and blades of grass. I stared down at my impeccable black brogues.

Apropos of nothing, apropos of absolutely fuck-all, Vincent said, 'How fast do you think a man could run if he was getting chased by a lion? Or a tiger? Or a cheetah? Which is fastest, do you reckon? Or maybe a white rhino?'

'Vincent,' I said. I shut my eyes.

'You all right?'

'Fine. Marvellous. Splendid.'

'Yeah? Really?'

'No, Vincent. Not really.'

'Oh. Sorry.' He made a sort of sad swallowing sound. I opened my eyes.

'I've to get back outside,' he said. 'Or I'll get bollocked as well.'

I sighed, and said, 'And we wouldn't want that, would we? Of

73

course not. You run along.'

Before he left, he paused in the doorway and said, 'Mister Connolly says if you've not brought your kit you've to wear whatever you can find in the box.'

Whatever you can find in the box. None of it fitted. All of it stank. There were not even two matching boots. Ten minutes later I tip-toed gingerly out into the unearthly cold of that January afternoon, dressed in a far too large red short-sleeved tee-shirt (with a white number twelve on the back, for some reason) a pair of skimpy sky-blue shorts, my own black socks, and colossal football boots, the left one too big, the right one even bigger.

Think of the worst thing and then make it even worse, and then transport it to Dewsbury, in January, and it's snowing. And you're outside and you should be inside, where it's warm and dry and safe. Yes, you should be inside, nibbling on a Cadbury's Flake, letting bits of Cadbury's Flake fall onto the silver lining of the wrapper you've stretched out onto the table for the specific purpose of catching them.

Which is the more satisfying: the act of eating the Cadbury's Flake itself, or the after-act, transferring the leftover tiny shards of chocolate to one's mouth with one's saliva-moistened fingerprint?

I dug my elbows into my sides, below my rib cage. My breath formed rather beautiful silvery clouds, each one different, each one the same.

Before I had made it to the playing area, thirty or so boys had stopped their warm-up exercises to look, point, laugh, jeer, chant, applaud, etc.

The PE teacher sauntered over, while nonchalantly yelling at the assembled throng to shut up. They all shut up. Now he stood before me, hands on hips, looking down at me. He was wearing a track-suit with a hooded top, with the hood up. He looked relatively warm in there. He pulled the hood down. He had short nondescript hair, and was of indeterminate age, as all teachers are. He was quite tall and thin and pale. He had a long face and, thus, a long nose, too. He smiled and gasped. He began to jog on the spot.

'You're just in time,' he said.

Oh, good, I thought. Lucky me.

'We're picking sides. Come on. All of you. Line up.'

He spoke with an accent that I couldn't place at the time, with my mind being jangled somewhat by the shock of my forcible ejection from the cosy book-lined common-room and into this hell-hole. I knew for certain, however, that he didn't sound like he came from Dewsbury. Neither did I, of course (thank God). But he didn't sound like me, either.

In his infinite wisdom, our new Physical Education guru had decided that the two team captains would be Mark Plascinsky and Anthony Knackle. These two apes stood proudly at either side of Teacher, and picked.

They began this process with real enthusiasm, selecting the strong and the tall and the fleet of foot, then moving on to the solid and the reliable (Vincent was in this category) and the not actually disabled, before finishing with cries of 'Sir, do we 'ave to 'ave 'im?' as they scraped the bottom of the barrel, and resignedly, wearily, 'chose' what they found down there: the skinny one, the giggling one, the obese one, the one who was almost crying, the one with the big plaster under one lens of his spectacles, the one who ate stuff out of bins, the one whose brother had tried to kill himself, the one with the ear-medicine (that unforgivable little know-it-all Bobby Snelling).

And me. I stood and shivered at the touchline. The whistle blew, the boys ran, the wind slapped my face. Somehow, the ball came into my possession. I threw it as far and as fast as I could.

Very soon after this, and for no reason that I could ascertain, several boys thrust me into the mud. One of my boots came off and was grabbed by someone and tossed into the distance. Vincent wandered off to retrieve the wretched thing.

Mister Connolly shouted, 'Tasker.'

Vincent stopped and looked.

'Where do you think you're going? Get back here. Keane. Is that your bloody boot? Go and get it yourself. Chop, chop.'

Vincent lolloped back, empty-handed. 'Sorry,' he said, his smile as mad as ever.

I wandered into No Man's Land, picked up my boot and struggled to put it back on. My numb fingers were fat and useless, like your fat useless lips after a visit to the dentist.

On the hill the school glowed in the fading light. The large windows of the sixth-form common-room blazed with inquiry and inspiration and imagination. I stood and breathed for a while, just staring at the lights, like a child in a Dickensian Christmas, pressing my nose against the glass.

What else needs to be said about the agony of that afternoon? My knees were soon jewelled with frozen blood. My shirt was torn and befouled. My shorts – so small, so stupidly tight around the waist and elsewhere – were temporarily removed during one especially hilarious fracas.

Upon hurriedly and nervously pulling them back up over my trembling legs, I noted, first with relief, and then with alarm, that my shorts were significantly less figure-hugging than before. Their elastic had been fatally wounded. I would be forced to hold the wretched things up around my waist with one hand for the rest of my time on the field.

No sooner had I noticed this than I noticed something else equally unpleasant: the ball was heading through the air towards me at incredible speed. I stepped nimbly to one side and let it go.

Connolly materialised and ordered me – *ordered* me, ordered *me* – to pick up the ball and throw it. I trotted pathetically to the spot where the ball had come to rest, and, still holding up my shorts, retrieved it as best I could.

I threw it. To where? To whom? It didn't matter. I threw it away, and tried to hide again. A voice said, 'Keane. You can throw better than that, can't you?'

Laughter, comments, jeers, etc. Oh, why can't you all please just leave me alone?

'Harrison. Chuck us that ball. Cheers. Now. Keane. Catch. Unbelievable. Pick it up. What's going on in the shorts department? Never mind. Throw it to Rourke. *Throw* it to him. Don't you understand basic *Eng*lish?'

Suddenly very hot, I threw the ball to Rourke. It sailed high and straight, and into Rourke's waiting hands.

'Not bad,' said Connolly, or 'Well done,' or 'Good throw.' Wasn't listening.

I'd get Connolly for this. I didn't know how, or when, or what I would do (there were so many things I could do) but I'd get him for this.

More running, more shouting, a blizzard of white limbs, a

stampede of black boots, a horde of raging mad fools running around to absolutely no purpose.

A whistle blew. The game appeared to be over, at last. Connolly was instantly surrounded by admiring fanatics, asking him questions, making jokes, bantering about football, about preferred football teams (perfectly fascinating and vital stuff about how the team from one town were nowhere near as good as the team from some other town). And, of course, the only subject anyone really cared about: 'Sir, that Yorkshire Ripper fella, do you think he's a queer?'

Laughter from everyone except Connolly. He just smiled a little and said, 'He's a very pathetic individual, I reckon. Nowt to do with being queer, or not. Or black or white or short or tall. Or a man, or a woman, if you think about it. Might be a woman. We don't know, do we? Nobody knows anything. Anyway, speaking of pathetic individuals: Joyce, carry that thing properly. God, how am I supposed to knock you lot into shape? I've had some challenges in me time, but this is summat else. And where's the bloody *ball*?'

I stopped and looked behind me as the raggle-taggle throng loped and jogged off to the changing rooms. The ball lay on the frozen grass, some twenty yards away. Another twenty yards behind it, or maybe even more, was Snelling.

I went to get the ball, keeping my eye on him. He was kneeling down, doing something with his shoes. As I picked up the ball, he got to his feet. He was still looking down at the frozen ground. No doubt he was lost in thought – struggling, perhaps, to remember his own name. I glanced over my shoulder. No-one was watching.

I threw the ball. It shivered a little as it flew in a good, long, high, perfect arc. Look at that. Outstanding.

It struck him on the side of the head, just above his right ear. Down the boy went, and away the ball bounced, its wintry work complete.

Dodging Gargoyles

Harriet Mercer

An excerpt from Chapter Four of Harriet Mercer's memoir

My thoughts about death first waved their podgy arms after a bedtime story on 27th December, my fourth Christmas. In the glow of a nightlight, I lay snug on my side, counting the tiny flowers edging the pale pink Paisley swirls that patterned my eiderdown; I was thinking about the blue painted nursery school, and how it was big enough, that it would fit everyone in… that everyone could die together. The chairs that we'd used for Nativity could be pushed back against the walls and everyone could sit there: Mummy, Daddy, Nom, Grandma, my aunts, and all the cousins. We would all sit there together and wait for it to happen, we could hold hands and tell stories, and when it did happen we would all go to Heaven together, no one would be left lonely or sad.

Die. I tried out my new word a couple more times… Die. Die. A journey that takes you past the moon and stars. I had learnt it that morning. *Why's the sofa in the garden?* I'd asked. Even though the sofa was flowery, it shouldn't be in the garden; it should be inside, opposite the fireplace. Honda was curled up asleep on one of the arms, she still purred like a motorbike in her sleep. Mummy, big with a baby, had taken my hand and led me back inside.

'Darling… listen, Granny Davy went to Heaven last night… she fell asleep on the sofa and didn't wake up. Poor Nom, she's very sad that Granny's gone.' Great Granny Davy was Nom's mother, and Nom was my father's mother. I didn't understand. Granny Davy *never* sat on the sofa, she was always on the tall chair with Candy the Pekingese on her lap, and I would sit on the footstool by her side, counting the blue, pink and yellow squares of the crocheted blanket that warmed her knees.

'But why did Granny Davy go to Heaven?'

'Well, when someone is very old… how old was Granny Davy, Harriet?'

'Ninety-three,' I say, proud of my numbers.

'Yes, there you are, when someone is very old and tired like Granny Davy was, or if they're terribly ill, there comes a time when they leave this world... and die... and go to Heaven.'

'Mummy, are you going to die?'

'We all die one day, darling. But hopefully not for a very long time.'

A few weeks later, I'm wearing a pink and purple corduroy pinafore dress, navy woollen tights and am sitting cross-legged on the floor of my bedroom. I've been doing my favourite book. Doing, because first of all you unfold its cardboard covers and secret flaps, then you bring them together, sliding them into one another so that the book stands up like a merry-go-round with pages instead of painted horses. Long bearded trolls stroll through the green leaves, on the lookout for a fairy to sweep their caves clean.

There's a buzz, a buzzing. It stops.

Hide up the tree, hide up the tree! I beg the fairy's wings to flee faster – knowing that they won't. The buzzing starts again. I look up, straight into the face of white sun. But the buzzing isn't blinded, on it goes, and it makes me think of when my lips hummed against a comb wrapped in tracing paper and the funny tickling bzzzzzzz. This buzz sounds like it's trying to run somewhere, and now like it's pushing someone over in the playground, it's angry. I can't see it. It must be a fly. Somewhere. I climb on to my bed and bounce, eyes jumping here and there over the ceiling. There in the corner, above the door, is a wisp of a spider's web, but no one is home, and there are no prisoners. I bounce higher, the eiderdown squidges up under my toes; Sweetieflower thumps to the floor. The buzzing stops for a second. *Oh poor Sweetieflower*, I say, jumping down. I sit and hug my naked dolly; the buzzing starts again but this time I feel it, the bzzzzzzz is tickling my chest. I hold Sweetieflower out in front of me. Sunlight spikes out her gold sticky-out hair; her eyelashes have grown spindly long in the light, fairy fingers on chubby cheeks. I shake my doll until her brown eyes open. I don't like them closed, for her to be dead like Granny Davy.

Bzzzzzzzz. Bzzz. BZZZZZZZZZZ. It's inside her. Something

is flying inside her head. I think that I would hate a fly zooming around my thoughts. I hold her on my lap and pull at her head. It doesn't take much. She has a weak neck; Daddy is always carrying Sweetieflower off to The Doll's Hospital to have her head reattached. In the second that her golden head parts from the body, a whirr of black and yellow flies into my cheek. I feel the soft burr of its wings push away from my face. I let out a scream, I don't want it in my hair; it's a giant beast, not a fly. How did it fit into her head? I crouch behind my bed, holding on to her body. Bzzzz bzzzzzzz the thing rushes round my room, it swoops up to the ceiling then drops down to my books, then it flies up again, and bashes straight into the window.

'What on earth happened?' My mother appears at the door; her eyes find the beast immediately. 'Did it sting you? No. Lucky girl. A wasp, at this time of the year!... It must've fallen asleep.' My mother opens the window and shoos it out. So easy. Then she picks up Sweetieflower's head that has rolled into the middle of the room.

'Let's get her back in one piece. And how about some clothes, she must be chilly.' But I'm stuck still, wondering how it can be, that the wasp can make a bed in my doll's head, and why Granny Davy couldn't be put back together in one piece.

Afterwards, I'm lonely. Sweetieflower sits all by herself on top of my bookshelves, she's still my best doll, but we don't play anymore. Daddy says it's raw gooseberries that give me the collywobbles but it isn't, my tummy hops around scary things, like when it's dark and ghosts are playing hide-and-seek, or when I think about leaving – like Granny Davy, or when I pick up Sweetieflower and hear the buzzing again. I can't touch her but I hope she's not crying inside.

When Emily was born, we were living in Somerset and both my parents worked long hours at their restaurant in Ilminster. We had a Norland Nanny, Jane, to help look after us; she was nineteen and newly qualified. Her surname, Tottle, used to make me laugh because her firm step was nothing like a totter or a toddle. Jane made everything fun, we danced between crocuses, built space ships with egg boxes, went for adventures in her maroon mini, her white gloves gripping the steering wheel as she sang with me. My parents would try and persuade Jane not to wear her uniform but she said she was proud to wear it. And there was something comforting about the fawn dress with its starched white collar and the soft brown cardi, and the nurse's watch on her chest, and more fundamentally, about her clothes not changing. When we went out, she looked like Mary Poppins; a brimmed hat perched on her carefully pinned bun, and a matching taupe coat that nearly reached her ankles.

Jane became part of the family, so much so that after our parent's marriage dissolved, she remained in touch, sharing her wedding plans and writing letters to me in her distinctive rounded handwriting that I found easy to read. When Emily and I were about seven and three, she came to visit us at Nom's during the Easter holiday with her husband Geoff whose slicked black hair made him look like a film star from the black and white films my father had been showing me. Nom had told us to be gentle, because Jane had been 'a little bit poorly'. But she was unrecognizable. Her eyes, nose and mouth were barely visible, her face was crowded with oozing, red and yellow crusted open sores; her long hair had almost all gone and she was so thin that she looked as if she might snap in half. She sat in Granny Davy's tall chair, her lap conspicuously empty. Normally I would have leapt up but I couldn't look at her. She wasn't Jane, and Emily and I jumped all over Geoff instead.

A couple of weeks later, when we were back in Hampstead, Geoff wrote to say that cancer had been too much for his beautiful, young wife; Jane had died. As Mummy read out the letter, my stomach felt hollow even though I had just swallowed sadness bigger than anything I could have imagined. Whenever I heard the word cancer thereafter, I would see Jane's open face and her smile that had twinkled me out of any sulk, and then Jane disfigured by the disease that stole her away. Her empty lap haunts me still.

'Mummy, Daddy, Emily, Grandma, Nom, Munroe (dog), Leo (cat), Enid, Robert, Timothy, Janice, Richard, Amanda, Peter, Jonesey... please God, keep them alive and well, let nothing bad happen to them.' I'd think this prayer as I huddled down in the mean sheets of my bed at Rookesbury Park School, before sleep took me. If I woke in the small hours freezing cold with the thought I'd left someone out, or put them in the wrong order, I'd apologise to God and pray again, making sure that I included everyone. Failure to do so would result in nausea creeping through my gut, whispering that something appalling would befall one of the listed. Poor them, it wasn't their fault that I'd included them in this list. My religious education more or less stuttered to a halt when I left Rookesbury at twelve, but I continued to pray, with gilded superstition.

Steph is the new babysitter. She's sitting in the armchair by the telephone, her blond hair scrunched back into a huge ponytail, her cheeks highlighted with stripes of yellow blusher that meet wings of pink eye shadow. But it's her mascara that fascinates me the most; both eyes are fringed with heavy legged centipedes. Emily's watching television.

'Are you going to draw their bodies?' I ask.

'Uh… no' Steph says, detailing pointy faces on a spiral notepad, strands of her backcombed fringe falling into the biro etchings. *You'll like Steph, she's doing 'A' Level Art*, my mum had said when I protested at having a babysitter at the age of thirteen.

The phone rings. Steph answers. 'Yuh… Oh no… Is she all right?… No, my dad's collecting me at ten. Yuh, ok. I'll see if I can. Yuh, I'll tell them. Ok. Bye.' She hangs up.

'That was your mum's boyfriend.'

'Peter?' I say, trying to ignore how nervousness has shouted down indifference in her voice. Emily has come to sit by me.

'Yuh. It's your mum. She's uh had a car accident. She's being x-rayed at the hospital now.' Steph picks up the phone again.

'Is my mum ok?'

She's dialing. 'He said she's having her neck x-rayed. Wait… Hello? Dad? Yuh it's me. Their Mum's had a crash; she's at the hospital. They want me to stay the night… no… ok, well can you come later then, to pick me up? I'm sorry, Dad… It's not my fault… Ok. Bye, Dad.' Her dad's angry voice had been leaping out of the receiver.

'Do you think my mum really is ok?' My heart is missing beats, and my fingers are icy. I hear the screech of tyres, the smash of car on car, and see a windscreen in smithereens, splinters of glass

82

made redder and more precious than rubies by my mother's blood. I see nothingness circling.

'Yuh. Look, don't worry. Don't you think you should go to bed now?' Steph goes back to her pointy faces. Emily and I sit close together, watching the TV screen; we jump at the sound of every car stopping outside the house. I squeeze her hand. The phone rings again. It's the first time I've ever wanted it to be Peter ringing.

'Hello, yuh... No my dad says I can't stay the night. He's picking me up at midnight, whatever. Oh. Ok. Yuh. I'll tell them. Ok. Bye.'

'What did he say?' I ask.

'He says that they're gonna let your mum out soon and then they'll come back.' A whoosh of lightness hits my head, my heart calms.

'Shall I make you some tea, Steph?' I ask with outsized brightness.

' Uh... yuh. Ok. Two sugars.'

'Can we make Mummy one too?' says Emily, reaching on tiptoes to get milk out of the fridge.

'It's probably just what she'll need.' I get down a couple more mugs.

When the keys rattle in the lock, we rush to the door. As it opens, Peter pulls out the keys. My mother is behind him; she's yellowy white and ghostly against the inky night.

'I'm fine.' Her smile wobbles above a foam collar. 'It's just a bit of whiplash,' she says as Peter helps her over the flood step that separates our house from the pavement.

'About time. C'mon Steph, get your cash.' Steph's dad, a small, balding man, had arrived a few minutes earlier. He pushes past Peter and my mum and disappears out of the front door.

Thank you for letting my mum be ok, I say when I eventually get to bed, before reciting my list of names to be safe. I had been trying to forget about the list, *if anyone got into your head and heard it, they'd think you so childish* I rebuke myself. *But if I hadn't've said it last night, who knows?*

Our 'O' level Biology teacher, Mrs Corney, was rosy cheeked and kindly faced; she leaned back against the edge of the whiteboard, her grey curls flattened into the medusa-mass of red and blue arrows demonstrating the heart's blood flow. We'd strayed from ventricular specifics to heart attacks and then to dying. The big full stop.

'I think... I think too much about dying.' I had said. Her rheumy blue eyes were deep in thought.

'What part of death worries you, Harriet?'

'Um... you know, the process, the moment of dying... the nothingness afterwards. What happens in nothingness... it happening suddenly... to me, and to my family, friends.'

'Actually, it's very difficult to die,' said Mrs Corney. The body has so many intricate lines of defence, it takes an awful lot to get past them.' Her words were an arm round my shoulder that I cozied into; *she was a nurse for twenty years, so she should know* I reminded myself, when I fought against the whirlpool lip threatening to curl over me, and swallow me down into forever swirling thoughts of nothingness.

'If I become ill, or start losing my marbles, I'll get in a boat and sail off... and that'll be that.' My father took another swig of cider. Lunchtimes with my father and Nom were intense. Ever since I could remember, a fat dictionary would be on hand for Emily and I to use when there was a word we didn't understand. There was never any chitchat; he was particularly scornful of his sister, my aunt Enid, who made a habit of mentioning the weather. At nine years old, I'd listen to his discourses on nature and nurture and conditioning; it was around then that I made the connection between cider and the colour of his language.

'But what would you eat? Who would look after you?' I asked, my head suddenly full of him starving, clinging to the rigging of a small boat being tossed high by monster waves.

'Harriet, how many times do I have to tell you, not to speak with your mouth full?' my father said too quietly.

'Sorry, Daddy. I was just thinking.'

'Well that'd be the whole bloody point, wouldn't it? I wouldn't need food, or anyone. I'd be sailing out to bloody die.'

And this is what my father chose to do some twenty-five years later. Only it wasn't in a boat.

Emily and I sit on crimson velour upright chairs in front of Mr Pidgeon's desk. In spite of the desert of bewilderment that's consumed me in the past few days, ever since my mother broke the news of my father's death, I am struggling hard not to laugh. I plug my mouth and nose with a tear sodden handkerchief, hoping that it will stifle the snorts that are sure to come. I am trembling with the effort of suppressing my laughter. *Oh Christopher... Really. Will you stop that awful guffawing!* Daddy's laugh exasperated Nom, especially when she was concentrating on her crossword. This would make him guffaw harder. My eyes slide sideways to Emily, she nudges my leg with her knee. Mr Pidgeon has produced a glossy brochure to show us the many varieties of coffin at our disposal. His sausage fingers are finding the shiny pages a palaver; he raises his right forefinger to his lips and finds his protruding tongue tip, whitened with a crest of saliva; his finger dips into the minute popping bubbles and the undertaker is able to turn the brochure's pages with wet alacrity. *There's nothing avian about Mr Pidgeon, ha ha ha... he looks like a butcher ha ha ha* I tell my father, knowing that if he were looking down on us at the Cardiff undertaker's, he'd be guffawing.

Bear Cove

Jennifer Howells

*This excerpt includes the opening chapters to the novel provisionally titled
Bear Cove. The year is 1927 and Bear Cove is located deep in the
Appalachian Mountains of North Carolina.*

Chapter 1

Talla Delve stood alone facing the strange wooden cabin, her
hands pushed into thin pockets, her shoulders slightly hunched.
It was stove hot, the sun white and high in a clear sky. Sweat
trickled down her back. She squinted in the bright light, looked
around. Chickens scratched at her feet and she nudged them away
with her foot. Her skin prickled and her nerves were up.

She had been walking since sunrise to get to Bear Cove. Fifteen
just a week, she was the furthest she'd ever been from home. Her
long brown hair was tied back, but a few strands had worked
loose on the journey and they stuck damp to her face. Dark, wet
patches spread out from under her arms where her faded yellow
dress pinched in too tight. The air was still and she fanned her
cheeks with her hands, grateful for even the briefest of breezes.

The cabin was sombre and solid. Its roof jutted over a wide,
dusty veranda, bare but for a rocker missing a curve and fixed to a
lean. Vines grew on its walls and they spread up from the floor
like dark veins, twisting round the frame of the door and two
small square windows which were draped shut. Sprigs of dried
herbs hung beneath the ledges and a fistful of dry basil was
pinned to the door. Talla knew it was to keep the ghosts away and
the sight of it stirred her belly. It fluttered and raced as if it could
see everything she was thinking and doing and she wrapped her
arms tight around her middle, trying to quell its rushing and
wishing it to hush.

She was miles from the road. The folk who lived out in these
parts had little wish to be found. Men holed up with a stock of
weapons and a survivor's gut, each of them scarred by a life lived
without polish. She had passed the edge of a number of rickety

homesteads on her way. Many seemed deserted but at one a man had stood bare-chested on his porch, his trousers held up with rope. A row of empty meat hooks hung from the beams above him and he slowly raised his shotgun and levelled it straight at her. It glinted in the sunlight like a wink and followed her along the path all the way into the shade of the tall pines.

There were women among them too. A rarer lot, they were spoken of with a wide-eyed mythical reverence. Tales of curses they had cast travelled far, drifting up over rocky ridges and down into lean valleys. Curses cast on unfortunate souls who meddled or strayed too close, curses cast on bible carrying redeemers who believed their God had a rightful place of business there. And with them went stories of magical cures, of sickly lives rescued from the edges of death, potions and concoctions brewed to save the unsaveable.

Talla watched a trail of white vapour spiral from the chimney and tail off into nothing. Her mouth was dry. In the fret to leave home, she had forgotten to bring her canteen and the last fresh spring had been an hour back. She could taste dirt and dust and her tongue felt thick as she stepped up onto the porch. Standing by the door, she rubbed her eyes, hesitated, then stepped forward and knocked twice. The cabin let out a low creak and she heard a body stir inside. The sound of feet on wood, the clink of a latch and the door opened to a slit.

'Yer better get right now,' came a woman's gruff voice through the slim opening and Talla found herself staring at the twin dark eyes of a shotgun poking through the gap. She lifted her hands up slightly, her fingers splayed and rigid.

'Please mam, I'm no harm.' She lowered her arms. 'I'm looking for the lady of the house.'

The door shifted a little, revealing more of the woman behind it. Her marble eyes peered out at Talla offering no warmth and she lifted the gun and pointed it at Talla's waist.

'I'm not hiring and not buying neither, so you best just skid child.'

'No, mam, That's not what I want.'

'I ain't got no scraps neither, be gone with yer.'

'Please mam, the tinker said you'd be able to help. He said the lady at Bear Cove could help.'

The woman lowered the gun a little.

Talla bit her bottom lip. The woman's dark eyes were locked firmly on her. Talla waited for her to speak but she made no sound and so Talla spoke again, taking care with her words so there could be no confusion.

'The tinker, mam, he said you'd be able to help. I really be needing your help, mam. I'm real needing it.' She lowered her eyes and put a hand to her belly. 'I got coins, I can pay yer.' She moved her hand to the pocket on her skirt, the coins inside, all dust and dirt money, jangled together.

'The tinker, ey?'

'Yes mam, he said you'd know what to do.'

'Yer on yer own?'

'Yes, mam.'

The woman moved so she was half in and half out of the doorway and rested the gun's muzzle on the floor. She was taller than Talla but not by much, her thin frame covered by a simple grey buttoned-down dress and a stained apron tied around her waist. Her nut brown hair was flecked with silver and pulled back into a braid. Her face was stony and set and she flitted her eyes between Talla and the trees in the distance.

'It's just me, mam. I promise yer.'

The woman's eyes focused on the trees.

'I promise, mam.'

The woman looked at Talla, her mouth twitched and she slowly nodded her head. She took took a last look into the distance and then stood to one side holding the door open.

'Yer better come in child.'

Chapter 2

It was dark inside and Talla stood waiting as her eyes adjusted to the light. The smell of aged smoke mixed with the faint smell of day old stew. Slits of sun streamed in through a badly boarded up window, lighting up dust motes in its thin strips of light.

The cabin was one big room. Against the back wall was a wide pallet bed covered with a faded quilt. Some cartoon strips cut out from the newspapers were pinned above it and a faded red rug that Talla recognised as Cherokee lay on the floor. A blackened cook stove was up against the rear wall and a large cooking pot sat on its top. Pans and pots of different sizes hung from the walls and a table with two chairs stood in the centre of the room. On the far side was a stool and a bookshelf, empty except for three books stacked on the middle shelf.

The woman stood in the corner with the shotgun propped by her side. It was old, probably from Mr Lincoln's war, but it was well oiled and gleamed in a thin beam of light coming from the window. She stood with her back to Talla looking at a shelf heavy with jars and bottles of varying shapes and sizes. Talla noticed now that her plait was thick and long and hung all the way to her waist.

'What have yer tried already, child?' Her voice was still gritty but its harshness had dampened.

'Mam?' Talla moved in closer.

'To rid yerself, what you tried already?' And she turned and faced the girl. Talla looked down at the floor. Her mouth felt gummed up. The past weeks stuck in her throat like a piece of gristle.

'No use being shy child, yer can't surprise me. What yer tried?'

Talla swallowed. 'I had real hot baths mam. I tried me some of that. But it won't quit.' Her eyes raised to the old woman but she couldn't meet her stare. 'I tried the tinker's powder too and his moonshine and nothing.' She paused. 'He said if it don't work to ask you.'

'That tinker's piss be better use to yer than his powder and moonshine and those steamers do nothing for yer.' The old woman's eyes flickered and she snorted, her nostrils flaring wide as bullet holes. 'He's right though, I got something. If it don't rid

89

yer, then not sure nothing will.' She wiped her hands on her apron. 'How far gone are yer?'

'Four months, mam.'

The woman looked at Talla's belly. 'And yer sure there's something sprouting in there? Yer ain't showing. Monthlies can just halt yer know, don't have to mean yer carrying.'

'I'm sure. I been like our Winnie was in the morning when she were carrying Innis.'

Just like it had been for Winnie, Talla hadn't been able to stomach even the sight of eggs. The food they had most plentiful and she couldn't even look at it without her belly turning over.

The woman nodded, 'Take a seat child. I'll get fixing.'

Talla sat down at the table. There was a jug of water next to her and she looked at it with longing.

'Yer thirsting? Help yerself child, it's not long pumped, should still be holding a chill.'

Talla lifted the jug. She poured the liquid into the tin mug next to it and drank the coolness down, not caring that it dribbled down the sides of her mouth, only stopping when it was empty and then she filled it again.

'What's yer name child?'

Talla gulped down the last of the water and wiped her mouth with the back of her wrist. 'Talla, mam,' she exhaled.

'Gidge,' said the woman, 'I'm Gidge,' and she turned and began taking jars down from the shelf one at a time and setting them on the table. They were filled with a circus of trappings. Inside one was a large bullfrog squashed whole into the jar, its skin swampy and knobbly like bark. Another smaller jar was full of grey rabbit's feet, others full of dried herbs and plants. One held just the heads of snakes, crammed in so close together it was as if they were greeting each other with kisses.

'Yer use all these?' Talla asked and reached out her hand and touched the glass jar. The scales shimmered in silvers, greens, blues and reds, all perfectly etched and layered in patterns.

'Not all child, but when I set about concocting, I keeps it all close. It's the herbs yer'll most be needing.'

The room fell quiet as the woman worked and with the warmth and the hush and the weary ache of everything sagging around her, Talla finally let her body soften. She was exhausted from

90

fretting and sorting and the constant want to not be thinking about either. Her eyes drooped and she let them close.

Her mind found comfort in the ordinary sounds of the kitchen. The gentle clink of pots being moved, the slice of knives on old wood, the gentle swish of Gidge's dress as she moved around the room. Without realising, Talla's hand moved to the nape of her neck searching for the reassuring touch of her necklace. The small wooden cross had once been her mother's and was polished smooth like a river stone. She stroked it slowly between her finger and thumb.

'What yer got there?' The old woman's voice pulled Talla back and she opened her eyes.

'This? It's just my necklace, mam.'

The old woman leaned in slowly to take a look.

'Yer best take that off child, no God been in this house for near on twenty years. I tell yer if Jesus himself come to my door asking for a sup he'd get a spit and no more. He ain't welcome here just as I'm sure I'm not welcome where ever he's at.'

Talla untied her necklace and let it trickle into her pocket. Her hand brushed where the necklace had been, feeling the loss in the empty space. She stared at the floor and felt the grip of trouble returning.

'Will it hurt?' She looked at the old woman. 'When I take it, will it hurt?'

'Child, it ain't no cherry tree that's for sure. That's if it works. But yer just as sooner throw it back up than keep it down and then, no, they'll be no pain. Just a wee one a few months down.' She leaned in and patted Talla's arm and then moved to the stove and began adding herbs to the pot.

Talla shivered. Her palms were damp and she wiped them on her dress but then wasn't sure where to place them. She held the edge of the table and her fingers began to pick at the dry wood, scraping off small splinters and letting them fall to the floor. After a while, she spoke, her words quiet but steady, 'I can't have this baby, mam. I just can't.'

Talla stood in the shade of the porch. She had come outside while the woman worked. The air was thick and still and the trees in the distance rippled in the heat. She leaned against the porch fence and watched a hawk circle above. It glided and dipped on the streams of warm air but the rabbits were too quick and eventually it drifted off, away and over the pines that stretched off into the east, reaching out to Tennessee.

Her closest brother, Bray, had tamed a hawk once. Had loved it more than any girl. He taught it to hunt for him, fed it from his hand, smoothed its feathers and whispered softly into its ear. It was a good hunter, kept the family well fed on rabbits. But their father had hated it. He claimed it was dirty vermin and wouldn't go near it. But she knew it wasn't that, he just couldn't stand seeing his son go all doe-eyed over a bird. The piercing hollering that morning, when Bray found the hooded bird dead in the barn, a bullet deep in its feather smooth belly, had cracked the cabin wide open. Before the morning coffee pot was boiled, Bray had packed a bag and left. She had been the one to bury the feathers. Carefully removing its hood, tucking in its spiny wings, feeling its heavy stillness. She had whispered to it, like she'd seen Bray do, a simple prayer she remembered from when she was young, then slipped her fingers beneath it. Clasping its thickness between two hands, she picked it up and held it out in front of her like a full pot, walking with it into the trees until it got too gawky and she had to cradle it in the nook of an arm. A few months later, a card arrived in the mail post-stamped Wyoming; *Mining in Black Thunder. Learning to ride horses in spare time. Tell the old man to go to hell. B.*

Talla stood straight, her eyes alert. She could see someone approaching. At the top of the valley, from between the trees, a girl. She was running at speed, her legs wheeling down the hill while her pale dress billowed up around her like washing in a breeze. In each hand, she held something long that flapped wildly as she moved.

'Mam. Mam, yer got a visitor approaching,' she called out to the woman.

The woman poked her head through the door. She had tied a scarf around her hair and her face was wet and red with sweat. Talla pointed to the child running down the hill.

'It's just Riss. She's been out trapping,' and she disappeared back inside.

Suddenly Riss was by the veranda, all hot and breathing fast, her eyes lively and wide.

'Where's Gidge?' she said, standing with her hands on her waist. The squirrels in her hand hung stiff past her hips, their bushy grey tails dangling past her grubby knees. Talla was silent. Riss shifted her position slightly, her head tilted to one side.

'She inside?' Her words came out fast like they were glued together.

Talla didn't answer.

'She cooking for yer?'

Talla looked to the floor and then nodded.

'Hey, yer ain't the first, ain't gonna be the last either. Gidge'll fix yer. Yer like squirrels? Trapped them this morning.'

She held up the two squirrels, one in each hand. Their heads lolled forward, their mouths slightly ajar. She laid them on their backs on the porch, their tiny arms stretched up towards the sky like they were reaching to the heavens.

'What's yer name?'

Talla didn't answer but looked at Riss. Her light brown hair was short and unruly, tufts stuck out at odd angles. It framed a red, sweaty face which was freckled and there was a smear of dirt streaked down one cheek. She wasn't wearing shoes, her feet were dusty and grey.

'Yer look thirsty.'

'Yer know what, I reckon I am.'

And Riss dropped the squirrels, turned and jumped down off the porch. She looked over her shoulder and called out, 'I'm Riss so yer know. I lives here too. Gidge is my Granmama,' then she ran off behind the cabin.

She was gone only a short while and came back with her hair wet and slick. Her face was freshly clean, droplets of water slid down her temples and she wiped them away with the heel of her palm. She stepped up on to the edge of the veranda, wrapped her arms around the porch post and looked at Talla.

'Yer not going to tell me your name then?'

'I'll tell yer. I'm Talla.'

'Talla.' She repeated the word slowly. 'I never met a Talla before. How old are yer, Talla?'

'Just turned fifteen.'

'I'm eleven. And nine months, to be true like Sue and exact like

93

Jack. So what is it, yer done run off from somewheres?'

'Yer sure ask a lot a questions.'

Riss leaned back, letting herself swing out in an arch from the porch post.

'I'm inquisitive that's all. I think of something and I gotta say it. Can't keep it in.' She pulled herself in and then swung back out again. 'Any words left inside, any words not said, well they just eat away at my gut 'til I have to spit 'em out. I tell yer its best they come out when they wants to. Anyhows ain't no crime in asking no questions is there?' She was quiet for a second. 'Yer planning on staying long?'

'No plans to, no.'

'Just wondered, some do. Girl stayed whole week few months back. Needed healing time. She was swelled good though, not like you. Poor thing near whimpered all the time when she were recovering, muttering on about how he said he was real sweet on her, said he'd buy her a new dress and wed her in Asheville.' She paused, 'So, did he tell you he was sweet on yer?'

Talla stiffened and her fingers curled. 'Yer sure like chewing words don't yer.'

'Don't mean nothing by it. Just wondering an all. It's just conversing right?'

Riss jumped down from the porch and looked up at Talla, her eyes glinting with concentration as she reviewed the older girl.

'Quit doing that,' said Talla.

'I'm just trying to see.'

'See what?'

'If yer a friend or foe. I can tell real quick about people. Gidge says it's a gift I been given.'

There was a silence between them as Riss looked Talla up and down like she was a colt at a sell-off. She stepped forward for a closer look and, standing on tiptoes, she peered into Talla's face.

'Yer need to stop that.'

Talla pushed her gently away.

'Yer ain't got no mean lines that I can see. Yer bite your nails?' Riss went to take Talla's hands in hers but Talla snatched them away behind her back.

'What's that gotta do with nothing?'

'Just helps with the decision making, that's all. No matters, I

94

think you're good anyhows. I can feel it. And Gidge always says to go with the feeling, says it speaks the truth in ways words and seeing just can't. So, friend, yer want to see something real special?'

'Only plan I got right now is standing here.'

'It's real good, swear it.'

'I'm fine just here.'

'Hey, come on, don't be biggety, it's worth it. I ain't lying. But I can't tell you what it is, you gotta see for yerself. Come on, follow me. I swear, yer'll want to see it.'

And she was off at a lick, running straight through the gathering of chickens, sending them scattering like flies round a carcass, raising a racket of screeching and flapping. Reaching the corner of the barn, she turned and beckoned at Talla with a wild, waving hand. She was grinning, her eyes wide and bright, 'Come on, Talla! Come on!'

Talla saw the excitement in her face and felt a rush of curiosity. She turned her gaze away, searching for any distraction in the distance but it was no good, the joy and the thrill in Riss's voice welled up inside her, and she lasted just a minute on the porch before she could stand it no longer and gave in to the pull, scurrying down the steps and hurrying after Riss.

Doubt

Liz Brown

The opening to a historical thriller set in 16th-century Sussex. Johanna Bachmann finds sanctuary in the Protestant England of Edward VI, until she is recognised by a man for whom her death is the only guarantee of safety.

Alone

Confession

I've written wills for many women over the years. Men prefer to use another man but women find a comfort in speaking to one of their own at the end. My father taught me my letters and they have served me well. Reading is a sixth sense giving free entry to another world and sure enough it's one that some godly men forbid their wives as the Devil's work.

An old woman knows when she will not see out the next spell of bad weather, never mind a winter still to come. Too old to work means the smallest portion of what food there is and a seat furthest from the fire. It's how it should be, the natural order, the old make way for the young. They are not long remembered and that is also as it should be.

My own will was written not when I was old but at a time when I had chosen Death over Life. I have it here still, unsigned.

Johanna Bachmann, My Last Will and Testament

I, Johanna, known also as Johann, Jehanne or Joan, leave all my worldly goods to the poor of the community to be distributed as the minister of the Church thinks fit. I do not commend my soul to God. In this my final testament and confession I tell the truth of my life.

I am here known as Joan but my true name is Johanna given for Grace as a child in Zurich where I was born. I was Jehanne for my husband in Geneva. There were times when I took the part of Johann for my own safety.

Such times began when I left my village with the first of the men that I

96

would pray for if I were a godly woman.

It was the spring of 1534 and the city of Muenster, where my sister lay with the Anabaptists, had not yet fallen to the forces of the Antichrist. My father died on his way to Muenster and I was left alone in the world. Born motherless into the Reformers' war against the Papists, it has been my part to live alongside Plague, War, Famine and Death.

I confess that what I saw in those years killed my belief in God. I have lived in a Godless world. Man is no better than any other animal. I carry this true secret with me like a death sentence or the mark of the Devil. There is no heresy greater than to deny God.

At the last I offer thanks for the Christian charity that has given me sweet Sanctuary here. May the Church in Lewes be spared the Evil that I have seen.

This is my true will, testament and confession.

In the fifth year of the reign of King Edward VI,
Lewes in the county of Sussex

Monday 12 October 1551 Day 1: Arrival

Sanctuary: refuge or safety from pursuit, persecution or other danger.

I

Today a preacher arrived. Ten days have passed since the Michaelmas goose and more than that since I went for blackberries in the hot sun up on the Downs. The berries have all been made into a fine fruit cordial with the pulp packed into fresh butter to keep a little longer. Yet this preacher makes me think of that day.

The rain started as he came through the door and is falling still. It throws a fine sheet of moisture over the yard, but is not yet enough to make the fire smoke. He is a good-looking man, tall and solid, but he has no smile, not even for the children, and he has a cold look to him. That cold look has been resting on me almost without a break but I am ignoring him. It is not for the woman I am to encourage the looks of a preacher.

The rain pauses and the children take the chance to run out and away from my teaching. I stand at the door waiting to see a rainbow. The grey clouds are low and dull, moving slowly from the west into position over the uplands. There will be more rain and I have little hope for my rainbow but I stay at the door so that I can keep my back turned against him. I think about that day when I went for berries, looking for clues. If I were a cat my ears would be up and swivelled back to catch any sound from the man behind me. I do not know why he makes me feel so under threat.

It was a stiff walk up onto the Downs that day. My knees ache now in remembrance of how they felt when I had climbed high enough above the valley to stop, and look south to the sea. It was a clear blue just like the sky above me. I had left the farm at dawn, and all that remained of the sunrise was a drift of rose pink stretched across the horizon. As I watched, the colour faded to that of old milk and melted into the sea. In between were the green folds of the sheep walk, layered turquoise and amber by the sun. I was sweating and breathless but it was worth it for the clean air without taint of wood smoke or animals. I wondered then, and I wonder now, if I will be able to climb so far next year.

Fastened to my belt, so that my two hands would be free to save me if I slipped on the thin grass, were a leather bucket and my knife. The knife was tight wrapped in a cloth so that it was hidden from the curious. Once I would have walked for miles before I settled to picking, but these days I head straight to the bramble bushes that I know. They are further from the village than most women care to stray, and higher than the sheep will climb. In spite of the birds that fled, calling a warning as I came near, they were still rich with berries.

I lined my leather bucket with leaves and began to pluck them with care so that no drop of juice should be lost. I am not so old as I would have people believe but I am old enough not to squander my energy on spoilt fruit. When the pail was full then I would pick to eat and not before. In the silence of the chalk hills I heard only the song of birds, the rustling of the lizards in the undergrowth, the sound of crickets and humming of bees. Even the flies had been left behind in the dirt of the village.

I saw the black clouds gathering long before their cargo reached me. There is no cover on the heath and no point in hiding from the rain on a day as hot and blowy as that one was. When it started it was sudden and heavy but beyond the clouds the sky was still as blue as cornflowers. There was an outcrop of white chalk nearby and when I had covered my bowl with the cloth from around the knife, I went and sat on it until the rain had passed. I balanced the half-full bucket between two rocks for safety and swept my skirts up under me like a fat damp cushion. I pulled the scarf off my head and turned my face up to the cleansing freshness pouring down on me.

My loosened hair smelt of smoke and food and I ran my fingers through it teasing out the tangles, but it soon became no more than a sodden mass tracking water down my back. The uncovered knife was in my right hand: with the left I bunched the stuff and tried to cut it through, hacking at it until my head felt light and free again. A memory, a pang of longing for lost freedom, was fast suppressed. The discarded hanks were the colour of roast chestnuts stuck with a little dirty grey ice. My neck was cold where they had lain. I rolled them into a ball and tucked them under the rock for nature to make use of.

The rain swept on propelled by the blustering wind, leaving me in sunshine, and I took my pail and my knife back to the bushes. I had drunk the rain as it fell but by choice I had eaten nothing that day and now I was eager to finish my task. My shortened hair dried fast to its natural bright auburn splintered with silver. My neck began to burn in the sun. And to this point I have no clue what link I make to the cold-eyed preacher.

I felt the presence of the riders before I heard or saw them. I sensed the cocoon of silence nature wove around them in the rain-thickened air as birds and insects waited for them to pass. The pail was full, my lips stained with the latest pickings, and my headscarf lay abandoned some distance away on the white chalk. I sank as low as I might amongst the bushes, bowing my head down as the little birds do when they see a sparrow hawk take to the air.

Rather than make their horses step through the briars, they called me over to the trail. I stood head bowed next to the lead horse ready to drop to my knees if it seemed wise. The pail of berries, leaf cover discarded, was ready as a sacrifice. A small offering might save much else, and I have never had a problem in abasing myself to those more powerful than me. These men might rape or maim me if they chose, but probably not now, not here. The local man, one I recognised as a buyer of Priory land, spoke first. Having identified me as too old and ugly to be of interest, he was already turning away.

He said to his companion, 'It's the French woman from the farm below Kingston.'

And to me, 'You, what are you doing up here on your own with your head all uncovered?'

I waved the pail towards him, eyes fixed on the ground, expecting him to knock it from my hand.

Moving on, he shouted back to me, 'Careful they don't take you for a witch doing your harvesting up here, strayed so far from home.'

The second rider, judged a churchman from the bottom of his gown, which was all I could see without raising my eyes and risking the charge of insolence, shifted his horse a little closer.

'French, you say?'

'Or from that direction. French, Flemish, all one up here.'

'She has the pelt of a vixen. Witch – or heretic perhaps?'

The level voice put me in his Christian scales and weighed me. The landowner had no desire, however, for a heretic to be found in his territory. He trotted on, shouting over his shoulder, 'Just a foolish old woman.'

I had to wait until my hands had stopped trembling before I could put fresh leaves on the pail of berries. It took three tries before I could tie my headscarf over my shortened hair. I hid my knife as before and turned back to the village. The folds of the Downs were in shadow in the early evening sun and the landscape seemed treacherous and alien.

The sharp new wood of the doorframe is digging into my side and reminds me where I am, ears still swivelled. I have my clue and I twist my hands together so that he cannot see that they are trembling as they did when the churchman called me a heretic. The preacher is not the man on the horse but he has the same smell: the smell of burning books and flesh.

II

I turn my trembling hands to kneading the dough that has been resting by the fire. There is always work on a farm and Alice, the mistress here, is happy enough to leave such indoor tasks to me while she helps her husband elsewhere.

I have chosen badly as I must work at the table where the visitor is sitting. He is a dark man, clean-shaven, hair cropped short, and dressed in black as his calling demands. I wonder indeed why he risks his fine clothes so close to my coarse white flour. I stand in front of him: a tall woman, gawky in my old and shapeless kirtle. I keep my eyes on my strong calloused hands as they work. His, I can see, are pale and unmarked, the nails neatly trimmed. I almost ask him if he has no work to do but then I think that I am perhaps the task he has been set.

I concentrate on the warm elasticity of the floured dough, knocking it back ready for the oven. It is his chance to catechise me in his well-trained voice, his words chosen with care.

'So you teach the children their letters from the Bible?'

He has been watching me earlier so he knows the answer to that one and follows it with, 'They do well?'

'Yes sir, for such little children.'

'Who learnt you your letters?'

'My father, sir.'

Into the silence that follows comes an image of my father as I saw him last. Foolishly I am distracted and the preacher's next question catches me out.

'From your accent I would guess it was from Luther's translation in the High German, his New Testament perhaps... Was your father a teacher of the Holy Word?'

I nod unthinking but press a floured hand to my mouth to stop any betraying words that might follow unintended. I do not know how the man could have guessed my thoughts or what calculations he has made to ask that question. My father's beliefs are best not discussed here.

He notes my alarm and presses home his advantage, 'You are from one of the German states perhaps? Or the Low Countries?'

And when I do not reply, he asks, 'Did you ever travel to the great Reform cities? Zurich or Strasburg? Or Geneva?'

His eyes, grey with a dark rim and black lashed, are fixed on me intently. I do not know why he attaches such importance to my travels. They will not tell him where I lost my soul. Still I detect a sense of doubt behind his fleeting passion and it attracts me. I have seen too many bigots and I know all about doubt.

The silence between us erupts into a cacophony of sound as the children burst in carrying hens' eggs and singing loudly. Alice, her voice strong above theirs, follows with a basket of big sour apples fresh picked from the tree just beyond the yard. This tree is the first in the orchard that she plans.

Alice is a comely, buxom woman. She was not born a farmer's wife but a stranger like this man would not know it. Her yellow hair is well hidden under her cap and her good red gown is cut short as suits a countrywoman who must contend with mud from dawn to dusk. She has a ready smile, a loud voice and the energy for two when it is required. It was her husband who brought the man here but she greets him warmly as if he were a guest of her own choosing.

The plain loaves should be in the oven and I have not checked the mutton pottage left to stew over the low fire. It will soon be time to eat and I am behind with my share of the work.

I quickly shape two loaves and put them to bake, stir the stew that thankfully has not boiled dry, and collect some apples to chop and bake inside the rest of the dough. I think I feel the preacher's stare following me but when I turn little Matthew is sitting in his place and the heretic hunter has gone from the room.

Tasks complete, I rest a moment, leaning my back against the wall furthest from the fire. I am out of Alice's way here.

The man has made me think back to my childhood, to my father in the main room of our home in a village not so very far from Muenster, before that city gained its evil reputation. I can see the printed letters of the High German script in front of me. There too are the pamphlets and the woodcuts, the pictures of the Pope as the Anti-Christ, the images of the corrupted priests and monks of the old Church. I think back over that time to try and guess what might interest or anger an English reformer.

III

When we come to eat, I find the only place left at table for me once the food has been brought out is at the preacher's side. I do not see how he can have engineered this arrangement but I am reluctant to believe that it is chance. After he has spoken the Grace he returns to the same vexed question of my travels but from another direction.

'They say you are from France. What makes them think that?'

I chew stolidly and do not answer.

He says, 'I was in Paris once. Were you ever there?'

'I've been to many places. Don't expect me to remember them all.'

I cannot soften my tone. I know that I should answer him plain and bold but I cannot do it. Why of all cities does he ask of Paris? Fear makes me defensive and he is so close to me that we are almost touching. He is looking directly at me and I know he is trying to guess my age. Alice and her family believe me to be past forty and maybe not so far off those years where a woman becomes a burden to her family. In fact I am four years short of two score and I think he is calculating the extent of my lie.

I pull Ann, near four years old and restless, on to my lap in a pretence of calming her. I swing her legs into the gap between us, forcing him to move further away from me. I bend my head over her so that my face is hidden or at least I cannot see him. Soon after, I use the child as a pretext to move away entirely, although she is puzzled because I am paying no attention at all to the tale that she is telling me.

Later I take my opportunity to do a little spying. While he is telling his hosts, farmer Matthew and sweet Alice, about his travels and his learning, I go to his room. As a guest and a man of God he has been given a small box of a space under the eaves. I take the precaution of laying a spare wool blanket over my arm. If anyone should see me they will approve of my consideration for the visitor.

He travels light this preacher, just a long leather pack that he can sling over the back of his horse and whatever he carries within his clothing. The pack is folded on a low table next to the wooden bed. A Bible rests on top of it. It is a fine Bible, well bound in smooth leather inlaid with gold, the corners protected with silver metal, and printed on fresh vellum; an exceptionally fine Bible for a travelling man.

I would like to search his pack but it is laced tight closed. The merest glance tells me that this is a careful man. Almost certainly he will notice if I unlace the leather roll. I put the blanket on the end of the bed for him to use if he chooses. The bed is very short for a man of his height.

While I hesitate over how far I dare to pry, I pull open the shutter on the tiny window. I slip my fingers out through the mullions to see if I can feel the strength of the rain. If he finds me in his room, I can plead my duties. If he finds me looking through his belongings, I am lost.

And yet later as I try to sleep, I think of him in the room under the eaves listening to the rain as I am listening to it. I think of him curled in the short bed, under the blanket that I placed there for him. I think of him as a woman thinks of a man. Restless, I peer through a part open shutter at the rain puddling in the yard below. I fear he will be obliged to stay another night.

The Sound of Sleep

Annabel L. Mountford

This is an excerpt from the first chapter of The Sound of Sleep.

Birth

I am born as a man of thirty-two, during the hanging of a gentleman named Victor Terrell. My new eyes squint against the glare of the dusty morning sun, my nose instantly clogged with the soot of the city and I spit and dribble and heave. And I gnaw my teeth at the blurred persistent chatter of the humans surrounding me, drowning me in their life. I dare to open my eyes further, drinking in my first sight – the silhouette of the condemned man shadowed by the apparatus that will enable him to tap dance on air.

I take my first breath and feel the sharpness of autumn biting to my lungs – the taste of excrement and fire sticking to my tongue. I am intoxicated, addicted to this sensation. I want more and more, dragging the air into my body until my chest expands and threatens to tear my ribs. The desperation to exhale and cough overwhelms me – my contracting muscles stab painfully at my ribs, the respired air scratching, clawing its way back up my throat. I struggle to keep the air in my lungs, breathing quickly, urgently, until a fit of dizziness overcomes me. Another satisfying feeling, in some ways, as if my bones have born their own gravity, shifting my axis.

My skin feels tight; I'm constricted, condensed, squeezed into this flesh, wrapped into this nauseating pink tissue. I flex my new muscles, working them in, making them stretch, trying to introduce some flexibility into this pulpy patterned prison, where I shall stay until I am told to go.

My birth is different every time – new eyes, new lungs, new tongue. I am always aware of what to expect, and yet each time I am still repulsed by this feeling of life. I had promised myself not to make a spectacle this time, but alas, I am human once more.

I compose myself and search the crowd for my source. It is a

105

crowd of rich and poor, of young and old. A crowd united only by the desire to see a man die. She knows I am here, of course. She is the one who created me. But she ignores my pain of birth, of this extraordinarily chaotic concoction of senses. She is preoccupied, I suppose, by the hangman placing the white hood over her father's head. His arms have already been tied by his side, and a young boy, no doubt the hangman's apprentice, positions the prisoner over the trap. The boy has to jump on his toes to get the noose over Mr Terrell's head; he lines the rope with his spine and runs back down the stairs.

The sun shines from the east making her father, Victor, glow around the edges, as if the angels he prays for are here, at this moment, extracting his soul prematurely. I feel sorry for the girl, and her mother, but perhaps care less than I should. I am distracted by the sight of the sun waltzing around me, stroking my jaw, teasing my fingers. The way the rays bounce from person to person, swirling, twisting into every crevice it can find. How it gleams on some, yet merely lulls on others. This warmth comforts my new form, yet I shiver. I shiver because my source has shivered. Because the priest has finished his final prayer.

I go to her, her body pulling me, drawing me to her. I stride with difficulty – the movement feels strange, a balancing act. Everything so stiff and unwilling – the joints, muscle and bone and cartilage fresh and unused. I feel like a new pocket watch, reluctant to turn my cogs for the first time, but moving with more ease with each new motion. With all the grace I can muster, I stand behind her and place my hand upon her shoulder, barely raising my elbow. She flinches, and then raises her own hand to grasp her mother's shaking fingers by her side. Both mother and daughter stand vibrating against the cool breeze that lifts their hair and gently places it behind their shoulders.

A Mr William Calcraft takes his place next to Victor. I tighten my grip on her shoulder. This will not be pleasant. I have seen this man perform before, many years ago for me, but just a few cycles of the sun for the rest. He was a crowd teaser, an entertainer of death. Calcraft sneers at the body that lies at his mercy then turns slowly, deliberately, striding with a visible skip to the bolt release. His hand hovers over it, his face to the crowd. A silence falls, those who have been gossiping and speaking idly of whims and weather turn their attention towards the scaffold. The silence thrills me, creating a chill at the nape of my neck that oozes like honey to my spine, my ribs, my groin. The girl's mother turns away, but the child stares on, resolved to watch the mercilessness of men.

This is what Calcraft has been waiting for. He grasps the bolt and pulls. I had expected the silence to continue. I had expected the crowd to stand in respect whilst they watched a man drained of his life. The crowd cheers. Men shout and women scream or sigh as they reach for their smelling salts and fans with a smirk upon their lips.

The wife and daughter stand in front of me, their breath hanging in the morning air as if in mockery of their own existence. It is in this static moment that the mother crumples into her skirts like a wax candle next to the hearth. A small gaggle of women surround us and take the poor breathless woman away. But the show is not over. The girl continues to watch as Mr Calcraft decides his victim is taking too long to die, and so jumps through the platform and hangs from Victor's legs. The crowd erupts – some cheer whilst others merely groan in disgust.

I have grown stiff watching, so as I place my other hand on the girl it slides from her shoulder awkwardly. I try again, and this time she raises her own hand to keep mine in place. She turns to see me for the first time. Her eyes are dry, but the memory of tears cling to her face, engraving gleaming trails between the layers of London filth. Her eyes are wide, in a way that only a child's can be, as if in a constant state of surprise. I notice the colours in those eyes, the brown with the yellow, like gold sparkling at the bottom of a muddy pond. I wonder what mine are like this time. I stroke her dirty blonde hair – it is the sort of blonde that is unsure of itself, that lacks confidence. My fingers feel like the breeze sauntering through her hair, a touch of comfort. She almost wants to smile. But her smiles have been stolen and she supposes she will never feel the muscles in her cheeks again. She looks back to her father with a quiver in her jaw.

'Edmund?' says the abandoned child.

'Yes, Harriet,' I reply.

'Take me home.'

'Yes,' I say. 'Harriet? What colour are my eyes?'

'Eyes?' she says, reluctant to tear her own glazed eyes from the view of her father, now limp and gently swaying in the morning zephyr. She inhales heavily, a sound sharp and soft at the same time, and turns to see me.

'I cannot see from here. You must crouch down.'

Bending down is difficult and requires more concentration than I initially thought. Harriet stands patiently whilst I manoeuvre my limbs, yielding to gravity, balancing my spine between hovering heels. She lays her hand on my shoulder to steady me. I am close enough to feel her breath mingle with mine; she bites her lips while she studies my eyes and contemplates the colours.

'Purple.'

'Purple? What kind of purple?'

'Come, let me show you.'

Harriet grabs my hand and runs into the filtering crowd. She weaves with ease between the rustle of skirts, the swaying bustles and crinolines, and so, of course, do I. She dances around horses strapped to their cabs; her feet steady on the cobbled ground. Ladies and gentlemen mutter of the insolence of children as they stroll out of the Newgate prison gates. They chatter enthusiastically about the fashionable topic of gossip – the scandal of the pharmacist. I run in tow of the girl – she cups her hands over her ears, protecting them from the airborne words:

'A good riddance to society!'

'He smoked the poppy's tears.'

'What a monster he was!'

'The wife was once of the night.'

'My brother-in-law's niece used to buy from that wicked man!'

'He drank.'

'"Sins of the father shall be visited upon tenfold unto the son." Or the daughter, so I hear.'

'He gambled.'

'I hear the child is illegitimate, born of sin.'

'An Indian street-walker.'

I feel the cold hard defiance of Harriet. I feel her face harden to stone and the coolness of her blood as it circulates her veins, because it is my blood too. The words whip through our hair and disintegrate to ash and dust, floating like fine snowflakes into the cracks of the cobbles. There they lay with the rest of the dirt and soot, fossilising.

Harriet knows her shortcuts, through the alleys and over the walls we run and run. Away from the words, away from the hanging body of her father, away. We run like the child she is, condensing the action to our fluid knees. We run down Warwick Lane, crossing over to Fleet Street where the fresh bundles of newspapers and penny dreadfuls are being hauled into the streets by boys shouting 'Terrell Dead at Dawn' to passers-by. Up Wych Street and onto Drury Lane, where the ominous sounds of consumption rattle every ribcage in sight, and where the beggars pull on Harriet's fine mourning skirts. We cross Broad Street, evading the waste left by horses and narrowly avoiding the whips and wheels of impatient cab-drivers. Crossing Oxford Street is equally as difficult, weaving in between the early morning tradesmen delivering fabrics from the orient.

We run north up the shadow-cast Hart Street where the sun is yet to touch, and halfway down, on the corner of Bury Street, we come to a rapid stop and catch our breath. How exhilarating it is to have acid pumping through me, the surge of energy and power. I gasp and hyperventilate, feeling the bitter taste of sweat and bile in my mouth. We hunch over, resting our slick palms on the curve of our knee caps, concentrating on circulating acrid air back into our bodies.

'Purple,' she breathes.

'Hm?'

'Purple, look.'

I follow her finger to a poster on a darkly varnished shop door – in fine calligraphy the poster reads:

'TERRELL'S THAUMATURGE'

The No. 1 Cure-All for All Ailments

With the mystical healing properties of the ingredients of the orient Mr Terrell presents a medicine that can cure all your problems as well as preventing those yet to come. One teaspoon before bed, and by morning all your ailments with be miraculously cured. Don't waste your pennies on quack medicine when you can have one remedy to cure them all! Soon to be available as a powder and pill.

Cures: Indigestion, Insomnia, Headaches, Women's Pain, Diarrhoea, Constipation, Toothache, Rheumatism, Gout, Fever, Miasma Poisoning, Typhoid, Typhus, Baldness, Cholera, Boils, Excessive Perspiration, Addiction, Alcoholism, Bad Blood, Bile, Phlegm, Paleness, Fatigue, Influenza, Measles, Tuberculosis, Dyspepsia, Hysteria, Swelling, Coughs, Colds, Bruises, Muscle pain, Inflammation, Brittle Bones, Nerves, Palpitations, Rashes and many more.

On the poster is the image of a fashionably attired family – a man, woman and child grinning as they pour the medicine onto spoons. In the middle is a large drawing of a bottle filled to the brim with a beautiful coloured liquid that seems to be radiating a blue-flamed hue. I step back and gaze up at the rest of the building. Crushed beneath four floors of red bricks and white windows is an ebony framed shop. TERRELL'S PHARMACY glows in gold above a window display of glass bottles, all containing colourful concoctions of every known cure. In the centre of the display, a bronze and glass display case sits empty.

'Purple?' I said, pointing to the potion on the poster.

'Papa asked what colour the magic medicine should be, and I said purple. Lavender kind of purple, like your eyes. Lav-en-der.'

Harriet pronounces the word carefully, but it sounds clumsy in her young mouth. She whispers it again under her breath to feel the shape of the word as she walks into the shop with a tinkling sound that makes me flinch. I follow her inside and feel a warmth flood my being. The shop is hot indeed, but the warmth comes from Mr Greene, the young apprentice. Mr Greene has scooped Harriet into his arms the moment she stepped into the shop, and now he is crushing her in his arms, deflating her. It is only now that she allows herself to cry again. Her feet dangle two feet above the floor whilst she dampens his coat with her tears.

Mr Greene is nearing the end of his adolescence but he looks like a man well into his twenties. If it had not been for the soft curve of his jaw you would have been easily deceived. He holds the weight of his trade on his broad hunched shoulders, stooping slightly as if constantly at the pill-grinder. He has dark hair and dark skin, which sparks the local gossip of 'Indian blood' in his

110

veins. As he crushes Harriet to calm her hysteria I feel his weight on my shoulders and wish to be held in such a way. I feel rather unnerved at this thought; we do not naturally crave physical companionship. What a curious idea that would be.

Despite having just witnessed the death of Harriet's father, this moment is much more intimate. I feel unwanted, unnecessary, and so I turn to wait outside, away from the warm sickly smell that's burning my new nostrils, and away from the indecently open familiarity of Elmer Greene.

'Edmund! Wait, where are you going?' says Harriet.

'Edmund? Miss Terrell, who is Edmund?' Mr Greene looks around the shop.

'Mr Greene, this is Mr Dewson.' And thus our introduction has been made.

'I can't see anyone, are you playing?'

'No! Stop being so silly, he's right here!'

'Miss, it's been an awful morning for you, why don't you have a little rest in your room and I'll bring up some bread and jam when it's lunch time.'

'Jam?'

Harriet's prospect of jam silences the protests shuffling through her mind, and so she agrees to go to her room. She slides between the counters and out the door in the back corner. I go to follow her, but find myself incapable. So far distracted by Mr Greene, I had not noticed the mesmerising interior of Mr Terrell's Pharmacy – but now I stand utterly bewitched.

I gaze at row upon row of glass phials filled to the brim with brightly coloured liquids, at the artistically stacked bottles of pills and the jars of herbs and spices neatly labelled on the counter. I am surrounded by languages of medicine; alchemical codes, chemist's symbols and periodic shorthand, all handwritten in the calligraphic hand of the pharmacist. A mahogany counter, dense with drawers, occupies the majority of the shop and is strewn with bronze objects that are delightfully mysterious to my untrained eye. Sitting to the left of this vast work surface is an ornate cash register, polished to a dull sheen, and next to that a set of weighing scales, which Mr Greene is currently using to package some sort of herb into jars. I walk over to him, with the intention of smelling the herb, when he looks up and stares straight at me.

111

Just as I begin to worry, he sneezes and continues with his employment.

Harriet walks back into the room, curious of my whereabouts. She sneaks behind Mr Greene, slyly opening one of the many drawers in the cabinet behind him, and grabs a handful of lavender before running down the hall. He knew she was there, of course, and he smirks when he hears the stomp of her small feet in the hall. This time I follow her. We go straight down the corridor, passing the sweet warm smell of a fire burning impatiently in the room to our right, a closed door to our left, and up the narrow stairwell that leads to the apartments above.

We wind around the stiff, square banisters – I clutch on to each one to support my body's defiance of gravity. The old dark-stained wood feels coarse and worn beneath my soft new hands, a new feeling for me to remember. I forget so much. I seize for the hem of Harriet's dress to feel the contrast. The dress is rough too, but in a subtle, delicate way; much like Harriet herself. I go from one to the other, fabric, wood, fabric, wood. I wonder if the colour of the fabric would make it feel different. Why have I forgotten this? Would a purple dress feel different to her black mourning one?

As Harriet reaches the final step she stops and sways. With each gentle rock the step creaks beneath her feet. She composes a two-note tune she knows by carefully distributing her weight from one foot to the other. She takes a step to the side and points at the floorboard. I carefully place my feet as she did and imitate her movements, mimicking the same tune she created. I wobble slightly, finding the rocking sensation unbalancing and disorientating. I reach out and rest my hand on her shoulder to ground myself.

She takes my hand and leads me across the worn waxed floorboards; I follow her feet so as not to step on the cracks. We pass her parents' rooms and slip straight into her own, closing the peeling white door behind us.

Harriet slumps like a rag doll on the crisp blue linen that suffocates her bed. I myself sit at the foot, staring around the bare white-washed room. There is the bed, of course, and a small wooden chair beside a desk in the corner next to the vast sash window. A cupboard looms at the end of the bed that contains her four gowns – two for weekdays, one for Sunday and one for school. She is wearing her new gown, her mourning dress, which is to be worn for at least a year. She hates it already. I extract her hard polished shoes from her feet and place them gently on the floor.

'I am sorry, Harriet, about your father,' I say, testing the fresh wound.

Harriet nods and looks at her hands.

'Why could he – why could Elmer not see you?' she asks, not wishing to dwell on the morning's events.

'Harriet, I'm just for you. I am *your* friend.'

'So none but I can see you?' She raises her eyebrows.

'No, just you.'

'Does that mean I'm special? Like Mary? Are you an angel come to protect me?'

'I'm here for you, yes,' I hesitate before I add, 'but I'm not an angel.'

'Are you going to stay?'

'Would you like me to stay?'

'Oh, yes!' She looks at her hands and furrows her brows. 'Are you a secret?'

'I suppose I am, yes.'

Harriet looks towards the window, wondering if her father has yet arrived in heaven.

'Good. I do like having secrets,' she says to the clouds. 'I'm really very good at keeping them.'

Selling Up

Eley McAinsh

This is the first chapter in a collection of essays entitled Mapping the Heart, *in which Eley returns to the formative places in her life; the places that have shaped her identity and consciousness and made her who she is today.*

The agent closes every door after every viewing. When I come back the house feels strange and I go from door to door, opening each one, reclaiming each room. I check for footprints and for scraps of leaves carried in on the soles of well-polished Oxfords. Today, I found a single dark hair, six inches long and thick as fuse wire, on the landing in front of the bathroom door.

It's a family house in a family garden in a hollow at the end of a cul-de-sac on the edge of a 1950s estate. The roads are named for a rural past, real or imagined: Fairfield, Longmeadow, Old Pasture. Detached but unassuming, on a large plot, the house is built of mottled brick, nine-inch solid walls of ochre and rose, with tile detail and a gable triangle of greyed-wood flashing. The white-framed replacement windows are diamond-paned and the front path crazy-paved. The front door is glass-panelled and not at all secure, but even after Mum was harangued on her own doorstep by a large unkempt stranger ('Why don't you want a free roof check? Are you too stupid to understand?'), and even after a visit from the community policeman, Vince, with kindly warnings and a sheaf of leaflets and stickers for the door ('No cold callers!'), the locks remained flimsy and the chain unused.

The drive slopes down to the garage and the carport, widening at the bottom. It has an awkward curve which even now recalls the fraught hours Dad spent teaching us all to drive. The terse command 'Straight back at that!', in a tone straining to be patient, became a family catch-phrase. I still don't know what it means. After I'd passed my test he would stand watching from the kitchen window as I reversed back up the drive. For almost forty years, if I knew he was there, I always, but always, misjudged the line, chewing up the lawn on one side or sidling into the beech hedge on the other, the sound of twigs on paintwork like nails on slate.

Under the kitchen window, where Dad stood watching and Mum spent large portions of each day at sink or hob, the drain blocks easily with blown leaves and now I keep watch with an old trowel, scraping out the stinking mulch so white suds and greasy scraps don't spill across the path and create a bad impression when prospective buyers come to view.

I always go out when there's a viewing and, depending on the weather and the time of day, rotate coffee shops, Costa, Nero, M&S, and parks: Virginia Water with its secret coves and totem pole and Savill Garden with its whale-back pavilion of larch shingle and oak levitating in the Surrey air. It seems best not to know who's looking, nor what they say to the agent, and what they whisper, rudely, conspiratorially, behind his back.

The sale is sad but necessary, and after one broken agreement and many wasted weeks, more pressing. In the space between the agreement being made and being broken, most of the furniture was loaded into an Italian removal van and taken away to my brother's home in Bergamo. It seemed impossible that everything would go in as more and more was piled up on the drive.

'Yes, that's to go.' I heard Rich's voice as he trailed the guys around the house and into the garage. 'Yes, that too. And that... and this, if there's room.' A complete Ducal bedroom suite: triple wardrobe, oak-fronted pine-backed, a dressing table with a curved, hinged mirror and two small drawers, baize-lined for jewellery, and a bed which needed to be dismantled to get it down the stairs. Two enormous settees, cushioned in a fine chenille of stippled beige and fawn, comfortable, quite new, but never really loved. The fridge and freezer from the garage, released from the insulating wooden huts Dad built round them the winter they stopped working because of the cold, leaning together leaking ice-melt onto the brick paving. Pictures, televisions, china and glass rough-wrapped in old waffle-weave tea-towels nesting in an odd array of cardboard fruit boxes and plastic crates. Green leather-topped desk and industrial drawing board, Admel office chair, its split grey plastic seat sutured with silver gaffer tape. A library of engineering textbooks and two boxes full of Dad's notes and files: patent applications for small but vital pieces of aero-engine and guided missile and cockpit gadgetry.

Among the pictures propped amidst the furniture, a copy of Tretchikoff's 'The Chinese Girl', recently retrieved from the loft. Dad's recollection of 'falling in love' with her one night in 1953 is more than vivid memory. Repeating the story, he relives the moment in every detail, seeing her for the first time, in an art shop window near Richmond Bridge, on the way home from the cinema with Mum. They had married earlier that summer, three weeks after the Coronation, and come south on the night train from Edinburgh, the contents of Mum's bottom drawer sent on ahead in two tea chests to furnished rooms in Twickenham.

Dad vowed that night in Richmond that one day he would buy 'the green lady' and so, some years later, he did, a Timothy Whites print for their second home, a new Bracknell Development Corporation house in Saffron Road. I hesitated to let her go and paused to take a picture of the picture on my phone before it was slotted into the van. The original sold for close to a million pounds in March 2013, the month we discovered that Mum had only weeks to live.

The removal men could have been Romanian, Rich reckoned, on account of their poor Italian and strong commitment to hard work. Between five o'clock and eight, as dusk then darkness fell, they laboured, ingenious and precise, sustained with pork pies and chocolate biscuits, till everything was loaded, tight-packed as a Rubik's cube.

After they'd gone, heading I believe to Dover via Birmingham, I set to cleaning: brushing swags of cobweb, grey and sticky, from newly-exposed walls and skirting boards, hoovering hairballs and Kirby grips and tiny chips of Lego from carpets where, until two hours ago, beds had stood unmoved for 20 years. The house three-quarters emptied, most rooms were bare. In the pine-panelled living room I kept moving the two remaining armchairs to try to fill the space and then reclaimed two yellow-shaded table lamps from the charity shop pile in the garage to soften the lighting. Once, practising *grand jetés* while everyone else was out, I broke a ceiling light in this room. Mum and Dad returned to find it shattered, hanging by a single wire. They were cross, my younger siblings wide-eyed and smug. The incident has been fixed in family legend ever since as the day I kicked the light off the ceiling.

The back bedroom was empty, but for a taped coil of brown co-ax hanging from the aerial point in one corner and a telephone extension on the floor in another. In Mum and Dad's room the brass-headed bed was still piled with flounced-pillows and spread with a thin cover in faded floral shades of pink and peach and apple green. Standing on the landing, looking in, you wouldn't know that the wardrobes and drawers, built by Dad over many weekends, were empty.

It was fine, quite satisfying in fact, to return the house to some kind of order after the removal men had gone and my brother, now bed-less, had left to stay with his daughter, my eldest niece, in Forest Hill. Fine, until I knelt to retrieve a card that had fallen down behind a radiator. A Christmas card, with a fairy-cum-angel swooping daintily over a Christmas tree, whimsical, in shades of blue and green and silver. Of all the cards it might have been, it was my Christmas card to Mum and Dad, last Christmas, wishing them a very happy Christmas, of course, and a New Year 'full of good things.'

I have been living back in the family home since the beginning of March, just two months into that New Year, when Mum finally capitulated and consulted her doctor about the stomach pain that had been becoming more bothersome over several weeks and which suddenly became acute. It was the week after her 85th birthday and the helium balloons still bobbed in the corner of the living room, pink and silver, a huge '8' and '5', two hearts and two stars, weighted with bells. GP Monday, consultant Friday, tests, and one week later results, crisis and emergency admission. My middle sister, Maxine, was with her, comforting and calming but shaken by the sudden descent into danger. I was at home, failing to distract Dad from his fear. An ambulance ride between hospitals and a long, long wait in A&E. Mack and I swapped over in late afternoon, in a curtained cubicle beside the check-in desk, where the queue of trolleys and joshing paramedics in green boiler-suits never seemed to get any shorter.

More tests, needles, samples, X-rays, ultrasound, questions, history, notes mislaid and recovered, endless repetition: Name? Address? Date-of-birth? Mum was exhausted and uncomfortable and fractious until, at about seven o'clock, a young A&E consultant pulled back the felted-paper curtain and came into the cubicle. The usual greetings, an apology for the wait, a surreptitious glance at notes to check his patient's name, and suddenly, with no whisper of warning, he was talking of 'this shadow on your lung.' They couldn't be sure, of course, until further tests, but it was there, quite clearly on the X-ray. He moved on with scarcely a pause, to arrangements for Mum's admission to a ward, to the drips and blood transfusions that would stabilise and strengthen her for further tests and treatment. As suddenly as he came, he left, leaving us confused. Lung? Shadow? Mass? The nurse who accompanied us to the ward at nine o'clock had QARANC epaulettes on her tunic and in the wide metal lift, filling the space with chat, we all agreed that Frimley Park was a very long way from Camp Bastion.

The hospital wasn't built when we moved to Frimley in 1967. It opened, just a quarter of a mile down the Portsmouth Road from the house, in 1974, the same year as the local section of the M3. The new motorway cut a swathe through ranges and pine woods from Sunbury to Basingstoke, but here in this far corner of Surrey it re-sectioned residential streets, leaving loose-ends of old roads – Brackendale and Waverley – stranded, like little ox-bow lakes. Dad remembers the ranges and pre-motorway A roads from army days: a motor-cycle training course in the icy January of 1946, and briefings at the tin shack Lupin Cafe on Bagshot Hill. The cafe closed in 1973 and a neat close of new houses – Lupin Close – was built on the site.

They held 'Come and See' days at the new hospital before it opened, for local residents to wander, soles squeaking on polished rubber floors, into theatres and maternity wards and stainless steel kitchens, before the final, pre-opening, deep clean. I had just started my last year of school and got an evening job in the cafeteria, two hours each day after class. I didn't last long, in my pink overalls and thin teenage skin, and it was many years before I had need to return, scooping one of my toddler nephews into A&E, his split lip bleeding onto the glazed rubber floor. The hospital has grown and grown, outwards, upwards, doubling in size in 40 years and now, in a crowning flourish, it sports a heli-pad on the roof. Commissioned just as Mum was admitted, with each take-off and landing of the bright yellow craft, noise and turbulent air beat down through walls and windows, ceilings and

118

floors, to the wards below.

Until this spring, I haven't lived 'at home' for over thirty years. My room is small, still pink, with a built-in white-louvered wardrobe and a large window with a now rickety venetian blind. Some of its wide slats had slipped where their ribbon hangings had rotted and frayed in the sun, but I patched them with masking tape and staples before the estate agent's viewings began and from the door, you'd never know. Nowadays the room is always too hot, the radiator control encrusted long-since with lime scale and rust. The drawers and wardrobe overflow. As the weeks have passed I've brought more and more from my own flat: in mid-March, extra jumpers, a warmer coat, then lighter tops for a late spring and cotton skirts for the tease of summer. Books, a printer, more books, sandals and scarves, a Kenyan coir basket for sunny days.

After I left for university in the autumn of 1975, the longest time ever between visits home was the summer I spent in India in 1982, when the slow and flimsy blue aerogramme was the only means of communication. Four months, the entire duration of the Falklands War. Like the hospital, home has grown and changed, extended out and up between 1973 and 74, with rooms for Grandma and a high new pointed gable. Changes since have been smaller, but cumulative: a kitchen here, a bathroom there, new banisters, new armchairs and settees, a different colour in the hall. And year by year, the small accretions in the geology of home. Gifts, celebratory pieces, memorial pieces; an illuminated globe, a Murano vase, a wind-up carriage clock with a tiny etched plaque, a dresser full of blue-and-white china, a bright bowl of papier-mâché eggs from Khan Market in Delhi, a framed gallery of grandchildren.

In the garden too, things have changed since we arrived, nearly half a century ago. The laurel hedge is four times higher and deeper, but almost all the trees have gone. The tallest went first, with the knotted climbing rope, an ancient beech condemned by disease, loosened by wind, then one by one, the other beeches, the sweet chestnut and the rowan, the silver birch, the willow and the huge but barren holly bush, with its hidden rat nest and fox hole. The metal swing of my childhood finally rusted away. The grandchildren's climbing frame and slide have come and gone,

119

and the turtle-shaped sandpit, bright green, smiley-faced. Only the trampoline remains, weeds clawing up through the circle of pebbles beneath.

Dad laid the curved terrace, built the low wall round it, like the bedroom wardrobes, single-handed over many weekends, once the extension was complete in the summer of 1974. Barrowing yards of sand and gravel and stacks of pink and yellow slabs from the top of the drive to the back of the house, he was lithe and strong and, bare-backed, grew browner by the week. Mapping the pattern with sticks and string, mixing the mortar by hand on a square of metal casing from an old washing machine, he fell into an easy rhythm, curving down-and-back, down-and-back, slicing and turning the sand and cement with a heavy garden spade.

The mortar is crumbling now and, weakened by frost, assaulted by football, the low wall wobbles. The paving stones are uneven, their sandy foundations undermined by ants and rain, their pinks and yellows faded and streaked black with mould. Last summer one of the garden sheds collapsed, rotten, and forgetting his own frailty Dad spoke of rebuilding it himself. Mum was non-committal, but in the evening, while he dozed, she searched the internet for companies who would do the work. Today, the concrete plinth stands bare, the shed unbuilt and a green wheelbarrow with a flat tyre leans against the fence, handles to the sky.

I miss a call from the agent but when I speak to him later in the day he is upbeat. There's been another offer on the house. In fact there have been three more offers, but one stands out, he advises, slightly lower than the others but 'chain-free' and, it appears, financially sound. I ask a question, then another, but know I'm an amateur, a weekend tyre-kicker in a used-car lot. I text the others and replies come back quickly from Bristol and Cambridge, but no word yet from Taiwan, where my brother is interrogating bicycle-makers. 'That sounds good,' both sisters agree. 'Can we push for a quick exchange?' asks Joanna.

We've worked well together, the three sisters, returning from our different lives. March, April, May, back in our old rooms. They made rich stews and shepherd's pies, slow-cooked and delicious, and I washed up while they phoned home, scrubbing away the dark crust of gravy inside Mum's cream Le Creuset casserole.

We clashed three times. Just three. Sudden and unforeseen moments when old resentments flared like long-buried shrapnel shifting to the surface to break the skin a second time. Friends assured me this is so common in the circumstances, it is normal, to be expected, but long-unused to the tantrums and huffs and reconciliations of family life, I remain shaken and fearful.

Mum came home from hospital just before Easter and the palliative care nurse came to call. She sat beside Mum on one of the chenille settees and in the nicest possible way asked her where she would like to die. She spoke to us together, professional but kind, in her navy cardigan and Ecco shoes, and then took Mum upstairs to talk to her alone. Afterwards, standing in the kitchen before she left, she told us that the one thing Mum wanted was for us to go through her jewellery with her. Mum knew it would be hard, the nurse said, but it was important to her. I felt guilty for I had been tearful when Mum broached the subject with us and she hadn't mentioned it again. Of course we would do as she wished.

There was a bottle of special Prosecco in the fridge in the garage and we planned to make a little occasion of the sorting of Mum's jewellery, all together, sitting on her bed clinking glasses, her precious things spread out on the floral cover in their satin-lined boxes from Mappin & Webb. Anniversary gifts from Dad, mainly, named in her mind even as she received them for her grand-daughters: fine gold for Katie, diamonds for Isobel and Isla, rubies for Imogen and Rowan. But we left it too late. Mum suddenly became too ill for home and was taken by ambulance to the hospice in Farnham. Backed on to the drive, departure was delayed for twenty-five minutes as Kirsty, the stout and reassuring paramedic, struggled to find a vein in Mum's arm, so thin you could see the hollow between the bones.

I call the agent again and ask Joanna's question about 'Exchange'. He'll check and call me back. We like him, Chris, clean-cut and newly-married, pleasant and as far as we can tell, straightforward. We accept the latest offer, and soon the 'Sold' sign is back. 'Sold!' A separate yellow strip covering the words 'For Sale', tacked easily in place and easily removed by the contractor circling the area in his white van, tracking mobilities.

121

I wait to hear from the new buyer's surveyor, but having survived one survey, I am no longer nervous of what they might find. I gather bits-and-pieces in the garage for one last trip to the tip: the mock-Tudor electric fire that fused and scorched its socket, a broken broom and a rusty hoe, and three panes of bevelled glass, removed for safety's sake from the nest of tables now in Dad's care home room.

It has taken weeks of sorting and sifting to reduce the house's contents to this. Forty-six years of 'stuff'. Clothes – thirty extra-strong black bin-bags full – linen, books, papers, gadgets, utensils, drawers stuffed with lists and receipts, photos, bills and statements. Enough socks for three lifetimes. Three half-finished baby shawls, fine as lace in two-ply wool, knitting needles and the old silver-grey patterns, folded and creased, still in the bags. A whole shelf of jam jars full of screws, graded, sized and sorted. Five unopened rolls of extra-wide kitchen foil. Four steam cleaners. A chest of crocheted table clothes, runners, antimacassars, in discoloured shades of oyster and cream, our grandma's and great-grandma's handiwork, their intricate skills lost in a single generation. Years and years of birthday cards we had no idea that Mum had kept and wept to find.

As each day's list grows shorter, the consolations of activity fail. 'It's only bricks and mortar.' Maxine is sensible, rational. 'Now that Mum and Dad aren't there it's just an empty shell. The sooner it's sold the better.' Perhaps she's right. I know at least in part she is, but I struggle to feel the same.

'If these walls could speak,' they say, 'what stories they could tell,' and I wonder how our stories will survive this scattering and diffusion. I wonder how we will connect, in future, without the house, and Mum, hub and heart of all our relating.

I cannot think of leaving, turning the key for the last time, without spiralling into distress and a kaleidoscope of loss. Never again to come home on Christmas Eve to decorate the tree with silver baubles and glitter balls and red satin ribbons. Never to sit chatting on Mum's bed on a Sunday morning while she curls her hair with 'The Archers' low in the background. Never to call Dad in from garden or garage for tea and Bakewell slices or to sit with them outside in summer with a misted jug of Pimms and ice and lemonade. Never again to watch them in the rear-view mirror, standing hand-in-hand at the top of the drive waving goodbye, confident of endless returns.

Standing in the doorways of empty and half-empty rooms, it is the world that has turned.

The Musical Musings of Frances Middleton

Melissa Elliotte

An excerpt from a novel-in-progress of the same name.

Chapter 1

When I first saw the name Mathieu de Lépinay on my student roster, no song came to mind which was strange. I was home at the time lounging on the sofa in my pajamas. My husband had just fixed me a cappuccino with a lovely clover design on the top, made by our own fancy barista machine. He was always thinking of some new way to pamper me – fresh roses strewn across the bed, a jasmine scented bubble bath, minstrels even came to our door once. It didn't matter that they played the polka. It's the thought that counts.

I suppose my life, just like a Cole Porter song, had become a bit cliché, so much in fact that I was now only able to conceptualize in platitudes and trite phrases. It's better than it sounds. Life is lighter, like I'm floating, gliding along from one day to the next. There are no potholes to trip on because I hover above the actual terrain. My feet don't touch down, they bear no weight at all.

Saying all that, seeing the name on my student roster sheet did jolt me. Half of the foamy clover spilled to the floor while the other half swayed back and forth inside the Paris Starbucks mug. It was another gift from my husband. He knows how much I love everything French. By the time the broken clover had settled, I was chiding myself for my reaction. Yes it surprised me. I hadn't heard the name Mathieu de Lépinay in almost twenty years. It was a name that had changed the direction of my life. But it was only a name after all, and Mathieu was common enough, at least in France. De Lépinay, however, was not.

But it had been easy enough to drink the rest of my coffee leisurely, smile at my husband from time to time while digging my feet under Skippy's furry belly for warmth. My toes are oddly cold all the time. My husband likes to joke 'cold feet, warm heart', which makes no sense of course so that's why it's funny. Our springer spaniel used to jump at the chill of them, but now he curls his paws stoically around my ankles. My husband named him Skippy, which we thought was perfect since the dog is quite fast and Skippy is also my husband's favorite peanut butter.

'It's a win-win!' he said jovially. I agreed of course. He's such a kind man, too kind for a silly disagreement over dogs and peanut butter.

I continued my morning ritual and went for a run. I'm quite fast too – Skippy should watch himself. I ran track all through school and have the medals to prove it. Maybe that's when my feet stopped touching the ground. I know that sounds quite dramatic, similar to my 'that name changed the direction of my life' declaration. But the truth is, that name would almost change the direction of my life yet again.

'Go get 'em marathon mama!' my husband called from the front porch; our dogwood banner blew in front of his face as he waved. It didn't even make sense. I'm a sprinter and I've never been a mother, although I came close once. But I don't talk about that, not to my husband, not to anyone.

Like many women, I fall victim to vanity. It was sobering when my wavy, golden hair and runner's legs were not causing the same stir as before. I was used to men letting me break in line at the Harris Teeter, opening doors as I entered the Bank of America Tower in Charlotte every morning, and offering grins or whistles when I crossed the street. That was my world as I knew it until about thirty-five as best I can recollect. None of this vanity served me well, still doesn't.

I decided on a sudden change. I wanted to embrace my decline, give in to my inevitable obscurity, but somewhere quiet and humdrum where I really would just be the status quo. I switched from the corporate world to academia. A small university just outside Charlotte wanted to add more practical experience to their Communications faculty. It was a department sinking from the weight of so many PhDs, or so the Academic Dean told me confidentially during my interview.

'I won't sugar coat it for you. There are a lot of egos in the department.'

He winced and dropped his chin to his shirt collar, as if ashamed he had admitted that out loud. The afternoon sun beamed across his office and through his hair, indicating where balding would begin shortly. It had been curious to me to see this tall man clearly in charge and yet so… soft. At the time, I couldn't decide if I found it endearing or pathetic. But here I am six years later, teaching *Digital Marketing in Practice, Introduction to Communications* and married to the Academic Dean.

My new job at Darby College infused me with buzz and verve. Those were the surprising words for it. I noticed it straight away after my first class. Although I was not a stunner among the masses anymore, once in a confined space for 60-90 minutes, spouting off knowledge about marketing and media, I somehow became alluring again. No one was more surprised than I. The expression MILF was even tossed around the other day in the hall. But I don't care for that for many reasons. My inevitable decline and decay was, well, *evitable.*

*

Sneakers squeaked and flip flops flapped as my newest class filled the room. It was the dawning of another year, another fall semester to discover which youth would adore me from afar. And it was from afar, I want to make that perfectly clear. It was all innocent enough and of mutual benefit no less. My vanity was soothed and, in return, I imparted knowledge.

With my female students in particular, I even began to provide a kind of parental guidance, or at least the kind of parenting that made sense to me. It started one day when a student ran into me in the ladies' restroom in the Chambers Building. Black smudges were under her eyes. At first I thought she was one of those Goth type girls, but then I realized she had been crying. A French language CD entitled *Ça va?* clattered to the floor. She must have come directly from the language lab as Phonetics class with Madame Pondeville would make anyone cry. I bent down and carefully inserted the CD back into its case with a click.

'Oh,' she sniffed. 'Thank you.'

I ripped a stream of tissue from a toilet roll and she dabbed it at her eyes.

126

'Is everything ok?'

She dropped her book bag on the sink counter and the CD fell out again, scraping against the tile before settling on top of the drain. She groaned and shoved it into her book bag, finishing with a violent tug of the zipper.

'I'm sorry. It's just a stupid boy.'

A few dark streaks still remained under her blue eyes, rendering the color more vivid in contrast. I've noticed that before, how sadness can reveal beauty. Normally it's because the tears reflect in the light, causing the eyes to actually glisten. I thought of my own tears around her age. Mine had been related to a stupid man rather than a stupid boy, but I kept this to myself.

I didn't reply, just held her gaze in the mirror while washing my hands, silently singing Happy Birthday to myself. I read somewhere that you should sing Happy Birthday twice while washing your hands in warm water to ensure good hygiene. I hadn't even made it to 'Happy Birthday Dear Frances' before she told me.

'My stupid boyfriend is a senior, a repeated senior.' She rolled her eyes and I couldn't help but think gosh, he really is quite stupid. 'And I'm a freshman and I just overheard that this is like, his *thing*. He just scores through as many freshies as he can. He has a running tally.'

I'm not sure why she told *me* this, but clearly she was distraught. Stupid boys and stupid men are very similar as it turns out, but I stopped myself before offering bitter advice that might be inauthentic for her. It certainly wasn't an effort to adhere to any professional, ethical code as a respectable teacher. But something about her struck a chord in me and that truly does sound banal given what I said next.

'Do nothing till you hear from me.'

'Excuse me?' she released my gaze in the mirror to turn and look directly at me.

'Do nothing till you hear from me.'

Taking a step back, she replied, 'Umm. What?'

'It's a standard from the 1940s, the great Duke Ellington. The music came first, but the words are thanks to Bob Russell, and that's my advice to you.'

That was all I had, so I left her there.

Days later, she found me outside my classroom after my Tuesday/Thursday class had finished. I was fiddling with the keys, inadvertently making them jangle as I tried to double lock the door.

'That Duke guy was right,' I heard behind me.

When I turned, she began to quote, '*Do nothing till you hear from me. At least consider our romance, if you should take the word of others you've heard, I haven't a chance.* Ha! It's dead on.' Her eyes were almost as pretty when she was happy. The twinkle lightened the hue.

It was actually Bob Russell who was the sage, not the Duke, but no matter. I never underestimate the music as the medium, how it allows the message to resonate and be remembered.

Even before I developed a cult following for my musical musings, I had always been good with female bonding. Historically being the prettiest girl in the room, there was never a need to be inconsiderate or vindictive, which put me in a unique position to simply be kind. Kindness feels good I should add. Kindness has never been a problem for me. And I could have easily taken a different path, like Lana I would soon come to learn. I first heard her high-pitched voice from the back of my classroom the same day Mathieu entered my life.

'Tommy wants to pledge SAE, but he's a Kappa Sig all the way, if you know what I mean.'

Her presence was elegant, almost regal, which was odd given her frayed jeans mini-skirt and distressed ankle boots. Her companion didn't seem to fathom the difference between an SAE and a Kappa Sig at all, but she tried to smooth her wrinkled brow before Lana noticed, swiftly tapping Lana's forearm as if she was totally in on the secret.

After shuffling some papers on my desk, I called, 'Mathieu De Lépinay?'

I wanted him to say in that precise Frenchy pout, 'Ici!' Not for any sexual reason, but sometimes I just missed hearing that Gallic language all around me, even after my junior year abroad had long since expired. But of course Mathieu responded, 'Here,' which was the right choice if he wanted to get along with his fresh-faced, basketball-loving peers. That's why he came to Darby College after all, basketball.

By then, I had forgotten all about the roster surprise over the weekend and only raised my head to give a new student a nod of welcome. *But there he was.*

It was Nicolas. He was sitting there glorious, his long limbs dwarfing the desk as he crouched, as if he could put things back into proportion in that position. It was *my* Nicolas. I hadn't known him when his floppy hair was jet black and the only crease on his face was a side dimple, when youth and uncertainty caused him to fidget. I knew him when he wore learned glasses and carried a battered, leather satchel. I knew him when he had a slight indention on his jaw from a mole that had to be removed. I knew him with a faced lined from living.

I exhaled a pent-up breath and waited for the excitement to subside from my body, like opening a bottle of Pepsi to release the fizz. I felt all flat until a powerful melancholy twisted my chest. It wasn't Nicolas though. It was his son, Mathieu.

Chapter 2

My office hours are Tuesdays 10 to 11.30am and Wednesdays 3 to 5pm. For the majority of these three and half hours, I am usually trying to dissuade another advisee from pursuing a double major with a double minor. Although Generation Z students have only just entered the college years, I find myself ready for all their fervour and intensity to move on. And yes, I recognize that my cynicism places me firmly in Generation X.

Back in my university days, it was rare to pursue a double major which made my choice slightly odd. I declared my intentions to my father, mother and grandfather post-game at Logan's Grill. The restaurant was located on the corner of 6th and Broadway, just caddy corner to my sophomore dorm. Like all the streets surrounding the campus that day, fans dressed in red and white were everywhere, weaving their way through cars stuck in traffic. An occasional horn beeped, not out of annoyance but rather in solidarity over the win. My mother always enjoyed a good visit over homecoming weekend: 'Oh how I loved the trombones during half-time.' As everyone was in such a jubilant mood, it seemed the right moment to announce that I would be studying

Marketing and Musicology.

My father smiled, deepening the creases on either side of his mouth. 'All this time and I never knew my baby was quirky.'

Being a piano teacher, my mother was enthusiastic, 'Marketing will take you far and musicology, I suppose it will give you something to talk about, you know at all those networking events.'

Dad chimed in, 'Hadn't thought of that. But gauge your audience Frances.'

'Oh yes, Gershwin isn't for everyone, dear.' Her compact clicked open and I couldn't understand why she was applying her red lipstick now. The four of us were about to eat, it would only come off again.

My mother's father was about to add his own verdict until his emphysema overwhelmed him with a coughing fit. When he finally spoke, his voice sounded like a low grumble, 'Your studies make no sense to me, no sense at all. Marketing and business? Sure. Marketing and learn a thing or two about those computers? Sure. Marketing and musical, what was it? Musicology? Well, I have no words for that.'

*

'Brand is everything and it must be consistent across all channels.' Now I had the words, but I barely knew what I was saying. 'Can anyone name different ways to communicate your theoretical company's message to potential customers?'

Several hands raised to respond. I turned towards the chalkboard much like a robot running through its program, albeit in a fitted pencil skirt with a chignon held up by a number 2 pencil. Oh how I loved to set a scene for them! I almost bought a pair of non-prescription glasses once, but that would have been taking it too far even for me.

I was poised, seemingly, with a piece of chalk ready to write down answers; until Mathieu raised his hand and the chalk snapped in mine. How ludicrous it was to teach a Comms class with a chalkboard and textbook. I had one of the last classrooms left to be renovated with a whiteboard and projector screen. My husband was always promising advocacy to the Vice Provost for improved resources.

'I'll invite him to play golf! Get the ole bulldog out of his suit and tie and onto a fresh green pitch in the open air. I'll even let him win.' Bless him but I couldn't see how his battered golf cap and favourite Augusta polo with the small hole under the arm would compensate for his gangly limbs on the golf course. He was very tall at 6 foot 4 inches and although a 45-year-old man, his legs and arms had still not caught onto the idea of becoming a grown-up. They seemed to enjoy being all elbows and knees, comfortable in the sharp angles of adolescence. His hairy chest and receding hairline were all man though and exuded strength and erudition respectively. We loved my pet name for him regardless; Grasshopper. When I was feeling particularly tender, I called him G. I suppose he really should have taken up basketball, like Mathieu.

Someone moved a desk and it rattled over the din of muffled giggles. Mathieu was seated closest to me in the front row. He stood up, his jeans hanging a bit low on his narrow hips and I believe I was shaking. He bent down past my knees and when I realized he was trying to pick up the broken chalk pieces, my torso jerked down as well. Our heads collided, knocking the pencil from my bun and my hair unceremoniously fell past my shoulders. More giggles. This would not do!

I must admit that the 'bend over-cascading hair' was an old favourite for livening up a particularly dull class, although I wouldn't dare try it with the upperclassmen who knew better. But the freshmen were too shiny and wide-eyed to recognize a shtick when they saw it. I know, I was shameless.

But again, this would not do. Nervous coughs were one thing, giggles and whispers another. I snatched the chalk from Mathieu, ignoring his long eyelashes, just like his father's. 'Please.' I extended my arm indicating he should return to his seat. He shrugged and obliged, a lone French boy in a foreign land. I knew he was just trying to be helpful but the first day of class was critical, the show must go on.

To compose myself, I dismissed the chalkboard and instead asked students to separate into small groups. Whichever group had the highest number of modes to communicate could opt out of a monthly quiz during the semester. This declaration was followed quickly by murmurs of assent.

Lana crossed the entire classroom, her Darby Wildcats T-shirt taut against her chest, and slid into a spare desk next to Mathieu. She twirled a lock of hair around her fingers as she introduced herself. Talk about shameless!

Her friend, abandoned in the far corner, chewed on the inside of her cheek while gripping her textbook. My eyes skimmed down the student roster until landing on a familiar name, like a card game of Memory where I stored information away for later – far right corner matches with...

'Mary! This group here could use a fourth person.' I pointed to some students in the front right corner opposite Lana and Mathieu. It was a lovely little group for her anyway. I could tell in the way all three of them twisted expectantly towards her. One was even quick to offer a pen once Mary realized she had left hers in the back. An awkward moment averted and I was relieved, as was she I'm sure.

A sea of heads settled down, huddled in their respective groups, hushed voices discussing answers and invigorated with purpose. It was the predictable order of a classroom, which didn't suit me at all, but it was still preferable to before. I sat behind my desk and gripped the stiff cover of *Dawn of the Digital Era*. There was a globe on the front with different types of people and buildings inside it, cultures and worlds overlapping each other and blending together.

I leaned back into my chair and lifted the textbook in a surreptitious peek-a-boo to stare at Mathieu. He looked kind, even gentle, something about his smooth forehead, and I thought of Nicolas. But his prominent forehead had been a shade darker than the rest of his face and split in two by a wrinkle deep from the Provence sun.

*

'Professor de Lépinay is fantastique!' fellow classmate Emily exclaimed. The school's gothic door closed behind us with a resounding bass clack. 'I see that strange crease across his forehead and it's like his head can't physically hold so much knowledge, it's literally coming apart at the seams. Ha!' She exhaled cigarette smoke. 'Until today's class, all this time we've been calling that gale force wind the Mistral and not even

132

questioning why it's called that.'

Emily chose to blend in with the French by smoking, I chose to wear scarves at all hours of the day. Fred, another classmate, participated in different *grèves* with local students. And of course, loads of girls were just sleeping around with French boys, tossing out phrases like, 'Oh really Frances, no one knows *l'amour* like the French' and 'they just have that *je ne sais quoi.*'

I leaned against the shady stone wall with Emily, cooling my skin during the heat of the day. 'I guess I just assumed *mistral* was some kind of *provençal* word for freaky wind. It never occurred to me it was an actual man.'

'Yeah, I thought about naming my first daughter Mireille after Mistral's poem, but her end is too tragic. So her dad says she can't marry her hot basketmaker guy and then she treks to some place by the sea to pray to the saints to change her father's mind and dies on the way. Did I get that right?'

I nodded that she did.

'Yeah, no way am I passing on that bad mojo'.

I stepped closer to the bike rack under the sole tree of the courtyard. Several boys from class walked stiffly over to join us. Fred didn't waste time before talking about a recent protest with his friend Guillaume for the rights of the farmer. Fred hailed from Philadelphia, so I wasn't sure from where his indignation came exactly. I still went slack-jawed and batted my eyelashes before I said, 'Wow, so like, cheaper cheese and wine for everyone.'

The boys relaxed and laughed. Fred put his arm around me. 'Oh Frannie,' he teased. 'It means le contraire I'm afraid, dear. We're talking about protecting the French way of life from foreign produce. That means keeping prices high enough for the farmers to thrive in their own backyards.'

'Vive la France!' another shouted and pumped his fist, although refusing to rid himself of his New York Yankees baseball cap.

I flipped my hair, 'Well if it doesn't mean cheaper wine and cheese parties for this girl's student budget, then who cares?'

The boys laughed, just like I knew they would.

'*Oh la pauvre. Elle ne comprend pas, mais nous l'aimons quand même.*' Fred pinched my cheek and continued to let his arm rest around my shoulders. The other boys waited for me to say something silly again. I didn't disappoint.

133

'Oho save your Frenchie French stuff for your farmers, it's all Greek to me.'

My boys laughed again. We all agreed to meet later at the Bistrot d'Aixois that night. Emily retreated with them, leaving the shade to traverse sun dappled cobblestones under the edges of the branches, until exposed completely to the hot light of the afternoon. I stooped down, scrunching my eyes in an effort to see my bike lock clearer.

'Why do you do that?'

I turned to see Professor de Lépinay.

'And don't flap your eyelashes at me, you forget I know how smart you are. I'm grading your papers, remember?'

I don't know why he talked to me so boldly that warm afternoon on rue Thiers. What did he care how I spent my time outside his classroom anyway? I let the artifice fall, stared hard at him and replied in perfect French, 'Stick to grading my papers cher Prof, won't you?'

He was surprised at my direct tone. I was too actually. But then he chuckled to himself and looked at me, like a child blowing on a paper pinwheel, fascinated how the colors change and turn. I had forgotten that. What it felt like to have someone really see me, it was only a glimpse, as long as it takes someone to blink really, before a strong gust of wind spins the colors into a blur.

Robert Kauffman on Jasmine Buchannan

Ed Sibley

Robert Kauffman is 38. His hairline has receded halfway to the back of his head. He is in good shape. For much of the evening, he is reluctant to talk about himself, preferring to explain his theories about the real functions of various government agencies. It is only in the dead of night, lying diagonally across the bed, naked and damp with perspiration, his head on a pillow and a lit cigarette in his hand, that he begins to talk about himself. Once he starts he carries on for over an hour. He has had a lot to drink by this point and he enjoys having someone listen to him. This is not something that happens to him very often.

I don't know if it was because I grew up on the top floor of a townhouse that meant in later life I came to associate misery with elevation. I like to look down at everything. You know how when you're good and sad, good and miserable, then that's alright. You don't want to get all low and listless. I always live as high up as I can. I love a good view. That's why I got this flat. It's also why I liked that hostel in Guatapé, probably why I stayed there so long. Guatapé is this town in Colombia. You should definitely go there. Geez, I was down.

The hostel was a kind of small mansion thing a little way outside of town. It had these huge handmade wooden bunk beds. There was a terrace out the back and past the terrace was a slope that led to a jetty. It was hard going, down that slope. No proper path, just lots of impromptu dirt tracks. To get there you had to go down one of these slopes and every time you'd get halfway you'd sort of realise you'd gone wrong, like somewhere between the terrace and the jetty you'd done a wrong turn and now you had to jump four feet down to the right bit, and you'd get to the bottom bruised and broken and then realise you'd forgotten the keys to the canoe and you'd have to climb right back to the terrace again, tripping all the way. It's completely possible to fall upwards. It's the only way you can get to the top of that goddamn hill.

So yeah, this one afternoon I got the small canoe and the

straightest of the oars out and I went out for a paddle. I'd been in the hostel for maybe three months and I'd seen a lot of people come and go. I started off just staying there but as time went by they kind of started giving me jobs, manning the front desk at night and this kind of thing, so I had all the keys. Not that the owner really gave a shit – he was this tremendous womanizer, it was all anyone ever talked about, so he was out a lot. He never approached the guests or anything like that, which was a good thing for me because I was, you know, recently single.

But look, it wasn't like I went out on the lake that morning looking for Jasmine or anything like that. She was a guest. Sure, I knew she was on the water, I'd been looking after the desk that morning so I knew she'd gone out, but it wasn't like that meant I was likely to bump into her. The lakes around Guatapé are pretty weird – I don't know if you've seen them. You kind of imagine a lake like this big round thing, like a fried egg, but the lakes around there are all mixed up, scrambled sort of thing. They're man-made, because of this dam. It's in the lowlands of the Andes, see, and so there are all these hills, but they feel more like islands, all melting in to one another. It's weird. This homeless guy in town, lovely guy, his name was Santi, he told me once that if the world was a perfect deck of cards, the oceans were red and the hills were black, then Guatapé is what it would look like after God shuffled it. Don't worry about the folk wisdom. It's free. It comes with the package.

So, this one morning I got my canoe into the water, just thinking I'd go for a paddle, burn some calories. Every day in Guatapé goes the same. The sun rises at 6am and hangs straight above your head until 6pm when it suddenly vanishes. The best thing to do is to get onto the water. It's mostly pretty clear and there's no one around during the week. You just sit there on your splinter and float. You're like, I don't even know. Breakfast cereal floating in a sink. Or a bit of pumpkin seed, maybe. Or a lardon.

So I've been on the water for maybe an hour, maybe more, and I'm looking up at the hills and I don't know whether I saw it first or heard it but there's something bundled up in one of these scraggly trees making this noise, like, I don't know. At first, this is ridiculous but I thought it was a bat, and then after a moment I wondered if it was some kind of machine up there, maybe it was busted, making this sound, but then I figured it out, so I shouted up in my broken-ass Spanish and she kind of yelped, like I'd surprised her.

Oh. No, wait, stop. I'm not doing this. I'm giving you my goddamn origin story. Listen. I'm not one of those sad bastards. Every fucking shithead has this story about the first time they met Jasmine. Bastards in bars talk for hours about the girl, they have this heavy fucking thing almost this parable about that first meeting, what it meant to them, where it led. Listen to me, I'm doing the same thing. The thing is, though, none of these people are really talking about her at all. Or, what I mean is that they're, you know, they're projecting. She has something. It must be tough. I mean, I've never driven another human being mad with lust or anything like that, which means at least that I think people are straight with me. But everyone had an agenda when it came to Jasmine. I'm the same. I admit it. She drove me mad.

I guess I was lonely. I never got anywhere much with the other guests in the hostel. They were young, they came in groups of three or four or five, they stayed for a couple of days. They were scenery, like the stray kittens that hung around under the beds. I saw things happen in that place, mundane things, things you just don't notice unless your headspace is working in this certain way. One day I was looking out of a window and I saw this pair of black nylons get snagged up in some railings. They just floated up, got tangled and stayed there. They're probably still there now. I saw that happen. I fucking remember that happening. It was a big deal that day.

I mean, of course I was feeling down about the whole Kristie situation, that goes without saying. I made that situation for myself, I fucked that girl on the aeroplane, I wanted it, I was an idiot, with the kids there and all. I deserved to get thrown out. She was trying to serve me with divorce papers. That's what I was doing down in Guatapé. I went there so she wouldn't know where I was. A powerful lady, my ex-wife. She had these people chasing me halfway around the world with court orders and decree nisi and all this other stuff. I thought I was doing it for the girls, like maybe I still had a chance to fix it if I bought myself some time. Or maybe I was just doing it because I'm a shithead.

Look, you probably don't want to hear all this crap about how I found Jasmine up a tree. She was stuck, basically. She'd climbed up to look at the view and couldn't get down, was pretty stressed out about it. Her canoe was parked on the other side of the hill. I helped her down, we paddled back together. We had a conversation, a good one, you know, which was rare. It's corny. The hostel was pretty quiet so we went into the town and drank beer and played pool. That night we had sex. You want me to say something about that? Something, I don't know, something that tells you something about her, that gives you some sense of what she was like when you were near to her? Something about her poise, about the way she carried herself? Bullshit. There was a storm that night. My clearest memory is of the whites of her eyes in the lightning. It was dark, I don't know.

A couple of days after that Jasmine left for Bogota. Her brother had arrived in town, apparently, and a couple of days after that I left as well. I felt like I was done with the place. I'd had what I wanted from it. I was restless and I knew some work would do me good. Purifies the soul.

The journey was about fifteen hours. I got a coach, which I hated, but I didn't have a car at that point. I knew somewhere good to stay in Bogota, a hostel I'd told Jasmine about so I thought maybe she'd be there, so that's where I went. I remember getting off that coach and heading for the old town, the Colonial pip in the middle of the city where the hostels are, and after I checked in I went and got a Juan Valdez, which is this shop all the Colombians love because it's basically a rip off of Starbucks, but it's Colombian and they love that. It was drizzling grey piss and the coffee tasted worse than the rain. In Bogota they say you get all four seasons at once in different parts of the city, so I guess the old town was stuck in fall. I read this book that I took from the hostel for the coach journey. *Notes on a Kidnapping.* It was shit. I hate books.

So I was all damp from the rain and keeping my hands warm on this Juan Valdez and sat under a concrete ledge, it was a library or something. All these new buildings in Colombia, they have these big exposed open areas and they're just great for moping about. I was the saddest bastard in town. I didn't have anyone to see or anything to do. There were these two young people, a couple, he was a small guy and she was pretty tall and he was kind of sat sideways on her lap, their foreheads were touching, their hair was all wet, and they were crooning this gibberish, I would have loved to have been one of those two. I felt about a billion miles away from that. This bald gringo.

So anyway a kind of cursory poke around told me that Jasmine was nowhere around, I guess I shouldn't have been upset about it. She hadn't taken my recommendation. I didn't know a single other person in Bogota. I got drunk, I went for a walk, 7th Avenue, *La Septima*, through the old town and then the financial bit with all the tall buildings and then out the other side into the strip suburbs where there are little bars above shops and little shops between bars. Ten years ago I would have been mugged to death out there, this pisco gringo staggering around, but these days all you get is haunting warnings from wide-eyed women who tell you to get a cab to bed in broken English, running fingers across their throats. They remember the old days. Fuck that, I thought. I walked the length of the town, I got to the saucy bit where the wealth goes to spend itself, nobody would let me in anywhere and so I got a cab home after all. Made a fuss back at the hostel over the music they were playing – some English guy, it really pissed me off – I wanted the Boss but they wouldn't let me have him and just as I was remonstrating with the flunky who was trying to toss me out, there she was. She seemed surprised to see me. I was certainly surprised. I was surprised as all hell. I threw up and passed out in the flunky's arms.

She was still there the next day, her and her brother. Gorilla of a kid named Arthur. They came into my room – I always cough up extra for a room for myself, if the hostel lets me – with some water and stuff. Thoughtful Arthur had this foil bag that he offered me. It was hot. It was full of these things that looked like yellow grapes but I figured out that they were tiny deep-fried potatoes, so that was pretty good. I had one and then another one, greasy and salty they were, and then I offered them back to Arthur and he took a handful in this weird way, sort of without looking, sort of pulled out a clump of them. Maybe it was just my head. This fistful of greasy potatoes. He looked around for somewhere to wipe his hand, saw one of my shirts on the floor and used that.

They asked me what I was doing in town. I don't think Arthur knew I'd fucked his sister. I told them I wasn't really sure what I was doing there, just that I was moving around. I'd told Jasmine about the whole decree nisi mess and she explained to Arthur what that was about. He asked me why I was staying in hostels when I could have been staying in hotels, which was a good question. The honest answer was that hostels are more fun, you know, less fussy, but I told them it was because I didn't know how long I was going to be skipping around for, which was also kind of true I guess. I don't find money a problem but you wouldn't think that if you saw the shoes I was wearing back then.

The main square in Bogota is a nightmare of pigeons. Jobless people sell breadcrumbs to kids and the kids throw the breadcrumbs around. There are thousands of them, coming at you as you walk across the place. We got some coffee in one of the little streets by the Palace of Justice. I must have looked like their dad: this balding white yankee and his twentysomething kids. Arthur was taller than Jasmine but he had the same black wavy hair around his shoulders. His was a little lighter than hers, I guess. Brownish. They had these cut-glass English accents like the villain in a Bond movie.

They told me they were going to visit some friends, Bogotano kids from the university, asked me if I wanted to come along, so I did. We got a cab. You get cabs everywhere in Colombia. I liked the University. It's this big open campus with graffiti everywhere. We sat in some lawn chairs that were lying around and peoplewatched until their friends turned up. Their friends were named Camilo, Camilito, Juan Camilo and Felipe. I kid you not. Camilito's girlfriend was there too, her name was Alejandra, and there was this other girl called Erica but she didn't speak much English so she kept quiet.

We bought some beer and went for a wander. Felipe found a bag of cannabis on the pavement and dumped most of it into a cigarette paper. We got more beers as the afternoon went on. We talked about punk music, about the buildings in the university, the library where I'd been hanging around was the same architect, apparently, a good one, I wrote down his name somewhere. I was lucky to meet these kids. I got a local view of the city. We sat in swings in the park. We ate empanadas on long trafficky roads. They had this affection for the place. Bogota has all kinds of problems, serious ones without even sticking-plaster solutions, but it was their city and they were proud of it. Jasmine could speak Spanish just fine but Arthur and I couldn't so most of the conversation was in English, as a courtesy. They wanted to impress us, me particularly because I'm from the States. Maybe that was because Colombia's got this colourful history of violence and they're trying to reclaim it. Maybe it's just because kids everywhere are proud of their cities. I don't know. They won me over. I thought to myself, 'It's a beautiful city, this Bogota.' Not my city. I wondered if I could settle down there, if it would still look as good in six months when I had my commute and my local shop, and when I'd already seen all the best graffiti already. Probably it would, that's the thing. Spending my evenings with the Camilos. Working on my Spanish. Getting to know Erica. Hm.

Still, I felt like an impostor. This wasn't really for me, I knew. I didn't know much about Jasmine and Arthur's background but certainly as far as I was concerned you get this odd feeling, being a rich guy slumming it. One time this dickhead hedge fund guy, not the head gardener, just one of his tools, we got in a row in a bar and he got so angry he spat at me and said, 'I could buy you, Kauffman.' I kept thinking that as we went around the city, the others buying juice or fags off these little people on the corners, or beer, I kept thinking, I couldn't help it, the thought just kept popping up into my head like some goddamn pink elephant, 'I could *buy* you.' I didn't want to. I never said it out loud, fuck no. But those words just kept coming through my head. I tried not to drink too much.

Anyway, it was a good day, that's why I'm dwelling on it. I had a good time. I missed my kids. I wondered if when they're older they'll feel the same way about Milwaukee as the Camilos felt about Bogota. But it was a good day. We ended up in Juan Camilo's apartment, which he shared with his mother, but we didn't see her that night. We had a bottle of this drink, it was from Peru, it was literally called Pisco. Tasted like salt whiskey. The evening gets fuzzy but I do remember Arthur and Jasmine and I taking a cab back to our hostel. Arthur vanished as soon as the cab got in, I guess to bed, who knows. Jasmine and I sat up for a couple of hours talking. She was excited, talking about the stuff we'd done that day, the buildings and the people. Glowing. Maybe you'd say she was glowing. She had this idea about studying, or teaching maybe, sometime the next year. She was excited about the idea, was trying to work out if they'd give her a job at the National University, talking about things she could teach. I felt conflicted about that. I hadn't seen her looking happy, before then, not really. In Guatapé she was tired, kind of depressed, I guess. I tried to get her to come to bed with me, obviously, but she wasn't interested.

The next day they were gone. I woke up pretty late on account of the Pisco and when I couldn't find them in the hostel I asked the front desk where they were. The lady told me they'd checked out, a last minute thing. Arthur left me a note. They had to go to a funeral back in sunny London. The friend was in prison and his dad had just died. They had to be there. Fuck. Suddenly, I had nothing again.

So Jasmine and Arthur were gone, for this funeral. First thing I did was get breakfast, this farmer's breakfast with chewy pig skin and ground beef and an avocado as big as my head. I had the idea to give Juan Camilo a call. He was working in the university that day but I talked him into letting me take him out for lunch. Juan Camilo was quite an impressive guy, actually. He was on the tall side, a good few inches taller than me, thoughtful. He had black hair to his ears and wore these thick black spectacles. Big teeth, toothy grin. He was studying international relations. He had a lot of opinions about things like educational policy. A socialist, but, you know, young. At least he wasn't an out-and-out communist. Lots of Colombians are, if you believe the graffiti. I met him at the cafeteria. He knew that Jasmine and Arthur were gone. Arthur had sent out an email, apparently, explaining things. Juan Camilo knew the friend, too – the one whose dad was dead. He blew out air between those enormous teeth of his and shook his head, saying 'real bad news, man'.

We got to talking about how he knew them. He said they'd been friends for years. They'd met as part of some of cultural exchange scheme. Juan Camilo's family had hosted a teenage Arthur for a couple of weeks and Alejandra had hosted Jasmine. Then later they'd done the reverse thing and all the Colombians had gone to stay in Britain. I asked him what Jasmine and Arthur's house had been like. Well, he said, they didn't live together,

142

Jasmine lived up in Edinburgh and Arthur was in London. But you know, he said, it was impressive. All these giant rooms, plush carpets. There was a swimming pool in Arthur's basement, he said, and they had all these servants, like you'd imagine.

I asked why I'd imagine that. They didn't come across like rich kids when you met them. Apart from their accents, I guess.

'Well,' he said. 'You know. Their dad.'

I asked who their dad was.

He raised an eyebrow. 'You really don't know?'

'No,' I said. 'I really don't know.'

'Dude,' he said. 'Their dad is Donald Greyson.'

My first thought was 'Oh shit. I fucked Donald Greyson's daughter.'

'Donald Greyson as in Donald Greyson?' I asked him.

'Yeah,' he said.

I had to let this sink in so I got up to get some coffee.

'So what was their life like in London?' I asked when I got back. 'Did you meet their friends?'

'Sure,' he said. 'Yeah, a bunch of them.'

'Did you meet the guy whose dad killed himself?'

He had met him. The kid's name was Henley, kind of a dumb name but there you go.

'Did you meet his dad?'

'No. He was another MG person, though. That's how Arthur and Jasmine knew him.' This is when I started making notes.

After lunch Juan Camilo went back to the library and I settled up and left. I couldn't believe it. Jasmine hadn't mentioned anything about any of this. I thought about those couple of days in Guatapé when I'd had her all to myself. We shared a goddamn bed, for Christ's sakes. What had we talked about? I thought we talked about everything. I know told her about myself. I told her how I'd come to Colombia because I knew my wife wouldn't follow me there. She's one of these people, Kristie, a lot of people are like this in the States, and in Britain, that have the idea that South America is this deathtrap. You talk about the place, all she hears is 'kidnappings, kidnappings, cocaine, kidnappings'. But yeah, Jasmine told me how when she started coming to Colombia after the first time she had to hide the fact from her mom, who'd been – and I quote – paralysed with worry when they did that

143

student exchange thing. Jasmine told me that as far as her mom knew, she was in Austria. So we were fugitives. Different reasons, sure, different ways. I didn't even know she was rich. I thought I was the rich one! I figured she was just some backpacker, not this billionairess. It was the most genuine thing to have happened to me in years. What a sham. What a fucking sham.

So I wandered through this fucking glazed sky and got back to the hostel and looked out of my window at this green mountain on the horizon and wondered if there was a single spot in this fucking city where you couldn't see a fucking mountain. I shipped out the next day.

The Way Things Go

Denise Bigio

The Way Things Go *tells the story of young Englishwoman Lucy Dalton, and the choice she faces as she encounters untrammelled desire, money and ambition in the Los Angeles art world.*

In this excerpt from an early chapter, Lucy and Mark are going to the Mojave Desert for the weekend. It is December 1989, and the early days of their relationship.

Mark picked her up in his old Peugeot two days later, and they looped around the city's tangle of freeways before heading out in a straight line for the vast flatness that lay to the east. A small silk pouch swung from the rear view mirror.

'I've had the car blessed,' he said. He had been in two accidents and had one car stolen, all in the last six months. 'There's a temple in east LA where some guy does it. A D-girl who works for a studio exec told me to go there. It was great.'

Lucy liked him even more for this idiocy, although she wondered about the D-girl. She bit down the impulse to sneer. Isn't everyone in development of some kind or another? Especially here, where if you weren't personally growing you might as well be digging your grave.

She suggested they stop for some coffee. There was a Denny's up ahead and she welcomed its soothing homogeneity.

Back on the road they drove past the tired strip malls, past the new houses clustered like Lego at the base of rust brown hills, past the gas stations and scrap yards, past the deceptively quiet military base, past the motels with missing light bulbs in their signs, wondering at everything, until at last the landscape sprang open, and Lucy felt a surge of relief. The ground and sky stretched endlessly, there was nothing else, just the small two-lane blacktop heading through the thin air towards a distant vanishing point.

They were quiet now, the silence between them full of easy grace. Lucy rested her hand on Mark's leg. She thought about calling Claire when they got back to LA, then decided against it; Claire was apt to cry at her friends' good fortune. She'd have to tone it down a bit when they did speak.

*

Mark glanced at Lucy from the corner of his eyes; it was a trick of his, not to look at people headlong – or if he did, it was a furtive dash in and out – but as he was driving, Lucy didn't mind.

'I think we're running out of gas.'

'We?' Lucy laughed. 'You mean, you, don't you?' But she loved the carelessness of it. 'We passed lots of gas stations, there'll be one soon.' How she relished that 'gas' – as if saying it almost single-handedly shot her out of constricted England with its cumbersome *petrol* (the weight of that extra syllable grew monstrous in her mind) and threw her, instantly, gloriously, into the effervescent promise of America.

'They've got to have diesel, that's the problem. Not many of them do. Sometimes it's hard to find. '

Lucy wound down her window. The car was making a heavy chugging sound. Was that new? Mark drove slowly now, hugging the side of the road, and she had time to take in the muted greys and purples of the rocks and scrub as they passed, and then with a faint judder the car stopped.

'Shit,' said Mark. 'I thought we could have gone a bit further.'

A passing car buffeted them with a blast of air. Mark rummaged in the glove compartment trying to find a map, but apart from some old Van Morrison cassettes, repair bills and a notebook – that would come to be referred to afterwards, long afterwards, as That Wretched Notebook – there wasn't anything there.

'I'd better start walking. Hopefully someone will give me a ride.'

'I'll come with you.'

'It's probably better if you stay with the car.' He laughed ruefully. 'Sorry about this, babes.' He kissed her. 'Don't deduce anything from it.'

It took a long time for Mark to disappear from sight. Another car shot past and Lucy wondered if it would stop for him. Everything was still and quiet in its wake. She took the keys and began walking into the desert, each step on the dry creosote a stifled bomb underfoot. When she turned to look back she was

146

surprised at how quickly the car had become a small white bump on the horizon. She stood still and let the air touch her. There's nothing here, she thought, it's like a sentence with no punctuation running on and on: no dunes, no trees, no interruptions.

She was about to turn back when suddenly all around her everything rose up, rose up with such presence that it hummed. The desert wasn't flat; it was so vertical it made Lucy's mind waver and stop. It had been lying down before, that was all, and had now stood up to greet her, radiant and shimmering. Lucy caught it, caught it all. Happiness exploded inside her. Where had her eyes been all this time?

And then, with a distinct visual snap – it was gone.

She remained still, her heart pulsing with wonder, until the long impatient note of a horn made her jump. Stones leapt away from her as she ran back to the car. Mark was filling the tank from a plastic can and she noticed a small dark spot on his shoe where the gas had spilled.

'I've just seen the most amazing thing, you've got to see it,' she said breathlessly as he screwed the cap back into place with a sharp clack. She pulled him after her, following her earlier steps as closely as possible, but it all looked the same and there were no traces of her anywhere. Still, they came to the same spot, she was sure of it. Lucy put her hands on his shoulders and turned him towards the way she had been facing earlier.

'Ok, now just… look.'

'Look at what?'

'Everything. The whole thing. See what happens.'

'I thought you'd like it. That's why I brought you here.'

'Yes, yes, but look… ' She steadied her breath. 'Just… look.'

They stood close together. Lucy could feel Mark looking, waiting. She could tell he wanted to ask her what she could see, but was holding back. Besides, what could she see? She closed her eyes, held them shut for a moment, opened them again. Silence, space, light. The ground running away from them in all directions. Far away mountains she hadn't noticed before. The solidity of Mark. Trembling air. Stillness.

After a while Mark pulled out his camera and took some pictures. 'It's beautiful,' he murmured, a faint tremor of anxiety in his voice.

147

A red-tailed hawk wheeled and hovered high above them, now and then letting out a sharp cry.

*

Mark was familiar with the inn they stayed in that weekend – it was a deceptively simple place screenwriters, aspiring and otherwise, went to hole up and finish their scripts, and merely staying there suggested that one was part of some cultural transformation about to take place. Lucy wondered how many times he had been there before, and who with, but didn't ask. She was still revelling in the new landscape of him, and didn't want to know about its previous inhabitants or what they had left behind.

Actually, it wasn't her first time there either. When she'd first become friends with Thea, she'd been thrilled when she'd suggested they go to the 29 Palms Inn.

'It's really cool. Just these little adobe cabins with an outside space where we can hang out. Be great to be by ourselves.' Thea was interested in a Mexican film director whom Lucy had met a couple of times, although nothing had come of it. But just as they were settling down on a couple of loungers, his shock of red hair suddenly popped up over the adjoining wall.

'Louis!' shrieked Thea, feigning surprise.

'Thea! Hi Lucy… '

Another face appeared over the wall, this one looking startled. Steven and Lucy looked at each other; their friends were really the limit. And yet Lucy found herself unable to chide Thea for her childish manoeuvring, or reveal how disappointed she was not to see much of her over the next two days.

She'd spent the weekend with Steven, who was a film editor, driving aimlessly around and listening to him rambling on in a nasal whine about the difficulty of working with a best friend (Louis) on a commercial film (*Night Raiders 2*) when really he wanted to work with Almodovar, or someone like that, but what was the likelihood of that happening, he was just a nice Jewish boy from the Upper West Side; um, would she like to go out with him? no, she wouldn't, although thanks for asking.

Lucy made this last bit up as she was telling Mark the story. She didn't tell him how Thea, an ex-model, once left a dinner when she thought Lucy liked a visiting filmmaker, 'just to be on the safe side', but she did tell him about her tendency to 'fall in love' with a certain type of girl, of which Thea was a prime example, and how she had fallen in love with certain houses too, in much the same way.

Mark laughed. 'Fall in love with me,' he said, 'fall in love with *me.*'

Behind him she could see water in the swimming pool dimly reflecting the lanterns strung overhead, little circles of light waiting for a breeze to set them free. They were the only diners sitting outside, and Lucy felt sorry for the other guests, cocooned inside in the warmth.

'Come on, let's go for a walk,' he said, taking her hand.

They walked over to the oasis of Mara, jostled up by one of the fault lines that ran through everything here, so still now it looked like an oil slick, then further into the desert where the darkness settled around them. The tips of their cigarettes sparked on and off like two fireflies in cahoots.

'Maybe we'll see a shooting star,' Lucy couldn't help saying. She had a superstitious streak she was deeply ashamed of, and knew if she saw one she would make a wish; although this usually came with a rush of confusion as the star shot across the sky, and left her feeling she had chosen badly.

They sat against a rock and scanned the winking metropolis above for signs of movement. Coyotes gathered somewhere in the distance, their yapping rising to a desperate pitch before it was quiet again. 'No gravitas,' said Mark.

He had brought a flask of whisky, and they passed it back and forth, grateful for the warmth. After a while she felt him pull something off a bush.

'Here.' He cupped her hands together, placed some leaves in them and blew. A faint smell rose up from Lucy's hands, like rain after a long dry spell.

'The smell is so familiar… '

'They're creosote leaves. It smells like rain, doesn't it? Or else rain smells like creosote.'

The desert night shifted around them in light cracklings. Mark kissed Lucy fleetingly, again and again, as if coming in from a great distance before flying off again. 'Desert kisses, but they will never dry up. I promise you that.'

Children, she thought, returning them, they were just children.

The next day they drove out to Kelso Dunes, and sat on the platform at the long abandoned railway station, swinging their legs over the overgrown tracks.

'Hey, Mark!'

Not here, surely.

Everywhere they went, someone knew Mark. They could be in the most out of the way place – like now – and there it would come – 'Hey, Mark!' Always with the same surprised delight of someone spotting a rare and precious object.

'Hey, Mark – unbelievable!'

'Hey, Fred! What are you doing here, man? This is Lucy.'

'Hey, Lucy.'

'Hello.'

Fred looked at her with real interest. If she was with Mark, then she must be somehow special. For all his easy-going charm, Mark was notoriously fastidious.

'So what are you doing here?' Mark said. 'Are you staying at the inn?'

'Just checked in. You know I've been developing this script? Thought this might be a good location for one of the scenes. I've got the idea of doing The Canterbury Tales on Harleys, bunch of bikers going from Seattle to Vegas.'

He directed this last part to Lucy, expecting her to pick up the thread. She was English, Chaucer must be in her DNA. Lucy frantically scanned her mind to locate anything she could remember – The Wife of Bath's Tale? Dirty? but Chaucer took himself off the radar – *pop!* like a missing airplane. She nodded. 'Sounds good,' a moment later.

'Lucy's trying to get an interview with Chris Marker, he's got a new film out,' said Mark.

'Really?' said Fred. 'That's amazing. He never gives interviews.'

Sunlight caught his glasses and gave his eyes an extra gleam.

'Well, who knows. I've asked anyway.'

'You'll get it, babes,' said Mark.

They traded cultural playing cards for a while, although Lucy felt her hand was a bit thin. Although if she *could* get Marker...

150

They met up with Fred again at dinner. Although there was the obligatory 'you guys probably want to be alone', he was a good friend of Mark's, the dining room was tiny and it would have been ridiculous not to. Mark had told her that Fred might be a bit depressed as he had just split up with his long-standing girlfriend, Helen, a fashion designer, when it turned out she didn't know at what speed the earth revolved around the sun. Lucy, who certainly couldn't be relied on for that sort of information, and who, in fact, believed that there were far more interesting revolutions to be aware of, such as what was happening between her and Mark, was shocked.

In any case, Fred didn't seem particularly depressed. He and Mark spent most of the meal discussing Fred's script, Mark's show, Lesley's new book and Kieslowski's latest, which they had all just seen. Lucy hadn't said anything for a while, although Mark kept glancing at her, waiting for her to speak. Finally, just as dessert arrived, chosen from a list ominously labelled Endings, she said:

'I think I killed Emile de Antonio.'

That was the problem with not saying anything for a long time. You were liable to come out with something crazy. She hoped her cheeks weren't as volcanic as they felt.

'Emile de Antonio? He died? When?' Fred's floppy blond hair swung about anxiously.

'Last week.'

'God. How did I miss that? He was a great filmmaker – a great, great filmmaker' – he turned to Mark – 'do you remember *Underground*, or *Painters Painting*? Warhol said everything he learned about painting, he learned from De.'

'Mmn,' said Mark. 'Amazing film.'

'And who's critiquing American culture and politics now – I mean, who's really doing it? Barbara Kopple with the coal miners, I guess, or what's her name – the one who did the film about Iran Contra – another Barbara I think – but it's not the same' – Fred turned back to Lucy – 'Wait, you killed him?'

De Antonio had sounded so pleased with himself, so unbearably, fantastically *pleased* with himself, when she called to interview him

151

at home on the Lower East Side. At least, that's how she explained it to herself afterwards. He was sure *Mr Hoover and I* would not win an Oscar, it was too subversive; he was sure audiences knew it was remarkable; he was sure his works were seminal, *seminal;* he was sure he deserved, even at seventy, yet another young wife, who could be seen cutting his hair in the movie; he was sure Lucy was fully on board with everything he was saying.

'I'm just wondering how you feel about the *Village Voice* review?' Lucy asked suddenly. She hadn't meant to bring it up.

'The *Voice* did a piece?' He sounded surprised. 'Can you read it to me?'

She made her voice non-committal when she came to the most damning part: 'He is charming, he is witty, he is tiresome, though "tired" seems more accurate and certainly more generous to a filmmaker at the end of a long life in dissent... '

There was a long silence. After a while De Antonio spoke. 'I hadn't seen that,' he said, and there was a new, faint tone to his voice.

Two days later he had a heart attack.

'It was a coincidence,' said Mark. 'Just one of those things. No one dies of a bad review.'

'No, but it was still one of the last things he heard,' said Fred.

Lucy thought of De Antonio's young wife, cutting his thinning hair as he sits on a stool recounting anecdotes she hasn't heard before, her easy incredulous laughter as she circles him, snipping here and there, pale tufts caught in the sunshine before drifting to the ground, and wished she could call her and ask for forgiveness. They listened to the Van Morrison, driving back at night, all their earlier landmarks invisible now. She leant back in her seat, closed her eyes, and tried to conjure the desert standing before her again. She knew it hadn't been a mystical or spiritual experience, as she'd explained to Mark afterwards, when they were lying in bed that night. Nothing like that. It was just that, for a moment, she'd been allowed to see the world as it really is, more beautiful really than it had any reason to be.

*

152

Five days later Erika buzzed her.

'Call for you on line two,' she squeaked in her Betty Boop voice.

Lucy picked up the phone.

'Hello?'

''Allo.'

'Who is this?'

'This is Chris Marker.' The ending of his surname sounded like air.

'Oh my gosh – I didn't think – thank you – are you – are you calling from Paris?'

'Mm.'

Lucy tried to formulate a thought.

'Englishwoman – fire first.'

'Oh yes of course, I'm sorry. Your film is called *The Owl's Legacy*. Why the owl?'

'Why the yowl?'

'Yes. The owl.'

'The yowl is' – pause – 'the yowl is a symbol of wisdom, of course. Minerva and all that' – longer pause and some bumping on the phone – Marker's voice came and went, muffled and indistinct – 'but as 'Egel said, the yowl spreads its wings only with the falling of the dusk.'

'So... we're in the dark and don't understand anything fully until it's too late? Until it's over? Is that what your film is saying?'

But the line abruptly went dead. She waited a while to see if Marker would call back; but that seemed as improbable as his calling in the first place.

'I can't believe it,' Lucy said to Erika. 'I cannot *believe* it. That was Chris Marker on the phone. This will make a great story.'

'What did he say?' asked Erika.

'He said... not much actually.'

Lucy walked up Robertson Boulevard to the bagel place, thinking about the call, and how she would spring it on Mark later. And from Mark it would no doubt bounce over to Fred. No, Marker hadn't said much, true. But that didn't matter. He had called. That was the important thing. He must have liked something about the magazine – maybe the fact that its circulation was so small? Or her writing perhaps? She'd sent him something she'd written about the Black Audio Film Collective and now she remembered one or two phrases she was quite pleased with.

The two sisters were behind the counter as always. They were in their late fifties, and although Lucy went there nearly every day, she never saw them speaking much to anybody. But she wanted to tell them that today had been a great day – a really great day. She wouldn't go into detail, obviously. Just that some days something you wouldn't dream possible happened, and well, today it was like that. She smiled and tried to catch the younger sister's eye, but as she leant into the counter to scoop up some cream cheese her sleeve rode up and Lucy noticed six dark grey numbers tattooed on her forearm. They had a slightly blurry quality, like a drawing that had been left out in the damp. Her sister must have them too. These numbers had once meant one thing; now they meant: survivors. Lucy paid and left. What was there to say? Belated wisdom wasn't much of an answer to anything, she thought, even supposing it came at all. Hegel, about whom she knew more or less nothing, except that he had called America the land of the future, where the burden of the world's history would reveal itself (for example at Best Bagels on Robertson Boulevard), was obviously an optimist; essentially a Californian.

When Lucy got back to the office she found a fax lying curled up on the floor. A computer-generated headshot of a gaunt man with compressed lips (*my work speaks for me*) appeared next to the top half of an owl's head. The owl stared out at Lucy with very round, very piercing black eyes. There was something unnerving in the steadiness of its highly pixilated gaze. The image was repeated six times, each time getting narrower and narrower, until just the owl's and the man's eyes remained, before they merged into a solid black line where the paper ended. A cover note said it was to illustrate the article as requested. Signed C.M. There was no mention that they had spoken earlier.

'He sent you a fax? Just after you spoke?' Mark was clearly amazed. 'From Paris... – are you sure?'

Lucy had gone straight to Mark's after work.

'Yes. It has the international prefix at the top of the page. 33–1. But why is that weirder than the fact that he called me? He loves all that digital stuff.'

Mark looked away. 'I don't know. I just find it very odd, that's all.'

What was odd was Mark's reaction. She'd longed all day for the moment when she could tell him about her coup, but he seemed strangely incurious about the conversation, and strangely interested in the matter of the fax.

'I'm sure I made a complete fool of myself. Maybe we didn't get cut off. Maybe he hung up because I was trying to figure out what he meant by that Hegel quote. But I must be doing something right if Chris Marker is calling me. The most people normally get from him is a picture of a cat. He sounded so... French. I mean, I know he *is* French, and Marker's not his real name – but to hear his voice – ' At this point Mark put his arms around Lucy and held her so tightly that she could no longer speak. He stroked her hair, and for a moment she had the impression that she was being consoled for something, and it was a relief when he began to kiss her and other, more straightforward feelings took over.

*

On Christmas Day Lucy bailed out of her various invitations, put the roof of the Mustang down, and drove up the coast. There was almost no traffic, the light was clear, and everything gleamed: the red bonnet of the car, the white beach coming and going, the blue sea widening into the blue sky. Even the houses on the cliffs seemed mesmerized, craning out on their stilts as if for a better view of the ocean, although poised and ready to fall at a moment's notice.

Lucy drove as fast as she could, relying on the faulty logic that speed restrictions didn't apply to foreigners (the same logic that suggested cancelling invitations at the last moment wasn't as rude as it was back home) but the car was old and shook dangerously at anything over 80 miles an hour. She pulled into Point Dume and made her way down to the beach. There were a few surfers in the water, but there were no good waves and they bobbed gently up and down like stranded seals, clinging to their boards.

Mark had flown back to New York to spend Christmas with his

mother two days earlier. He had wanted Lucy to go with him, but she said it was too soon; maybe she was conscious too that her reticence didn't exactly decrease her stock. She had discussed this with Claire.

'Definitely don't go,' Claire confirmed.

'Plus his mother sounds ghastly. Apparently she only likes tall thin flat-chested women for her son.'

'*Eww*, that counts you out, then. Although not me.'

At the airport they had both somehow been surprised to discover that there were other people in the world, holding on and not letting go, just as they were. Before he went through the gate Mark handed her a small, badly wrapped present, which Lucy now opened. He had bought her a gold heart on a chain, sweet and delicate, with an amethyst in the centre. She put it around her neck, lay back on the sand, and closed her eyes. She could hear the surfers calling to each other, their high-pitched voices ending in a rising question mark. It was, she thought, a perfect Christmas.

When it came down to it, the story of Marker calling her took up only a few lines, and got relegated to a sidebar. She got an ambitious film student at UCS to write an in-depth analysis of *The Owls' Legacy*, which he did with commendable enthusiasm, considering the quick turn-around time and poor pay.

Mark returned, and they rediscovered the exhilaration of being found, of reaching for each other at odd moments, any moment, the sight of the other's clothes tangled on the floor, or hanging on the back of the chair, a coat or a scarf, containing within their folds the absolute *themness* of them. Shoes lying alone or apart – everything spoke with extraordinary poignancy about its wearer. Every object became a portal to the other's world, a reason to open up and say, *it was like this.* This sweater belonged to my father, Mark said. Beige, triple-ply cashmere, moth-eaten; somehow it represented a fortune made and lost, and Lucy saw the rents in the fabric as gaping holes through which the family had been forced to look and wonder, before gradually reconstructing their lives. Each revelation now appeared in a different light: So this is what it was all for – it brought me here to you. Together they created imaginary maps, pinpointing all the intersections, crossings and diversions that had finally led them to meet. Mark bought two racoon hats and nailed them to the wall. 'Love pioneers, conquering new territory.'

For the first time in her life Lucy could say, I am completely happy.

'Yes,' wept Claire, over the phone. 'I can see that.'

Six months and it still hadn't abated. Everything was backdrop – dinners, movies, walks – it didn't matter what they were doing, the world that lay behind these things was muted, the sound switched off. 'You guys are impossible to be with,' Fred complained. 'Does anyone else exist?'

The remorseless summer pushed on well into September. Lucy couldn't find the usual signs to suggest that a new season was on its way; the windows of her apartment were thrown open, but there was no cooling of the night air. There was the occasional dry rattling from the palm outside, and the wail of a siren racing to an emergency in the distance, but otherwise the dark was almost oppressively quiet and still.

Living Death

Harley Carnell

These are the opening chapters from a novel of the same name.

Pre-Prologue

On March 3rd 2014, at 23:23, Scott English died during an operation to remove his appendix.

Prologue

Apart from his dying, Scott's operation was a success. And, now that his appendix had been taken care of, he was in perfect health; with the minor exception of the irreversible scar running across his stomach.

The next morning, one of the surgeons – Dr Joy Nurse – spoke to Scott. As well as being a doctor, Dr Nurse wrote popular medicine books, for which she had been awarded the moniker: 'The Brian Cox of Medicine'. This experience always proved useful when Dr Nurse explained complicated medical facts to patients, and did so again as she told Scott how unserious his death was.

'Put simply,' she said, 'the word "death" means something different in the medical community than it does in general talk. When you're talking normally, you think of the word "death" and you think of that being the end. You think of a corpse. But in medicine, a person can be declared dead if their heart stops pumping blood properly or does so irregularly – when this happens they are what is known as "clinically dead". If this goes untreated for long enough, then you would be in trouble: you would actually die. This is what is known as "legal death" or "brain death", which is where the phrase "brain dead" comes from. You were dead in the medical sense, but obviously not in the colloquial sense. And, because we were able to fix the problem quickly enough, there was no damage done. So really, when I say you were dead, you have nothing to worry about. It's like if I call my friend in Australia at nine o'clock this evening, which for her would be 7am. You wouldn't say that I was talking to her in the future, or she was talking to me in the past, would you? In the same way, when I say that you died during your operation, I don't actually mean that you were dead.'

1

For many years, Scott had been embarrassed that his parents were stereotypes. When he was at university, taking a degree in The Sociology of Psychology, he had left one of his four yearly modules open for Creative Writing. The stories and the characters that appeared in his Creative Writing submissions were drawn directly and unfiltered from his life, and were essentially non-fictional. He had tried to write invented characters, and place them in fictional scenarios, but he found it too difficult. Making up stories was, he conceded, an alien concept to him.

In one of these submissions, his parents had appeared as characters. His lecturer had written in the feedback that his parents were 'flat and unbelievable' and that 'people just aren't like this in real life. You read the characters of the parents and you think to yourself, ironically enough, that these read like characters in a book, not actual people.' He added that 'when you read a character or an event in a book that doesn't seem plausible, you lose interest in the whole story. You feel like you can't trust the author, and you don't want to continue with the book.'

The comments were for the draft of the story, and were made one week before the final submission date. Scott was able to salvage his story by the last minute exclusion of his parents and inclusion of his sister, Rachel, who became the new protagonist. Rachel was a lawyer, who spent her evenings singing K-Pop songs in various London karaoke bars wearing a purple wig. She was renowned locally for winning numerous karaoke competitions. She had once even made the national news when she had prevented a man she saw trying to steal someone's phone from their jacket pocket by throwing a microphone at him, tying him up with the microphone cord, calling the police with the phone she had saved from being stolen, and then sitting on the thwarted thief until the police arrived. Scott's lecturer had been so impressed with the inclusion of Rachel – 'one of the most original and imaginative characters I've ever read' – that he had given Scott a 72 for the story which had been previously destined for a 56.

Scott hadn't seen his parents for a few months, so he was looking forward to their visit. But he was also dreading it at the same time. Their behaving and acting like stereotypes was fine behind closed doors, but in front of other people it still embarrassed him even though he was now in his thirties. He didn't mind being embarrassed by his parents when he was a teenager. Doing it then was fine. So normal that it was stereotypical itself. Now that he was in his thirties, he felt stupid, ashamed even, to still feel like this. At the same time, though, his parents *were* embarrassing. He couldn't help worrying that one of them might say something stupid to one of the doctors or nurses, and that it would reflect badly on him.

As if summoned by him thinking about them, his parents entered the room. Visiting hours began at two, and now that it was two, they were here. Over the years, they had managed to perfect being on time to a science. They were never late, never early. As his father had said once, 'If I say I'm going to be at a party at 7pm, that's when I'll be there. Not six fifty-nine, not seven oh-one, but seven.'

Scott's mother was shrunken by worry. She held in one hand a wad of tear-sodden tissues. In the other she clutched his father's hand. When she, Rose English, saw her son, bedridden and pale, draped in a hospital gown that looked more like a shower curtain, she started crying again.

'Now really Rose, this is too much!' said Scott's father, John English, shaking his head.

Ignoring his admonishment, Rose continued to cry and ran over to Scott. She threw herself on to the floor by his bed, wrapping her arms around his body. Positioning her head on his chest, she cried muffled tears.

'Sorry about this, son,' his father said, tutting. 'I told her you wouldn't want all this blubbing first thing out of an operation. But, you know how it is: there's no telling them. It's like talking to a brick wall. I mean, you're not a child – you're thirty years old for heaven's sake. And look at you, you're fine. In the old days, they held you down with a belt and gave you a piece of wood to bite down on and it didn't do anyone any harm. Nowadays, an operation's as easy as claiming benefits.'

For the next five minutes, his mother continued to cry. Her weeping was interspersed by his father's unsolicited views on various subjects. He had just managed to inform Scott why best before end dates were a scam – 'I once ate a piece of bread that was covered in mould and I didn't die, did I? Well, did I?' – when Scott's mother lifted her head up.

'I'm sorry,' she said. 'It was just seeing you like that: looking so helpless. As a mother it's the worst sight you can see. You never want to see your child ill. It would just be the worst thing in the world if you were to outlive your child.' The thought almost introduced more tears, but she was able to suppress them.

'Oh come off it, Rose,' his father said, 'he's fine. Fit as an ox.' He slapped Scott's shoulder. 'See. You'll make him soft if you keep up with all this nonsense.'

With her almost uncanny ability to tune out his father, his mother said:

'Before I forget, Rachel said that she'll come and see you tonight, after work.'

'Thanks, Mum.'

'Is Michaela coming?' she asked, referring to Scott's girlfriend.

He nodded, still feeling his father's slap tingling against his shoulder. 'Yeah, she's coming after work too.'

'And how are you feeling, darling?' she asked. 'Are you warm? Do you want another blanket? You look like you need another blanket. John, go and call a nurse and ask for another blanket – Scott, darling, is there a button you press for you to call a nurse, or do you just call them?'

'Mum, I'm fine really. I'm not cold.'

'And you're eating right?'

'I'm eating left,' he said, smiling in apology for the awful joke. His mother, usually receptive to this kind of humour, barely managed to smile.

'Scott, this is no time for joking,' she said solemnly.

'No, Mum it's fine. I'm fine. It's a hospital; they know what's good for you.'

'You say that Scott, but I was reading this thing on the Internet last night, about hospital food. You never know what's being put into what you eat.'

'Well I'm sure I'll be fine, Mum. If the food made people ill, there'd be complaints and stuff. And anyway, I'm not even in here for a week. I'm getting let out next Monday.'

At this, his mother visibly relaxed: her facial muscles unknotted and she leaned back in her chair. In his experience, his mother was rarely worried about the thing she claimed to be. Usually, she liked to focus on a small issue to worry about, to avoid having to focus on the much larger issues that framed it. She was undoubtedly concerned more about his contracting a virus, or there being complications from his operation, than whether he was being properly fed. Now that she knew he was getting out soon, all of her worry was gone.

'Oh that's wonderful news,' she said. 'Such *wonder*ful news!'

'I'm absolutely fine,' Scott said. 'And the operation went well. The doctor said it couldn't have gone better.'

'Oh, yes,' his mother said, smiling and sitting up. 'We spoke to Dr Nurse on the way in. Such a nice woman. A bit small, though. I think that she really needs feeding up. But then I guess if you're a doctor you know how to watch your weight and still be healthy.'

'Strong handshake,' his father added.

'And look,' his mother said, reaching into her handbag and taking out Nurse's bestselling book *How to Keep the Doctor Away: Simple Steps for a Healthier Life*. The front cover saw a cross-armed Dr Nurse, in a white doctor's jacket, smiling at the reader/browser. Her head was a few centimetres under her name, large-printed in gold letters, and her feet hovered slightly above the title, which itself sat atop the tagline: *The book doctors don't want you to know about!!!*

His mother opened the book, slid through a few pages, and then stopped.

'Look,' she said, turning the page in Scott's direction. The page she indicated was blank, except for a scrawl in the centre which, with a squint – he really needed to get glasses – he realised was Dr Nurse's signature. 'When I saw her I just had to get something signed,' his mother said. 'Luckily, the WH Smith's across the road was open so I went and bought this. She waited for me to go and get it as well. Isn't that nice of her? I've never seen a celebrity before. It's so weird to see someone you've seen on television in the flesh. And to think, not only have I met *the* Joy Nurse, and spoken to her, and got her signature, but she operated on my son! I can't wait to tell them at my book club.'

'How is your book club, Mum?'

His mother's book club met weekly to read and discuss books, and to gossip about the members of the book club who were away on a given week. The book club only had two rules. The first rule was that everyone had to have fun. The second rule was that they could only read books that had been television shows first. Graham had chosen one of Dr Nurse's books last year (*Better or Nurse*) and everyone in the book club had adored it. Since then, they had all become massive Dr Nurse fans.

'Oh bloody hell,' his father said. 'I'm going outside for a cigarette. If I had a pound for every time I've had to hear about the book club, then I'd have... well I'd be a bloody rich man I can tell you that much.' His father left the room, patting his chest to see if his cigarettes were still in his pocket. Once he was outside, Scott's mother said: 'What were we talking about?'

'I can't remember,' Scott said.

Ten minutes after his father returned from his cigarette, Scott's parents left. Despite his death, operation, and meeting of Dr Nurse, the fact remained that they still didn't really have anything to talk to each other about. Once they had covered the minutiae of their extended family – Aunt This had won ten pounds in the Lottery; Uncle That still wasn't dead – they had all known that it was time to leave. Scott, utilising his C in GCSE Drama, produced a yawn that was convincing enough to successfully conjure one from his father. Seeing this, his mother said that they needed to go, to let Scott rest.

2

The yawn was fake, but it did make Scott realise that he was in fact quite tired. When his parents left, he decided to sleep until Michaela arrived.

He woke up four hours later, with Michaela running her hands across his forehead.

'Scott,' she said, 'Scott.'

'What time is it?' he asked. When he opened his eyes, he winced, and quickly shut them again

'Seven,' she said.

He remembered now that she had come straight from work, which finished at six. For a moment, he had thought it was a Saturday.

Work for Michaela was being a senior lecturer at the University of Camden, where she taught a course called '*Hard Times*: Literature and Porn', which was so popular that UO Camden had been forced to hire two guest lecturers to take seminars for it, and had to move the lecture to the main lecture hall. A keen Freudian, she also taught a course on Freudian and psychoanalytic interpretations of literature, which had seen a modicum of popularity when she had changed its name to '*From Oedipus to Twilight*: Freud and Literature', but it still lagged way behind the porn module in terms of number of students. She also contributed regularly to the *Journal of Post-Freud Freudian Studies,* for which she was currently writing an article which applied Slavoj Žižek's notion of the unconscious manifesting itself externally (if covertly) in the forces of ideology to the *Goosebumps* novels of R.L. Stine.

Monday was her busiest day, in which she had a lecture, two seminars, and had to supervise one of her three PhD students. Scott had told her yesterday that she didn't have to come, knowing how busy she was. But she had dismissed it, saying that she'd be 'happy to'. (She was the only person he knew who used the phrase 'I'll be happy to' literally.)

'While you wake up,' she said, 'I'll just show you what I brought you. I saw that you didn't bring anything from home, so I got you your crossword books. And I didn't know what book you were reading at the moment, so I brought this because it had a bookmark in it.' She handed him Clive Johnson's *Mansfield Park and Mole People*.

'I read a bit of it on the bus here,' she said.

'Yeah? What did you think about it?'

'I thought it was great,' she said.

164

'Really?'

'No, of course not really! They can't perform their play because the mole-people have burrowed under the stage! It's just stupid.'

'But look,' said Scott, pointing at the cover. '*Bloodbath Magazine* gave it six stars out of five. Can't argue with that.'

'That's true enough,' she said. 'I also brought you these.' She put down a four-pack of iced-fingers, which had begun to stick to the bag. 'What's the food like in here?'

'I don't really like it,' he said, 'but I don't know if that's just because I'm in hospital. Maybe if I'd bought the exact same things in a shop and eaten them at home I'd've liked them.'

'I'll bring you some food when I come tomorrow if you want.' She looked into her bag, but there was nothing else in there. 'And how are you feeling?' she asked.

He took a moment to think before answering her question. When it came to his mother, it was obvious that he shouldn't tell her that he had died during the operation. Doing so would only worry her, and it would be the sort of worry that would be hard to erase. With Michaela, he was less sure. She was not a worrier like his mother, but that didn't mean that she wouldn't be in regards to this. In his years of going out with her, hearing her talk about Freud, watching Freud documentaries with her, reading her papers on Freud, attending Freud conferences, visiting Freud's house, and wearing her Freud slippers, he had come to develop a quite impressive working knowledge of the Father of Psychology. In one of his essays (he couldn't remember which), Freud had written something about old superstitions being hard to completely erase from people living in even the most rational societies. According to Freud, this was most apparent in regards to the fear of death. Michaela was a rational person, but that was not to say that she would take his death rationally.

It made sense, then, not to tell her. Just to be safe. But at the same time, he didn't want to lie to her. Even if lying by omission was to actual lying what his own death was to actual Death. When he promised her a few years ago that he wouldn't ever lie to her, he had meant it. He had also meant it when he said that he didn't *want* to lie to her; and wouldn't do so even if there was no chance of his being caught. Whenever he did lie – no matter how innocuous the lie itself – he felt bad; it was a betrayal of her trust.

He would have to tell her.

He first told her about waking up from the operation and speaking with Dr Nurse. Then, he said: 'And, funny thing, but Dr Nurse told me that – '

'Mr English,' said one of two men who had just entered the room. He was good-looking, with a sprinkling of black stubble lining his jaw, and lightly-spiked hair of the same hue. If he had been a bit taller, he could easily have starred as a handsome villain in an adaptation of a Victorian novel.

'Yes?' said Scott.

'Mr English, nice to meet you,' the man said. 'My name is Stephen Penn, I write for the *Chronicle* newspaper.' As he spoke he maintained a smile which seemed as sincere as a shop assistant's. He swivelled his head in the direction of Michaela.

'And this must be Mrs English?'

'It mustn't,' she said. 'I'm Dr Michaela Reynolds.'

At this, Penn's smile got even wider. 'Of course. My sincere apologies Dr Reynolds.' Turning back to Scott, Penn said, 'Mr English, would it be possible to borrow a moment of your time. Although I suppose you can't really borrow time, can you!' He punctuated his joke with a short, unreciprocated laugh. 'Can I *have* a moment of your time would be better.'

'Well, I mean – '

'As I said, Mr English, I work for the *Chronicle*. I am here with my photographer, Len Simpson.' He indicated the man next to him, who nodded at Scott without smiling. 'We really just wanted to ask you a few questions, speak to you for a bit. We wouldn't be long.'

'You mean like an interview?'

'I suppose you could call it that, yes.'

Fall

Zahra Mulroy

Narrated by twenty-something oddball Cassandra, Fall *is set in London. Cassandra starts talking to us on January 1ˢᵗ 2013. Troy, her oldest friend, has killed himself, and her only other friend, Reuben, says that she is responsible for his death. Cass tells us she is a seer, albeit one who will never be believed and who cannot alter fate in any way. Her story cuts back and forth from her childhood to how she came to be responsible for her friend's death, and is about self-fulfilling prophecy and insanity.*

Part One: Chapter One

You mortals love them, but romantic comedies make me want to self-immolate. Especially the painfully formulaic ones – you know the kind I mean. Because there is no comedy in affairs of the heart. Only the inexorability of something breaking – like someone's hairlined, fibreglass hopes. Or that all-too human heart. What's so comedic about that? Little mortals, tell me where the comedy is in *this*?

It's 4pm on New Year's Day 2013 and my first and truest friend has just shuffled off this hatefully finite coil. Swung off it, in fact, and with ties he ham-fistedly struggled to knot in life. I may have seen this coming, and not only did I see the Man with the Scythe lumbering towards us, I did nothing. But no, that's not quite right. I did do something. I was responsible – I bade the Man with the Scythe *'come hither'*. And he did.

Now, indifferent winter daylight is bidding us all good-bye. It barely has time to drool through the kitchen window onto me, utilitarian in flannel pyjamas and shivering because Troy was always the one to put money in the meter. Now his body is stiffening two floors above me. The absence of life is palpable. It deafens me, so I run a glass of water and try not to retch as it hits the stomachic void. I drink slowly and gaze with blank maggot-eyes out of the window. London is really no place to find yourself without an ally. Thus it is with relief, as the last stale crust of sunlight gets eaten by the houses facing us, I catch Ms One For Sorrow dancing for worms on the freshly frozen turf outside. Fellow harbinger of doom and bearer of bad press – the sight of one makes the more superstitious among you soil yourselves, peering over your shoulder for the man with the scythe. Or your P45. Or something. And collectively they don't fare much better; *more* than one is Murder. Yet giraffes get Journey, which I like. Although admittedly Baboons get Flange, which is disgraceful. I am glad of the company.

Have you ever woken up to an ebb so low you wish it would just drown you, then weeks later deposit your turgid cadaver somewhere everyone could see, just to rub it in their faces? Well if you do, get thee to a quack. I jest. I never did, until today. And I certainly only ever rarely fantasise about dying and even then only on special occasions. A psychiatrist acquaintance told me that fascination with death is natural, albeit less socially acceptable than fascination with fornication. And I remember pondering what kind of person dances with the void on a regular basis, just for the hell of it. Certainly not I. Though my friend Roo frequently updated his obituary, much as a saner member of society might update their CV. The two might have even been one and the same and although in a different time, place and dimension I may have laughed at this thought, I am alas me, circa now and Troy is dead and Roo will never speak to me again. I know this because the future talks to me.

To be honest, lots of things talk to me.

Daniel Day Lewis talks to me. Not the Irish alpha-actor with a heaving trophy cabinet, but a homeless ex-serviceman who circuits SE's 13, 10, 8, 14 and 15. He talks to me because the future also talks to him. Mr Opposite – pervert and local eccentric – he talks to me. Primarily because he is a pervert but also because he is eccentric. He appeared to me in a dream twice – the deities like to use the flotsam and jetsam from my day-to-day life. They like their little joke. But between you and me, their sense of humour is – at best – dated. At worst – it's crueller than clamping a hearse. I mean, *Calliope*, for fuck's sake…

If you don't believe me about the future thing, I'll show you. In ten seconds, Mr Opposite's outside light will go on as he steps

168

into his garden to water his plants. There. Please imagine the sound of his knees pistoning and popping as he crouches to fanny around with the hose. Ooof. Study the anal puckering of his lips as he starts to whistle. Last week it was Prefab Sprout, 'The King of Rock and Roll'. Ad nauseam. Now watch as his head flashes round to the direction of the street.

Sirens are smashing their way through the hung-over, sleepy stillness of the day. He drops the hose in excitement, sniffing the air, smelling blood on the wind. A lifetime of voyeurism has honed his senses to a police-dog level of formidability. He's figured out they're pulling up outside my flat. Try not to snigger as he trips on the hose, eagerness rendering him slapstick. The emergency services will soon be clamouring for entry, and a long night of questioning awaits me.

So as we are all now on the same page, let me go to the lounge and gather my thoughts as best I can.

You might be wondering – and you'd be right to – why doesn't this loser *do* anything? Why is she fraternizing with hobos and perverts whilst her only friends are either leisurely measuring out enough rope to hang themselves with or striking her from their lives? Why all this existentialist, fatalistic bullshit? Does she even know women have the vote? Well, I do. And I'll tell you why.

When I was eleven, it happened for the first time. Up till that point, life had been paint-by-numbers, contented. We weren't exactly the Waltons. But nor were we the Mansons. If I lacked for anything, I was not aware of it. If I had too much of something, I did not know of it. And the onset of puberty, up until that point, had been quite formulaic; I knew all about periods before my mother told me; I used my father's Bics the wrong way, lacerating my legs; I was curious enough about sex, but it did not consume me. I'd found my parents' copy of 'The Joy Of…' hidden behind their Readers' Digests and would flick through it, trying to imagine what was going through that hirsute, retro couple's minds.

So far so anyone's story. And it still seems somewhat incongruous that what brought on my fit of the foresights was something as arbitrary as the body ticking an evolutionary box.

Our teeny tiny terraced house ensured two familial

developments. The first was that my father promptly got the snip after Helen's birth, and the second was that my sister and I were sentenced to sharing a bedroom – each witness to the other's every night terror, instance of somnambulance and bed fart. I had been feeling crampy and strange all day. I had had swimming practice, and found the water distorting and claustrophobic, whereas usually, I had always marvelled at how well the water and I seemed to mesh. I submitted myself, day after day, medal after medal. Because swimming made me special. A girl like me – your common garden Plain Jane (or Butch Cass, as was my pithy moniker) – needs something to make her special. But I quit my session early, self-consciously scuttled back home, went straight to bed and fell into a cautious, viscid sleep.

With this all taking place seven years prior to moving to London, I had not yet *really* met Mr Opposite. But *eh voila* – there he was, sat on the edge of my bed.

Marbelline with fear, I blinked rapidly over the top of my sheet at him. My mother had told me about all bad men, about *stranger danger;* enticements into cars with promises and sweeties. At eleven, I was beginning to grasp that under the sunny, warm face of the rock we inhabited there lived unspeakable creatures who revelled in darkness and slime. Here was such a creature, come to take me away. Tears itched down my face. Other than that, I could only manage paralysis and muteness.

Then he shrugged, which at the time I found weird, but now I can appreciate that the situation must have been as awkward for him as it was for me. He cleared his throat. He was going to talk! He was going to say – in a voice darker than hell – that he was going to kill me. Or worse. He cleared his throat with bronchial *'hrrm'* and spoke.

'Don't drink, don't fuck – these mortal whatnots tamper with the astral signal. Oh, and try not to give a fuck that no one will ever believe you.'

Although I winced at this (we had a swear jar at home, and heavy penalties for profanity dropping), I remember his t-glotalling and h-dropping took the edge off his threat. It made me relax a little.

'Did you hear me?' he whined. The poor bastard sounded like he just wanted to get back to his flora, away from this strange girlhood bedroom.

I nodded.

'Good,' he rubbed his hands on his thighs, as if psyching himself to get up and leave. 'Good... Erm, any questions?'

'Yes,' my voice was hoarse with feelings vying for supremacy. 'I don't understand.' My abdomen ached and moaned. 'Who are you? And, sorry – astral signal?'

For although he hadn't yet told me he was going to murder me in cold blood, I still felt it wise to stall for time, until someone or something could wake me, could rescue me.

Mr Opposite raised his hands impatiently.

'Christ, I'm no good at this, am I? I had it all mapped out. Right – in my mind's eye I wanted the conversation to go a little something like this: I'd say, *'Guess what, Cass, you can see the future!'* Then *you* – all grateful like – would say something along the lines of *'Great, I can't wait to get started. First stop – a EuroMillions ticket.'* Then *I'd* remember something and have to say, *'Stop you right there, Cass, We forgot to mention... no one will ever believe you, so don't bother tinkering with fate.'* And you'd be teed off, but you'd get your head around it eventually.'

He stared at me.

'So... so I'll see everything that's going to happen, like, in the world?'

'No, no, no – there's only so much time in the day my girl. You'd go mad! Plus you'll be needing to hold down a job, have a life and all of that shit. No, you'll know when you get a, a – whatsit – a premonition. Mostly to do with people you know, keep it simple, personal like.'

'But no one's going to believe me – isn't that what you said?'

'Alack, yes. Don't ask me why.'

'Well then,' I struggled to sit up in bed, half laughing into the stupidity of it all, 'what's the point?'

'There is none. That – you'll see – *is* the point.'

Childhood is pitted with illogical parental maxims. *Do as I say, not do as I do; because I say so; would you jump off a cliff if so-and-so did; you'll understand when you're older.* But this one seemed more asinine, more unfair than any other. Life was all about 'point', right? Being good yielded rewards. If you had something and could share it, it was your duty to do so. I didn't know about drinking and fucking

171

but I had an inclination that one day I might like to. And if these things had to be forfeited for foresight, then that trade-off didn't seem too shabby. But if sacrifices were to be made for this… gift… and yet it had to remain a secret, turned inward away from the world, then even as an eleven-year-old I sensed a life of grey.

'How do I know you're telling the truth?'

'You'll be tested tomorrow,' he said, gesturing to my sleeping sister.

'What about Helen?' All remaining saliva evaporated from my mouth.

'Hrrm,' he wiped something he found in his ear on my duvet. She's going to get rather badly hurt. Sorry.'

'What? How – will she be OK? This isn't funny anymore.' My cramp started to beat a hot tattoo.

'Now, don't go shooting this here messenger,' began Mr Opposite, ''cause it pains me to say this. Truly. Hrrm. *You're* the cause of it. But remember Cass – not a word of it to *anyone.*'

And with that, he got up and left the room.

Hot and sly and complex – womanhood seeped through the membrane of my girlhood and that last, innocent sleep was no match for my abdominal pains. I awoke to twisted sheets, warm, wet and tangy with sweat and blood. I lay with my eyes closed for a beat, waiting for a tide of 'womanly' feelings to wash over me. Nothing. I could not have felt more 'eleven' if I had tried. Disgust was followed by more practical feelings; how was I to change the sheets without waking my sister? Should I wake my mother up? But turning on to my side, I saw Helen sitting up in bed across from me in the darkness. Awake, and a furious little fairy in her white night dress, arms folded.

'What's your problem?' I asked, eventually giving in to her hackneyed dramatics.

She yanked her bed-side lamp on.

'You're my problem!' she hissed.

Even in an infantile rage, my sister could have won child modelling contests. My mother delighted in the anomaly of Helen's genes, and was always finding or making her some kind of trinket to enhance her prettiness. I think it worried my father though, as he saw the local neighbourhood wolves circle ever closer.

'Either tell me what I'm meant to have done or shut up,' I said, rolling back over and willing her to tire of this fledgling tantrum so I could sort my bedding out. I didn't think she'd been given 'the talk' yet.

'If you don't know then I'm not going to tell you!'

'Fine,' I shrugged. That said, Helen wasn't always – cerebrally – the most worthy of opponents. Her comeback *du choix* was 'I know you are, you said you are, so what am I?'

'Fine! I'll tell you!' she hissed.

I switched sides again so I could look at her. But I was distracted. There was a tempest raging in my ears, perhaps adrenaline, or perhaps, *'There is none. That – you'll see – is the point'*. Waking up in my own menses to one of Helen's paddies seemed to reinforce that. Swimming made me special, yes. But there was an irrefutably dark glamour to Mr Opposite's visit. Surely I was the only eleven-year-old to adopt the mantra 'Don't drink, don't fuck – these mortal whatnots tamper with the astral signal. Oh, and try not to give a fuck that no one will ever believe you.'

Helen pinged out of bed and got right up in my face. I closed my eyes.

'You were mean just then, you woke me up saying dead mean things about me!' Her eyes were feverish with working herself up.

'Mean things about you to *who*?' I made a sarcastic show of peering around the room for some invisible interlocutor. Helen loathed my rookie dalliances with the lowest form of wit, as she most often could not match them. Instead, she preferred to shout...

'I dunno! You were dreaming or something! But not like normal... '

'Well then what was I saying that was so bad?' I felt gummy and disorientated. I swallowed heavily and opened my eyes to take her in.

('But remember Cass – not a word of it to anyone.')

'Idiot smelly cow things about me. How I was gonna get hurt, badly hurt... and...and... '

This was not a common Helen shitfit; there was disquiet in her eyes and heart, rendered more frantic by her childish inarticulacy, preventing her from gaining purchase on the questions and concerns she really wanted to throw at me. I interrupted her.

173

'You stupid pig, it's just a dream. Everyone has them and they literally never come true. Mum has them, Dad has them… '

But she just shook her head.

'This was different. You're not listening to me you, you… ' She paused, cocking her ear for signs that yet another nocturnal spat had woken our parents. The coast was clear ' …ugly bahstarred!'

She garnished her malapropism with a poison nod. I assumed that she had only ever seen the word in writing (for as I said, our house was a rare thing in its lack of profanity dropping).

I opened my mouth to speak, but another emotion kicked in. One which came far easier to my girlish self than it does to me today. It was love. Love for this furious, frustrating sharer of my DNA. Certainly, she had just pissed me off by simply being herself. But here was the incontrovertible fact that (dark glamour or not) I still had to grapple with: a strange man had just sat on my bed and told me my first ally and friend was going to get badly hurt, and because of me. I wanted to commit to the path set out for me, but if this accident of which he spoke was the first step then I wasn't so sure.

My umbrage at this gift then unfolded further. Who exactly was this governing body, bestowing powers all willy-nilly, but then imprisoning me within them? And could I even trust that my gift was true? That Mr Opposite had had a decidedly shifty look in his eyes, just like that old man in the park everyone's parents told them not to talk to. These questions then engendered a new feeling: defiance.

For, looking back, it was a flaw, shoving this all on an eleven-year-old girl. A girl who everyone called Butch Cass and thought was weird. A girl who could count her friends on one finger…

My thoughts were tripping over themselves. If nothing else, then this otherworldly entanglement could be a solution to my commonplace problem of unpopularity. Ex-best friend Lois O'Shea hadn't spoken to me in over two years, and her influence was such that all other playmates had followed suit. But if I confided in her this most dazzling of truths, then that would make me special, worthy of being included once more in the joyous motions of childhood.

I looked across at Helen, violently rearranging her teddies, fussing with her duvet and casting me uncompromising daggers. I

174

wobbled, thinking it really ought to be her I let in on my secret. But no. There was nothing to be gained from that. Not really. I turned to her.

'Soz if you got a bad night's sleep, but I don't know what you want me to say.'

I shut my eyes again and rolled on to my back. Impassive and tomb-like. I felt her continue to stare at me, the stranger in her sister's nightie.

Chapter Two

The next morning tasted a little of Christmas. With an apologetic grin and an armful of bedclothes, I imparted my fleshly news to my mother. I luxuriated in her embrace.

'Darling! Now you're a *woman,*' she sang.

She scanned me with excitement. Then her gaze snagged on something. A little sadness? A moue of worry? I wasn't sure. And I refused to let it bother me. For this was something we could share, just the two of us. It caused me to shine a little brighter, to need my mother that little bit more than Helen.

Then there was the unfleshly secret I had to share, the winning move in the (thus far) thankless slog at having friends. Effervescence charged through me, and it was heightened by how much it pissed Helen off. She did not cope well without her eight hours. Her daggers continued on the walk to school, but they were weighed down by the shadows under her eyes.

'Why are you grinning like an idiot?' she spat.

'None of your business' I chirped, my voice hitting an ear-splitting note of sanctimony.

'You've got Weetabix still stuck in your brace, did you know that? You look like you've got furry teeth.'

And with that she stalked off down the street ahead of me, attracting drunk-in-love glances from all who saw her.

I faltered a second, my bonfire slightly pissed on. I wanted us to be friends. My guilt at my part in what was to transpire could not be ignored. But then I remembered that I had an important day ahead of me, and I could quickly sort out my orthodontic malfunction in the toilets before registration. And I'll say it again:

the fates are capricious beasts. For who else was in the toilet, but ex-best friend, Lois O'Shea. Alone. Her entourage of Shauna Hislop, Becca and other assorted minions must have been elsewhere. It was an unprecedented piece of good fortune and it caused me to stop in my tracks, just for a pause, to watch ex-best friend Lois O'Shea leaning over the sinks towards the mirrors to expertly tarmac her lips in an unctuous cherry gloss.

I walked slowly toward her, shy. Suddenly she saw me in the mirror, and gave a little yelp, dropping the cosmetic freebie into the sink. A metallic smile split my face, before I remembered the gatecrashing Weetabix nugget, and snapped my mouth shut. I gave a small wave. She stared at me in the mirror, wavering between hard and soft, before throwing back her paraphernalia back into her rucksack and making to leave the toilets.

'Lois, wait.' I grabbed her arm, the imploring widening of my eyes mirroring that of hers.

'What do you want, Cass?' she muttered, slowly trying to pull her arm away and looking over my shoulder, away from the steam of my gaze.

'Just, please, hang on a second.' I scrabbled for words. I had not thought to rehearse what I might say to ex-best friend Lois O'Shea. 'I have to tell you something!'

Eye-rolling was a recent developmental phenomenon amongst us year six girls. I had not mastered the art, as all attempts to practice at home were met with no cartoons and early tea and bed. Clearly, Mrs O'Shea did not employ the same iron fist of discipline in her own home, and thus my ex-best friend Lois O'Shea could crush you with a casual revolution of her baby blues. She did that now.

'Come off it. We're going to be late for register.'

'We've got five minutes, at least. Please? I've got a secret, and you, you're the only person I can tell.'

I winced as I tried to forget that by cutting all contact with me two years ago she may not have had the right to my girlish confidences. But I remembered the plan, and screwed my courage to the sticking place.

Lois met my gaze, and I knew I had her. Or at least partly. Secrets are valuable currency amongst eleven-year-old girls. When I think about it, any girls, really. But it also felt like a hollow

176

victory, and thus I raked her face for any sign of nostalgia, of hopscotch and French cricket and our secret made-up language and that time we stole her mother's Milk Tray and scoffed it behind her shed so gluttonously that I vomited over my father's back the moment I got home.

However, whilst not discouraging, her look nonetheless could not be read. It's what made her such a stone-cold ex-best friend.

Then it happened again.

Pinioned by her poker-face, quick as a flash I saw ten years later; this stasis in her emotional rage, this clumsiness of her expressions, were what would make her such an unsuccessful actress. And that's what would ultimately drive her to a lonely death in an empty garage. A stream of lacklustre and painful auditions trickled into my mind. With every false-start and with every failure, the tumescent dewiness of her youth shrank and hardened, the clothes got cheaper, the eyes sad and confused, as if she could not quite swallow that bitterest of fallacies; that she, Lois O'Shea, could *not* in fact turn to gold whatever it was she touched. Then lastly, before these images faded, I saw that the same impassivity would be cemented on her grey, stiff face when her boyfriend found her in her make-shift monoxide spa. There was a local newspaper unopened on the passenger seat next to her. I was allowed to see the date. She had ten years left to live.

The Wrestler

Jamie Michaels

An excerpt from the novel Tales from the Fart Warehouse. *The story follows the misadventures of an absurdist short story writer and his deadbeat friends hustling to make art and a few bucks to live off.*

No one was home at Paul's place. The lights in the apartment were mostly burnt out. No one bought new bulbs. Everyone was waiting to see who would crack first, to see who really needed the light.

It was the same with the garbage. Everyone just added their piece to the pile. It was always falling over and leaving a greasy stain on the floor. Even when it splattered out, no one would take it outside, they would just pile it up again. It was like a pathetic game of Jenga. The garbage made the apartment smell like rotten banana skins.

I took some toilet paper from the bathroom and cleaned the dust off the desk. I looked around the apartment. The desk was right next to the futon. Beside the futon was the roof rack from a '91 Wagoneer. It was leaned up against the wall. A bunch of clothes were hanging off of the hangers on the roof rack: t-shirts, jeans, and a winter parka. There was a hockey bag on the floor, and a couple of hockey sticks leaned up against the corner of the room.

Beside the desk there was a stack of VHS tapes. The tapes were a mix of old hockey fights recorded off of the television and pornographies. It was the entire worldly wealth of Peric Erez, who had racked up a six-fight win streak and fought for the belt, the best bantamweight Winnipeg had ever produced. An artist in his own right. He had been the big winner. Now Peric slept on the futon. I slept on the couch. Neither of us could make rent.

It was sad to look around the apartment. It was sad to look at where we were heading. Fuck, it was sad to look at where we were now. On my side of the apartment there wasn't much; a couple of old Hudson's Bay Company blankets, a couch, the few books I'd had time to grab before being thrown out, along with my boxing gloves and laundry baskets. The baskets held my clothes. I was jealous of the roof rack but didn't have the heart to steal one. It was okay. The laundry baskets were alright.

I went to the fridge. There were a couple of wrinkly apples on the bottom shelf. I ate the apples and stacked the cores on the top of the pile of garbage. This time it didn't tip over. I was a lucky guy.

There were a few of cans of beer in the fridge. I took one of the beers and cracked it open. I took a sip. It was good. I drank the rest. I cracked a fresh can. The beer made me feel a little better.

I went to my laundry basket and took out my copy of the five books of Moses. I sat at the desk with it. I flipped open to the story of Jacob. It was a great story. My favourite part was when Jacob sends his family and his servants across the ford of Jabbok. Everyone got sent over, the kids, the wives, the servants, everyone except Jacob.

Jacob is all by himself, all alone on his side or the river. He is approached by a man, and the two of them get down to wrestling. Not the cartoon watered-down wrestling you see on the television, but the real, old style wrestling. The biblical wrestling, the wrestling with guts. Near the end of it, the man delivers a fierce blow to Jacob, nails him right in the hip. Wrecks it. Jacob just keeps wrestling.

The two of them wrestle until the dawn, busted hip and all. The bible doesn't describe the whole thing so well, but it's easy to picture. The two of them sweating under the setting sun, feeling for traction with their toes in the earth; grappling the length of the night, pulling ragged breaths from the cool desert air. Cold sweat. They wrestle until the sun comes up. The man tried to leave but Jacob wouldn't let him. He held onto him, and demanded a blessing.

It's a good story, real gritty. My favourite part is the end, the blessing, when everything gets its true name. Jacob is renamed Israel, the one that wrestles with god. The place they wrestle gets renamed Peniel, the place where god is seen face-to-face. The naming reveals everything. It lets everyone see things as they actually are. It lets Jacob be more than a shepherd clutching at his brother's heel. It's a good story. Everyone wrestles god alone.

Afterwards everyone wonders what their true name will be.

Maybe our true names were still out there, hidden under the laundry baskets and the piles of garbage.

I sat down at the desk, beside the futon, beside the stacks of hockey videos and porno tapes. I took a pull of beer and started to write a story.

It was the story of a man who had an incredible power. He was able to reveal things, as they were in their one true nature. He was able to reveal the essence of a person, cut to the soul of them. Once he'd done that everyone could see them. See them as they were. It didn't matter how much a company thought they were worth. It wasn't something you could measure in bucks an hour. It didn't matter if they slept on a futon, or even if they ate shit for breakfast. This man measured the grain of a person, their true worth. He measured them in a way that after they'd been measured, it was the only way the world would ever see them again.

This man was like the man in the story of Jacob. People didn't realize they were wresting with an angel until after he named them. This story was for a different time though. This man didn't have the time to wrestle everyone from dusk until dawn. The world was a big place, and so many people needed to be named; to be seen as they truly were.

The first stop that the Angel made on earth was a visit to the liquor store on Route 60.

It had been a long trip to earth.

The angel was thirsty.

The angel ordered a twelve-pack of Moosehead. There was a guy behind the register. The name of the guy was Jimmy. He was a thirty-two-year-old loser. His job was to put the money in the register and get the beer from the back. The angel handed Jimmy a twenty. Jimmy put the twenty in the register. Jimmy handed the change over the counter. He went to get the beer from the back. The angel put the change in his pocket and waited.

Jimmy was a pretty average loser. He shorted people on the cash deposits for bringing back empties for recycling and pocketed the difference.

He played pick-up hockey on the river during the weekends. When he got lucky, the boss would find expired beers at the back

180

of liquor store and let Jimmy take them home. When those lucky days rolled around, Jimmy would call up a couple of buddies and they would drink the expired beers until they puked or passed out. Jimmy was alright.

Jimmy wasn't just a regular old till jockey. Not on the inside. In fact Jimmy was planning on becoming something more. He'd been taking night classes down at the university. Jimmy was planning on becoming the greatest architect the world had ever known. He stayed up until dawn broke going over schematics, studying the works of Frank Lloyd Wright and Filippo Brunelleschi. He worked late into the night on his drafting board, recreating the works of the greats and improving upon their already formidable designs.

Sure, the long hours and the liquor store weren't great, but during all that time he was dreaming, scheming, designing, and fiending. He had blueprints on the brain. He knew he was worth more than 10 bucks an hour. Not that he cared about the money. No, Jimmy cared only for the design. For art and beauty. Jimmy was a man who understood that the structure of a building could alter the way a man felt, it could inspire a dream or end a marriage. No one appreciated the emotional content of architecture in the same way as liquor store Jimmy. If Ruskin were alive today, the contents of Jimmy's notebook would have made him ejaculate on the spot.

It had taken Jimmy ten years, but he'd finished architecture school. He went at nights, one class at a time. He was close to making it, to seeing the designs he had dreamed of in waking life. It had been a long ten years. Long days at the liquor store, long nights at the drafting board. The expired booze helped. It kept him going. Now it was all behind him. No more jamming the buttons on the register and shoving around crates of booze for a slave's wage. Jimmy submitted his portfolio to several prominent engineering firms in New York, Dubai, and Sydney. He didn't hear anything back.

Jimmy kept applying, the months turned to years. Jimmy kept punching buttons on the till and drinking expired booze. The cider was the worst. It tasted like rotten apples and newspaper. He drank it anyway. It took off some of the weight of the day.

Now Jimmy was thirty-two years old. He was in the back

181

getting a case of beer for an angel. Jimmy came back with the case.

'Here you go, pal,' he said. He put the beer on the counter.

The angel dove across the counter and tackled Jimmy to the ground.

'YARGHHH!' yelled Jimmy.

Jimmy and the angel wrestled across the floor of the liquor store. The floor was sticky with booze. It gave their feet traction. The angel fought with all the grace of timeless heavenly experience. Jimmy fought with the bitter desperation of a man who had nothing to lose.

The angel picked up the cash register and smashed it over Jimmy's head. Jimmy crumpled to the floor and didn't move. The angel blessed him on his way out of the automatic doors, the twelve pack under his arm.

When Jimmy came to it was dark. The phone was ringing.

'Urghhh,' said Jimmy. He sat on the floor behind the counter and picked up the phone.

'Hello, I'm trying to locate Jimmy Nickels,' said the voice on the phone.

'Speaking,' said Jimmy.

'Excellent,' said the voice on the phone. 'This is Adrian Smith calling from Skidmore, Owings and Merril.'

'Yeah?' said Jimmy. He rubbed his hand across the lump forming on top of his head.

'Indeed,' said Adrian Smith from Skidmore, Owings, and Merril.

'What can I do for you?' asked Jimmy, gingerly touching two fingers to the cut running across his temple.

'Your portfolio came across my desk this morning, I'm not entirely sure how.'

'Yeah?' said Jimmy.

'Yes,' said Adrian Smith. 'We're looking to begin a new project. A tower in Dubai. It's going to make the Word Trade Centre look like kid stuff. I've seen your work and to be honest, we need you on this team.'

'You do?'

'We do. It's a long-term project. Can you free yourself from your current employment obligations?'

182

Jimmy looked around the store. The register was empty. The fridges had been robbed bare while he had been K-O'd. The floor was sticky with beer and blood from his head.

'I could probably make myself available.'

'Marvellous, I'll send over the paperwork first thing in the morning.'

'Marvellous,' said Jimmy.

He smiled. The world was finally going to know what he was actually worth.

Meanwhile the angel was across town. He'd already made twelve bums real estate moguls, and transformed one investment banker into a steaming pile of dogshit. He had also made a successful but rude artist a dishwasher. When he was wrestling that one, he got a little carried away and stuffed a smelly sock into his mouth. Oh well, a small mistake. Besides, when you do that much wrestling you need to introduce a little variety.

Everything had been going according to plan. Everyone was being named. Everyone was being seen for who they truly were. The angel decided to take a little break. Just a short one. It was a lot of wrestling for one day.

The angel stopped over at the Woodbine Hotel on Main Street.

It was dark inside. There were a couple of old timers who had come in from the North End. They were playing pool for pocket change at the back. There was a toothless old whore waiting for the bus just inside the door.

The angel walked up to the bar.

'Yep,' said the bartender. He had a long ponytail, a fat gut and tattoos all over his knuckles.

'Moosehead,' said the angel.

'Three-fifty,' said the bartender.

The angel passed a handful of change over the table.

The bartender cracked open the beer and slid it across the counter. The angel took a pull. It was pretty good.

The bartender went back to scratching his scrotum.

The angel took a seat at the back of the bar. He drank his beer by himself and listened to the stereo. It was nice.

'Hey, pal,' said one of the old timers. His name was Ernie.

'Hey,' said the angel.

'You shoot stick?' asked Ernie.

'Sure,' said the angel.

'Play ya for a buck?' offered Ernie.

'Sure,' said the angel. 'Let me get another drink.'

He sidled up to the bar and ordered another Moosehead. He came back to the table and pumped some change into the slot. The angel played pool with the old timers. They traded quarters and dimes back and forth. No one talked too much. It was nice.

He had a few more beers. The old timers went to go smoke outside underneath the neon sign. The angel went with them and bummed a smoke. The angel was dehydrated from all the wrestling. He could feel the beers now. It was a nice feeling. The angel decided to go in for one more beer and then wrestle the bartender. Those tattooed fingers had an unrecognized talent for the cello that had never been appreciated. The world could always use a little more cello.

'You sticking around for the band?' asked the bartender.

'Who's playing?' asked the angel.

'Wandering Indians,' said the bartender.

'Any good?' asked the angel.

'Not bad.'

'Sure,' said the angel. 'By the way, how much is a room upstairs?'

'Depends. How long you staying?'

The angel looked around. It was dark. The beer wasn't expensive. The old timers had come in from their smoke and were playing another round of pool.

'A month,' said the angel.

'I can do 290,' said the bartender.

'Sure.'

'Cash,' said the bartender.

'Sure,' said the angel.

He paid for the room with the money form the liquor store register. The bartender passed him his key. He put it in his pocket, sat down by the back and waited for the Wandering Indians to start their set.

The angel had things pretty good. His room was just above the bar. He could suck back a few beers during the day, catch the band at night, and stumble up the flight of stairs to his room. Yep, at 290 a month you couldn't complain. The angel thought about this wrestling business. There were 7 billion people in the world, and there were more every day. Wrestling all of them seemed like a hassle.

In fact, the angel decided, the whole wrestling business wasn't for the time we lived in. It had been fine back when the earth had been younger. When wrestling was in the desert, under the hot sun, besides the banks of the ford of Jabbok. The angel smiled as he remembered back and took a pull of his beer. He remembered the good wrestling. He remembered the mighty blow he had struck into the hip of Jacob. He remembered blessing him, remembered watching him sire what would become a nation. Those were the good old days. When men were men and blessing were blessings. The angel took another pull of beer. He decided not to do any wrestling for a while.

The angel stayed in the Woodbine Hotel. He only drank beer. He only ate the hardboiled eggs that sat in a jar of pickled brine on top the bar counter. The only time he went outside was to stand underneath the neon sign in front of the hotel and try to bum smokes from the people walking down Main Street. He didn't do much wrestling anymore. On extraordinarily rare occasions, when he'd had too many, he'd roll up his sleeves and get back to it. Strange stories came from the Woodbine Hotel. People said there was a bartender there who had been recruited by the London Symphony Orchestra to play the cello at the age of forty. It was altogether more remarkable because he was recovering, at the time from a severe concussion after having his head slammed through a ceramic urinal. The LSO rang him up at the hospital. Either way, the guy could play the cello.

The angel took a big pull of beer. He decided that people would have to wrestle god in a new way. It wouldn't be overt. The wrestling would take more than a night. They would wrestle with god everyday of their lives. They would wrestle with him as they painted canvases they couldn't sell. When they played the guitar in the hotel lobby for forty bucks a night and waited for life to hand them what they were owed. They would wrestle with god at 4am after working a double when they were mopping puke off the Woodbine floor. And even then, sometimes, even after they wrestled their hardest, there would be no one to bless them. No one to proclaim their one true name. Even so it was important to wrestle, even if you had a busted hip. If you weren't going to wrestle, you might as well lay down and die. The angel took another pull of beer and got up to put a loonie in the jukebox.

Oh, Mexico

Molly Wyer

Oh, Mexico is the story of two brothers in their twenties sailing down to Mexico after their father dies. When the estranged brothers discover that their father had been planning a sailing trip for the three of them down the coast of Mexico to Panama, they decide to make the trip in his memory. Their resolution is tested, however, when a woman joins their crew and they encounter an unseasonably early hurricane. This novel explores the ways we face loss, as well as the complicated loves and resentments between siblings.

We were at my dad's wake talking to Uncle Ernie when he sprung the fateful words on us. 'You know, it kills me that your dad died before the trip panned out.' He took a long drink of Stella and cocked an eyebrow toward the ceiling. 'No pun intended, Dave.'

'What trip?' I said, swallowing beer faster.

'His birthday trip to Panama – ' He looked at Dylan and me, his blue eyes needle-sharp. 'He didn't tell you? He wanted the three of you to sail down there as a kind of early birthday celebration. And also to – you know.'

I could see my own blank stare clearly reflected on Dylan's face.

Uncle Ernie valued honesty; he was its brutal prophet at times: 'He wanted you two to get over your Jacob and Esau complex and family harmony to be restored.'

Dylan snorted. I was preparing my outraged face for him, but then his grin melted in weird directions. I looked away.

Uncle Ernie pressed on: 'He even bought the boat.'

I inhaled beer bubbles, which gave my eyes a reason for watering. By the time I was done gasping for breath the conversation had moved on, but the boat was out there, drifting through all our thoughts.

The seminal phone conversation had gone something like this:

'Hey Jim.'

'Hey Dylan.' A sticky silence. ' …What's up?'

'Want to go sailing? I was thinking you could meet me in San

Diego, since Panama is kind of a ways south.'

I pulled the cell phone away from my ear and stared at the number. It really was Dylan.

'What?' I said.

'Panama.'

'Panama? Like, Dad's sailing trip?'

'Why not?' Dylan said.

'You're crazy.'

'Is that a no?'

I drew a long breath in through my nose. 'Let me think about it.'

'Really? You'll think about it?'

'Yeah. I'll think about it. But – *if* we did go – do you think we can sail the boat he bought? It's been years since I've sailed at all.'

'Well, you read up on navigation and I'll make sure we have what we need on board. But we're doing this old school. No GPS and shit.'

'Okay.'

'Uncle Ernie said the boat's docked down in Mission Bay, so that makes life easier. And my boss says I can get six months off, no problem.'

'You're crazy,' I said again.

'I'll take that as assent.'

'Well, it's not. I'll get back to you.'

'Put in for some time off work.'

I didn't bother telling him I'd quit my job a week before, when I found out about Leslie and Stefan.

I watched the streaks of blue on blue flashing past the train window. Today the ocean's blue was the kind you could stare at for hours – a thirst-quenching blue. The sky was pale by contrast, but so clear you almost expected to see through to the stars. The train snaked closer to the coast and I spotted two dolphins weaving through the swells. It was 10am on a weekday and not many surfers were out at Rincon, but one man on a paddleboard caught a wave and sliced toward the shore at a diagonal, using his paddle like a rudder. Oil rigs, Channel Islands, dolphins, surfers, all began to blur together. The gentle hush and roll of the train soothed me faster than a sleeping pill.

When I climbed out of the train in San Diego, I felt like I'd been drugged. The hours of sleep on the train had only whet my appetite for more, reminding me how bone-achingly tired I was.

Dylan was pulled up to the curb, waiting for me in his Ray-Bans and his red-hot Porsche convertible. I slung my bag into the trunk to the accompaniment of Girl Talk; the bass was up so loud that the car shuddered back and forth. I barely had time to make contact with the passenger seat before we squealed away from the station.

'Hey.'

'Hey.' Dylan kept his eyes on the traffic. 'Glad you made it.'

There were a few minutes of silence as we merged onto the freeway. Then Dylan started talking again, over the wind rushing into our faces: 'I saw the boat. It's a sweet 44-footer. And Uncle Ernie's letting us borrow some of his spearfishing gear. So we can live off the land – I mean, ocean.' He smiled without much commitment.

'Cool. So, we'll pick her up in Mission Bay and head straight for Baja?'

I tried to keep the scepticism to a minimum. But I hadn't been on a full-fledged sailing trip since one summer in college when we sailed down to Catalina Island – and I didn't think Dylan had, either.

'Glad you're so convinced this is going to work.'

We set off with the morning tide two days later. The coastline began to recede. I looked at Dylan. I should probably be worried, but I had the bittersweet tang of the sea in my nostrils and now its siren call was upon me. I couldn't resist a smile.

'How about some music?' Dylan pulled out a dusty, battery-powered stereo and stuck a cassette in the tape deck. James Taylor started singing about Mexico, and I dug a couple bottles of Pacifico out of the ice chest. James crooned on, his words a love song to the country we were venturing back to after so many years.

'Remember when Dad used to sing that song?'

My eyes jerked away from the front of the boat to my brother. Dylan was scanning the horizon carefully, even though I was the

189

one steering.

I nodded. 'Yeah.' I took a long drink, feeling the golden beer tickle the corners of my mouth before I swallowed. 'Remember driving in that ratty old suburban through those Baja towns – Mexicali, San Felipe, Puertecitos – and that one mix tape playing over and over? What else was on there?'

'Let's see,' Dylan scratched the back of his head; his hair stood out like it had when he was a kid. 'Margaritaville … Take It to the Limit … Operator … Surfin' USA.'

Just hearing the names of those songs, I could smell the diesel and burning trash and feel that corduroy road bumping along beneath us all over again.

Then the song changed and I stopped smiling. Leslie and I had slow-danced to this one. Her lips had brushed my cheek, murmuring something about poison and blood. I leaned over to the cassette player. 'Don't really like that song. Mind if I fast forward?'

Dylan shrugged.

Once we made it through customs in Ensenada, I felt like this might really be happening. We didn't know when we'd next anchor near civilization, so we stocked up on ice, beer, limes, tortillas, cilantro, and avocados. Dylan also insisted that we stop at a *panadería* on our way back to the boat, even though our hands were full with the groceries we already had.

We walked out with arms and mouths stuffed with fresh *bolios*. 'See?' said Dylan. 'Worth it.'

I conceded between bites of warm bread: 'Okay, so you were right. This time. Don't let it go to your head.'

'I'll take what I can get.'

I had too much stuff in my arms to get a stealthy look at his face. Was he was joking?

Dylan elbowed me – a little harder than necessary – after a minute: 'Food coma, already?'

I drew a long breath. 'No, I'm good… Actually, I was just remembering how much Baja used to intimidate me as a kid.'

'As a kid, huh?'

'What's that supposed to mean?'

'Oh, nothing. I just noticed you getting a little tense when we

190

saw those *Federales* packing – whatever those guns were they were packing.'

'Well I don't come from the hood like you do. I'm from San Luis Obispo County, where you're more likely to see a man self-immolate than someone get shot.'

Dylan frowned: 'Yeah, I heard about that.'

I didn't know why I'd mentioned that grisly incident.

Dylan latched onto another phrase: 'What do you mean I live in "the hood" anyway? Last time I checked, Solana Beach isn't the hood.'

I kicked at the dirt, then backpedalled: 'Pretty much anything is going to be more "hood" than where I live. But I'm more concerned about what to call this boat of ours. I don't like Nelly. Can we at least rename her unofficially?'

Dylan took the bait.

I woke up the next morning feeling sticky. I crawled out of my hammock and up the few steps to the deck. We should really start sleeping on deck; it was too hot in the cabin. The sky was dusty pink over warm brown mountains. I'd wrestled out of my shirt in the night, so I jumped right over the side, boxers and all. The water only felt cold for a few seconds. I ducked my head under and swam a few laps around the boat. Then, treading water and slapping the hull, I hollered for Dylan. A couple of muttered curses preceded his tousled head up from the cabin.

'Damn it, Jim! Haven't you heard of sleep?'

I spat an arc of water in Dylan's direction and backstroked a few feet as a precaution: 'Fine, go back to bed if you want.'

'Well, I'm up now.' Dylan gave me an accusatory look. Then, running forward, he cannonballed into the water just beside me.

'I thought I was far enough away.' I blew water out of my nose.

Dylan smiled a little: 'That's your problem – you always underestimate me.'

We trod water in silence for a moment, watching the sun burst over the mountains like it was the first time.

Dylan spoke again after a couple of minutes: 'So, what's for breakfast?'

'Who says I'm making breakfast?'

'Well, you woke me up – I figured you *must* have had a good

191

reason.'

After we ate what I would consider exceptional eggs and bacon – it was time to use up all the bacon, anyway – I suggested taking the dinghy around the bay to see if the fish were biting.

I still remember the first time I caught a fish all by myself. Of course there were plenty of trips to Hume Lake or the Lopez trout farm when Dylan and I were little, but we'd always had help reeling the fish in, or at least hooking the fish, once we got a little older. But when I was nine or ten and Dylan was eight or nine, Dad decided we were ready for the real thing.

We crammed Dad's old silver Volvo with sleeping bags and tackle and PBR and headed down to visit Uncle Ernie, who had – still has – a place in Baja, not too far south of Puertecitos. Don't get the wrong idea, though: 'vacation home' would be an overstatement. Uncle Ernie's place is a trailer that he's lovingly embellished over the years with scrap lumber and plywood and spare toilet bowls – anything he can put his hands on and thinks he can repurpose. It took Dylan and I a little while to get over the fact that we had to flush the toilet with a bucket of saltwater and that our beds were cots on the sand. ('Don't let the coyotes get you!' Uncle Ernie whispered.)

But pretty soon we couldn't get enough of it all. Digging for clams, watching for shooting stars at night, sitting around the fire pit listening to Dad and Uncle Ernie swapping stories about Baja in their young and lawless days, kayaking, swimming... But best of all, fishing.

We'd get up when the sun was blazing too strongly on our sleeping bags from across the bay (and the flies were buzzing too persistently) for us to sleep anymore, eat cold cereal on the patio while Dad and Uncle Ernie woke up over coffee and then – if the wind was down – we'd 'help' get the aluminium dinghy down to the water.

The sun had you sweating as you waited in the boat, but then the engine would catch and the boat would purr out into the bay. Maybe you went hunting for a whale shark or maybe you sped straight off for the bass hole. Either way, you weren't hot anymore, because the wind caught you in the face and then you had to hold on to your hat. The water was smooth and shiny as silk, and you seemed to be flying away from the multi-coloured houses along the horseshoe of the bay, towards the great unknown of the eastern horizon.

The boat stopped when Uncle Ernie 'smelled' the fish and you dropped your line in and tried not to catch the bottom, and the sun was hot again on your shoulders and time seemed to hold its breath – until the line wriggled. The first few times I felt that tug, I panicked and didn't reel in nice and easy, so I lost at least three fish. I could hear the irritation in Dad's voice, asking if I wanted help reeling in the next one.

'Give him another chance – he's getting it,' said Uncle Ernie, who'd been hollering just as loud when I had the last one on the line. 'Why don't you take my pole, Dave, and I'll get Dylan's line off the bottom?'

Then it happened. While my line was still dropping back down to the bottom it gave a shiver and started pulling away, and I started reeling firm but not too fast, fighting to keep the pole up off the side of the boat. The butt of the pole dug into my stomach and my arms shook but I kept reeling, spurred on by yells from Dad, Ernie and Dylan.

At last Dad said, 'Stop! Now bring him this way!' He scooped the struggling fish up with the net, untangled the hook from his jaw, and held him up for everyone to see. He was whitish with dapples of brown and big eyes and heaving gills.

'I thought he'd be bigger,' I said, trying not to sound as disappointed as I felt.

'No, he's solid! Two pounder, I bet. We can have fish tacos if we catch a few more!' Uncle Ernie gave me a nod of approval.

I felt sorry for my fish as it was thrown into the bucket instead of back into the ocean, but I also felt a warm glow of pride. We would eat *my* fish tonight! And I had caught it by myself. With an inward thrill, I let the line spin out past my thumb and into the water again.

'Think we'll catch some corvina?' said Dylan.

'Sure, yeah!' I shrugged out of the memory, still so tangible I could feel the weight of the pole in my hand, even though Dylan and I hadn't picked a spot to drop our lines down yet.

'*Someone* hasn't been reading up on their banned fish.'

I looked up in surprise.

'So I finally have your attention, huh?' Dylan gave his smirkiest smirk.

'Wait. You can't keep corvina anymore?'

'Nope. They're protected now – too many people raping the ecosystem down here for too long, I guess.'

'I can't believe it!' I said. 'Those were the first – '

' …First big fish we caught. Yeah, I remember that day.' Dylan cut the motor and handed me a rod. 'I think there's something here.'

We cast and reeled, cast and reeled for a while in silence.

'Think we've drifted off the spot,' I said.

Dylan cast again: 'Have a little faith.'

I rolled my eyes and cast. A minute later, I felt that exhilarating tug on the line. I forgot about Leslie, forgot what had dragged us down here – even forgot to be peeved that Dylan had been right after all.

'Not too fast, Jimmy! You're gonna – '

'*Damn.*'

'Don't worry, there'll be – oh!' Dylan's line jerked. 'I think I've got a bite.'

The line twitched and then ceased moving.

'Shit!' He spat the word into the glassy water.

I turned away to hide a graceless smile, but Dylan must have caught me out of the corner of his eye. He reeled his line in carefully, turned the dinghy around, and motored back to the sailboat without a word.

I flopped onto the sand panting. I hadn't swum in a couple of years, and my muscles felt rubbery from the exertion, although the boat wasn't anchored *that* far away. I let the sun compete with the lapping waves to see whether I would dry out or not. Idiot! Here I was, flirting with the past that I'd told myself to avoid. Dylan had seemed willing to play nice – so why was I making it harder? I closed my eyes. I needed a few minutes of not thinking at all, of just feeling the sun on my shoulders and hearing the eternal whisper of the ocean against the beach's breast.

I rolled onto my back and blinked up at the sky. I must have slept.

194

The sand beneath me was still damp, although the tide had retreated and left the rest of me to crisp in the sun. I lifted my head up just far enough to look out at *Nelly*. (We still hadn't renamed her.) No movement on board. Dylan was probably sprawled out in a hammock in the sun with a PBR – the Pacifico was just about gone at the moment – not giving our earlier skirmish a thought. I should do the same. Filial harmony: that's what Dad had wanted for us.

Dylan had always been better at separating his emotional responses from the rest of his life. He refused, for example, to let his fear of stingrays keep him from learning to snorkel. Of course I learned to snorkel too, but I wasn't deathly afraid of stingrays like he was.

Anyway, it was easier for Dylan to be cool about our past because he had always come out ahead. Just one example: upon my graduation from Cal Poly, I landed a job with a green energy startup in San Luis Obispo; when Dylan graduated from USC, he got hired by Veolia in San Diego. Sure, it was unfair to blame Dylan for being more successful, but it also seemed unfair that Dylan's bigger achievements had always impressed Dad more.

I sat up. This was pointless. I waded back into the water: the cold felt good against my sunbaked skin.

I had relied on the swim back to clear my head. Instead it had dredged up other unwelcome thoughts. I still hadn't told Dylan about Leslie and I. Granted, he and I hadn't shared many personal details over the past ten years, but I *had* been engaged and now I wasn't.

I don't want to think about this. Focus on your breathing. Breathing. Yoga. Leslie had been good at yoga. Shit.

I knew that no matter how long I lived and how 'whole' I eventually became, I would never be able to forget the first time I met Leslie. It was one of the memories I wanted to keep, despite the ache that came with it.

Leslie had come riding down the street in a green sundress, her hair flying out like a sunburst of brown and gold around her face. She parked her bike in front of the café and I decided I was better off studying here on my own, rather than meeting up with my study group over at Kreuzberg. She ordered a tall soy chai latte and I wanted to order something hip and organic too, but all I could think of was how her honey-coloured hands moved when she told the barista about her cocker spaniel, and how her lips formed each word with such love.

She passed me with a smile, and my brain seized up and I didn't know what to do. So I ordered black coffee, which I never drank, and a day-old scone. I seated myself a couple of tables away from her and pulled out one of my textbooks at random. Great. Physics. Now she would think I was a freshman or something, just because I'd left a GE requirement till my last quarter.

As I sat there, drawing cubes in my notebook instead of solving for buoyancy, I ran through possible scenarios. The most obvious solution was to walk over there, introduce myself, and ask her out. But that was *so* obvious. And terrifying. I needed a more subtle approach. Ask her if she knew the internet password? I glanced furtively over at her. She didn't have a computer. She was reading a book – of *course* – because she was perfect. Pretend to want to know the price of the artwork on the wall above her? Could work – but what if she made some comment about the medium the artist had used and I couldn't respond because I didn't know crap about art? I tried to swallow another bite of scone, but it stuck to the back of my throat and I had to take a swig of coffee, which – undiluted by milk – was so strong that it made my eyes water.

I looked around for my napkin, but it had disappeared at this critical juncture, just as my nose began to run. I was getting ready for an inconspicuous sprint to the bathroom when I felt a tap on my shoulder. She stood smiling down at me, holding out a napkin.

'I'm here to ingratiate myself by any means necessary, with the devious plan of convincing you to help me with my physics homework.'

I stared up at her, my nose buried in the napkin. There were several beats of silence before I remembered to say yes, I would be happy to help her. By this point, she was probably regretting that she had chosen me as her physics tutor. Couldn't maintain basic hygiene, couldn't handle social situations... But I wasn't about to let her take it back.

'So. What section are you in?' I said.

'8am Monday, Wednesday, Friday.' She made a face.

'11:30, Tuesday, Thursday. I'm Jim, by the way.' I offered my hand.

She took it: 'Leslie.'

When she smiled I realized that her eyes were green, that she was still holding my hand, and that I was barely breathing, all at the same time.

When I got back to the sailboat, Dylan had just hauled himself up over the other side, his ditty bag heavy with two or three large sea bass he'd speared. I offered to clean them as a kind of peace offering – and also because I didn't want to feel I had contributed nothing to our first meal where we were actually 'living off the ocean'. I filleted the fish, remembering the many times I'd watched Dad and Uncle Ernie do the same thing. I ran the knife from tail to gills along either side of the spine, separating the meat from the bones, and being careful not to puncture the gut.

Dylan reemerged from the cabin, a frying pan in one hand. 'Thanks for cleaning the fish.' He picked up the pile of pink flesh.

'Sure,' I said to his back.

That evening, Dylan made margaritas and we sat on the deck, watching the sun journey towards the limitless blue of the horizon. The silence between us was rendered more profound by the soft lapping of the waves against *Nelly*'s hull. The Pacific was living up to its name tonight.

'Remember that time we saw the green flash?' Dylan said after several minutes.

I took a generous swallow from my Dixie cup. 'I didn't see it that time, remember? I was driving and I looked over too late, because you guys didn't bother mentioning that it was a good night for a green flash to begin with.'

The memory still tasted sour after all these years.

Dylan shrugged: 'Guess we thought, who'd be watching the road when they could be looking at the ocean? Anyway, you've seen one since then, right?'

I nodded: 'It was at a restaurant on La Jolla Shores – right after we came to see your new place, I think.' I tried not to think about that 'we'. 'I remember the restaurant got really quiet as the sun was going down, and everyone staring out the windows. The last sliver of sun disappeared, and then there was a green glow on the horizon where the sun had been, and everyone in the room started clapping.'

'I wonder if we'll see anything tonight.' Dylan nodded towards the bronzing sky.

'It's clear enough.'

I figured that would be a sort of benediction on the trip if we saw a green flash. Like Noah and his rainbow. But the last mandarin section of sun slipped below the water and nothing happened. Well, maybe 'nothing' was the wrong word. The sky still blazed in its final, dying glory, turning the mountains and the farthest corners of the compass a breathy pink.

I stared at the darkening water where it licked at the boat and took a last sip: 'Well, that was good, but how about some dinner? You know, if that Veolia thing doesn't work out for you, there's always bartending.'

Dylan punched my arm hard.

The next morning I was headachy, and Dylan wasn't far behind, judging by his bitter stare at the cereal box. We'd followed up dinner with more margaritas, PBR, and any other beer we could find lying around. Now we slouched around the boat, united in our hostility towards life.

Dylan first spoke about an hour after we got up: 'Wanna go find some waves? They were saying something on the radio earlier about a big swell coming in. I've heard there's a spot just south of here where the surf's pretty good, when there are any waves at all.'

I poured myself more coffee. 'I haven't surfed in years.'

'Don't worry, it'll come back to you. Like riding a bike – except, completely different.'

I grinned. Why *had* it been so long since I'd done something I loved so much? In college, I'd sooner surf than eat – although I usually came out of the water as hungry as a shark. Some evenings I'd stay in the water till the final blush of sunset was gone from the sky, till there was no one on the beach, till the only way to see at all was to surf within range of the lights on the pier. I remembered the freeness of the cold water, the rush as I flung myself onto my board and started to paddle; then, sitting outside and waiting for the next set to come in, and seeing the mountains, the cliffs, the beach, the crumby beach town as if I'd never seen them before. A gull would swoop low or a curious seal would pop up next to me or a pair of dolphins would jump, and I'd be at peace with the world. Why on earth did I quit?

'I didn't bring a board though,' I said.

'No worries; I brought an extra,' Dylan said.

'Can we anchor nearby, or – '

'Seriously, Jim: relax. I've got it covered.'

By the time we moored *Nelly* in her new spot, it was early afternoon. 'No point going out right now,' Dylan said. 'Surfing will be crappy, with the tide as it is. Let's take a nap and then go.'

Waking up in the afternoon heat was disorienting, but the best thing about naps is getting a second chance at the day. It felt weird to be wearing only a spring suit to go surfing – I had to keep reminding myself that the water was warmer here. Still, the weight of the board under my arm and the sweet, coconut smell of the wax were pleasantly familiar. We jumped over the side and paddled ashore, then followed directions Dylan had got from a surfer he'd talked to back in Ensenada. I shifted my board from one arm to the other. Dylan had given me Dad's old board, which had seemed like a nice gesture until I realized how far we were going to be carrying our boards – Dad's was substantially bigger than Dylan's.

Finally, we rounded a bend and the dirt track dumped us out on a lonely beach. The sand was grey-white and coarse, and the waves were *big*. I watched a set come in, waves peeling off to left or right. Dylan gave a whoop and plunged into the surf. I followed, devoutly praying I wouldn't eat it the entire time.

I looked at the jade water suds-ing around my ankles. Probably warm enough for stingrays. Better shuffle. I didn't have much time for thinking or shuffling, though, because a wave broke right on top of me long before I'd made it out past the whitewater, and I got sucked under. The wave took me, forced me into a somersault, and held me down long enough to get my heart rate up. My arms flailed for the surface. It was hard to find for a minute. When at last I emerged, gasping for air, it was just in time to see the next wave coming. I grabbed for Dad's board and managed not to fall over this time as the wave broke. My mouth tasted like I'd just eaten a spoonful of salt. I threw myself forward onto my board and paddled hard.

It took a couple of attempts, but I finally made it out to where Dylan sat, rolling with the swells, his face towards the horizon as he watched for the next set.

'Glad you could join us.'

'Hey, I told you it's been a while – and some of these have got to be ten-footers.'

'I wouldn't say double overheads, but maybe eight feet or so, with a few standouts.' Dylan talked like a surf report.

I didn't bother arguing. Now that we were out here, I felt that remembered rush of calm – but interrupted by a boost of adrenaline whenever I saw a wave that looked like it wanted to break too early. We bobbed for a couple of minutes with nothing but the surf and a few hungry gulls to interrupt the quiet.

'Here we go!' Dylan shouted.

'You get this one,' I said.

I watched Dylan's board angle in toward the shore, watched Dylan paddle like he was an Olympic swimmer in his final sprint, watched as the board and the wave caught and bonded.

Dylan whooped again as he stood, he and his board racing out of my line of sight. Just in time, I turned to look at the swell. The next wave would be a good one, too. My breathing quickened. Then, as I swung my board around, memory locked in. By the time I was in the wave, I forgot to worry about when to stand and when to turn. I felt the power of the water hurtling me forward, heard the rush of the wave building behind me. I crouched, and the barrel was around me. My hand skimmed the wall of water to my right; for a moment the whole world was suspended and at rest. Then I realized that I wasn't going to make it out before the wave folded over me completely, and I went back to being present-day Jim, who hated getting water down his nose – which of course I proceeded to do.

'Dude, nice one! Saw you get barrelled! Did you make it through?' Dylan said.

I rolled my eyes. I was still breathing hard from the fight to make it back outside.

Dylan grinned: 'Don't worry – plenty more where that came from!' He turned his board and started paddling again.

I sat bobbing on my board, trying to slow my breathing and

spit out as much of the salt taste as I could. I thought about the first time Dylan and I had gone boogie boarding with our cousins. We'd come home, excited to tell Dad all about it. Dad snorted, threw his long board on the roof of the Volvo, and took us back down to Pismo Beach so we could see how *real* Californians rode waves. Watching Dad catch a wave for the first time, I thought he was probably the best surfer in the state – maybe in the world. Dylan just kept shouting that he wanted to try it. We were both surprised when we couldn't stand up the first time.

We surfed through the golden light of sunset and into its rosy afterglow. Pelicans and gulls became nothing more than moving silhouettes above the horizon. The evening star appeared in the gathering dark of the sky. When the lesser stars began to show up, Dylan and I finally propped our boards against a bleached log and sprawled out on the beach. The surface of the sand had already lost its heat, but when I burrowed down further, a little warmth remained in the moist sand beneath. I turned my head to look at Dylan. Dylan's eyes were wide, taking in the growing constellations of the night sky. We lay there in silence for a moment. Then my stomach gurgled.

In my peripheral vision, I saw Dylan's head turn: '*¿Tienes hambre?*'

'*Sí. ¿Cómo se dice* "starving"?'

'Well, since we didn't go fishing today, how about some beans and rice?' Dylan said.

'I was kind of thinking steak, but there probably aren't any wild cattle to slaughter around here, so that works too.'

Flyer's Remorse

Bonnie McDonald

The following is an excerpt from a collection of non-fiction short stories exploring the quest to fit in and how astray it can go.

Slathered in SPF and the burdens of an early puberty, I leaned toward the gold speckled bathroom mirror to inspect the fireworks-like display of eyeliner I had managed to skid across my face all before 9am on a Sunday. The gallon of Tommy Girl perfume I had released in a series of 10 sprays settled on my hair, adding a sweet sheen, not unlike an angel's or that of an Abercrombie and Fitch employee. I attempted to rub out the eyeliner and flashed my best metal-ridden smile to myself. Josh was gonna love it.

Although we had relocated about a year ago to a neighbourhood so dilapidated that Denver had refused to include the area in its county lines, Dad and I had spent every Sunday that summer learning to fly private two-seater planes. Josh was the twenty-something, blonde-haired, hilarious, charming, instructor I had spent the last nine Sundays falling in love with. Sue me. *Who ever loved that loved not at first sight?*

He may have been a full-fledged adult, but I was practically there myself. I had long stood recipient of comments from unsuspecting adults such as, 'Your favourite show is the news? My, you're mature for your age!' and, 'Goodness, I don't know a child who behaves so well, you're like a small grown-up!'

If my intellectual maturity was arguable, my physical maturity was definite. I topped out at five foot six by age 11. I had to forego the dainty, daisy-clad bras my classmates were purchasing and go straight for the industrial support strap contraptions. My physique had gone from that of a pale jaunty 10-year-old to that of a pale burlesque dancer in a matter of months. Outings with my toddler sister and my pocket sized pre-pubescent best friend, Leia, often resulted in moms approaching me at the park to ask if our children might like to play. I was as close to an adult as a person could be without actually being one, and once Josh saw my prowess on both fronts, it would only be a matter of time before we were galavanting through the skies as soul mates. Besides, it just made sense. Josh got on with Dad. He laughed at all of his jokes, even the one about the Pirates of Penzance. Josh had his own car and he listened to 93.3 FM just like I did. He loved Jim Carrey movies and Mexican food. Plus, he always asked me about my summer camp and how I was doing. Crucially, he said 'may' instead of 'can' at all the right moments. He wasn't arrogant about it, just classy. Not to mention, he could fly a plane. It really was not that hard to imagine spending weekends flitting from town to town together, accidentally crossing state borders, and seeing the Grand Canyon on a whim. We were basically made for each other and Josh seemed like the kind of guy who wouldn't mind waiting five years until I was 18 to legally consummate our love. What's five years when we've got a pilot's licence and *The Mask* on VHS?

I adjusted my pooka shells and butterfly hair clips as the bathroom fan gasped back on.

'Are you prepared to disembark, dear daughter? The skies await!' Dad yelled from the living room.

Dad had always enjoyed sounding as if he were a high member of a royal court. We had moved into our shanty one bedroom apartment about a year before while he and my stepmom finalised their split. The brown brick building, compliments of the 70s, emitted a permanent mouldy musk. The walls were prickly and smeared in white paint. We even had a chandelier comprised of eccentrically shaped lightbulbs and a telephone cord that hung over the main room. Still, Dad did not hesitate to refer to our apartment as 'Chateau du Cherry Street'. Dad slept on the trundle bed in the living room when I was over and allowed me to decorate the bedroom with the many pieces I created during my watercolour phase. The neighbours weren't the kind of people who waited around for an excuse like the Fourth of July to set off fireworks in the street. For most of our first year there, we used old green lawn chairs as furniture in the living room, holding hot dinner plates in our laps, pretending to be on a camping trip. We had fashioned our TV antenna with tinfoil and wire hangers, and had quickly mastered contorting our bodies at a moment's notice to herd the fleeting signal back to the television in time to see final

Jeopardy!

Some nights, we would plug in the teal boom box I had received for my 10th birthday. I'd spread out our tape collection on the beige carpet, pretending to consider Dad's jazz collection and old people music, and quietly select Don McLean's tape for the 400+ time. I would fast forward to the last song, and *Bye Bye Miss American Pie* would begin to play, standing as a soundtrack to the light show starting in the street. Occasionally, Dad would look up from his book, squeaking in his plastic chair, exclaiming, 'What stars do spangle heaven with such beauty!'

The spring after the divorce, Dad received a settlement cheque from my stepmom. Seeing as Dad was an aspiring actor, stuck in a job as a (failing) insurance man, and she was an established, successful, dentist, Dad had inadvertently become a progressive male receiving a settlement cheque from a woman. A badge he was determined to wear proudly as a forward-minded, staunch feminist.

Dad proceeded to spend the money with a princely flair, just as one might after being under the extended duress of a thorny queen. We became regulars at the two French restaurants in town and at a few of the jazz clubs. I tried foie gras and the snails. He bought me a soft brown leather purse from Coach that I had no idea what to do with. Then he bought me a slew of Abercrombie shirts that I definitely did know what to do with and proceeded to wear every day. Dad began receiving catalogues from a company in New York called Steuben that makes glass figurines for rich people to hold when they want to cool their hands or to remind them of the nice person who bought it for them. Dad would leaf through them like the Sunday paper, while I looked over his shoulder.

He said that by Fall, we would be moving to a new place, close to my middle school. Mostly though, our summer money went to Shakespeare and small aircraft pilots. Dad had long loved Shakespeare, and shared as much, whether or not it particularly fit into conversation. So, when he could actually afford to enrol me in a Shakespeare summer day camp at the same private school he attended while growing up, he jumped on it. On the other hand, neither Dad nor I had ever previously even feigned interest in small aircrafts or flying, or anything remotely aeronautical. And yet, with the big-to-us bank roll in Dad's pocket, we found ourselves learning to navigate the skies in the smallest plane you could rent for an hour with an instructor.

Dad started taking lessons before I did. I got to go along with him to his second lesson one day after camp.

Dad was sporting a blue golf shirt I got him a few Father's Days ago and sunglasses from the Qwik-Stop across from our apartment. He had poured a half of a bottle of sunscreen onto his sparsely haired head and rubbed in about 60 percent. His head was so big his hats could easily double as bowling ball bags. Dad was about six foot two and had a fair amount of softness, particularly in the belly region. A classmate of mine politely called him 'jolly-looking' after seeing him on the stretching mats at the gym, meditating in a red shirt.

Dad picked me up in his red Saturn sedan and we found the narrow highway that led to the airport. Dad put in the Rod Stewart tape we had bought the weekend before and opened the sunroof.

The road turned to dirt and the sky grew wide in all directions. I pivoted in my seat to see what the mountains looked like from so far away. They were still there, standing like a row of teeth against the sky. Denver was thumb-sized through the back window, covered by a brown cloud of pollution.

After we crossed over a dry riverbed, we came to an empty parking lot in front of a small one-storey white brick building, with 'Front Range Airport' spelled out in blue block letters across the front.

Dad parked the car, and led me across the lot toward a waist high metal fence near the back of the building. His walk transformed into a stately swagger. As we approached, I could see little planes parked in rows behind the fence. I had never seen so many small planes in one place. They looked like shiny white birds with stripes on their ends.

Dad's flight instructor came out from behind one of the planes to let us through the gate. Rick was a small man. He had a policeman's mustachio and the physique of a 13-year-old gymnast stuck in an engineer's short-sleeve button down. Rick had square glasses with clip-on dark lenses. His pleated khakis rustled against his spindly legs in the growing wind.

Dad's burly left hand rapped Rick on the back, and they shook hands.

'Rick, my man. It is good to see you, fine sir.'

'John, nice to see you again.'

'May I introduce you to my daughter? We're hoping to get her into lessons soon too.'

Rick put out his teeny hand to shake mine and smiled.

'Nice to meet you, Kate. Your Dad here has said some very nice things about you.'

Rick looked at Dad.

'My client roster is full, but there's a new teacher, Josh, I could set her up with.'

Rick reached for his shirt pocket, complete with pocket protector and mechanical pencils. He pulled out a small piece of paper and wrote down Josh's information for Dad.

'Thank you, Sir Rick,' Dad said as he slightly bowed in gratitude.

Rick darted his gaze to the ground. 'Well, should we get going? I assume you'll sit on the right side of plane again today? Now, I don't want to offend, John, but the fact of the matter is, well, there is a difference in kilos between the left and the right side of the plane when we're sitting in it.' Rick's brow furrowed as he clasped his hands together. 'It creates a bit of a tilt when we're flying. Well, it just isn't safe.'

Rick's eyes stayed glued to the ground, looking like he was trying to remember lines he had rehearsed in the mirror. 'We can't compensate up in the air, but we can fix it with some extra weight on the left side. There are some cinder blocks at the end of the lot that would work, if you don't mind helping me load 'em into the plane, John?'

Dad smiled and let out a laugh. 'Rick, it would be my pleasure. Show me the blocks and tell me which plane to put them in, and we'll be on our way.'

'Thanks, John. Now, Kate, you are welcome to sit in the airport while we have our lesson. It should be unlocked.'

Dad looked to Rick, ready to haul the cinder blocks. 'Now

which plane is ours again?'

'The blue and white one. Kilo Romeo. Two rows back over there. Let me take ya over to the blocks.'

Dad turned to Rick as they walked away from me. 'Kilo Romeo huh? Say, Rick. What do you say to a little Shakespeare?'

The first time I remember Dad inserting Shakespeare into normal life was when he fell in love with my stepmom. It was 1994 and Dad was making it work as a single parent, taking me to church on our weekends together. Dad was more of a 'spiritualist', complete with wishing crystals, but he said the ritual of church would add structure and texture to the tapestry of my childhood. It also happened to be a better place to pick up insurance clients than by the amethyst bucket at Ms Cleo's Emporium.

He met my future ex stepmom when they were both volunteering as Sunday School teachers. Karen had beach-y brown hair and electric white teeth. She dressed as if winter might strike at any moment, wearing arctic sweaters and thermal leggings. Karen liked to add 'geeze' and 'gall' to most of her sentences. Dad said that's just how Michigan people express themselves. She had a son named Nate my age. He was short, wore turtlenecks, and had a shark tooth necklace.

I don't know if it was her tundra-ready wardrobe or the way she made even the gentlest of words rhyme with the scream of a steam engine, but love's arrow struck.

We spent our weekends together doing family-type activities. The merest mention of anything remotely related to, well, anything, inspired Dad.

During a riveting viewing of a Michigan football game, Karen might put her face in her hands, contemplating a game Dad nor I completely understood. And to this Dad would look to Nate and I with a smile, saying,

'See how she leans her cheek upon her hand.

O that I were a glove upon that hand,

That I might touch that cheek!'

A couple of years later, love's arrow had broken in half. The fights were steeped in theatrics. They all but hired a choreographer for their renditions of 'What do you mean you forgot to take out the

207

trash?!' and 'Don't make me sit through another brunch with your parents, or I will kill myself!'

Dad and Karen were in their room fighting one summer night, while Nate and I sat listening in my baby sister's room.

The shouting stopped and Dad's footsteps pounded toward us. Dad slowly turned the knob to our room. His red face peered through as he tried to smile at us,

'Kate, darling, shall we find some dinner, you and me?'

Dad grabbed my sandals from the front door and said I could put them on in the car. We walked out the front door.

Karen opened the door. 'You get back here, you son of a… '

Dad shouted, 'Wrath make me deaf, you ignorant shrew!'

On the day of my tenth lesson with Josh, Dad and I arrived at Front Range Airport enveloped in my perfume. I refused to let Dad roll down the windows so my flutter of butterfly clips would stay in place.

I sat strapped into the weathered passenger seat of the Cessna 180. The sun penetrated the two-seater plane, prodding out the faint scent of summer afternoon sweat that I had caked myself in strawberry deodorant to avoid. I glanced left and flashed my bracket-smile to Josh, sitting next to me.

'Ya ready over there?' His green eyes met mine and we put on our headsets. 'Let's get going since we're running a bit behind schedule, okay?'

'Okay, Josh!'

He surveyed the sky, rattling take off procedures into the mic. 'Let's put the flaps at zero. Okay, now, get the RPM to read twenty-three hundred. How's the oil? Okay, now, I'll apply the power. Let's take the nose up, shall we?'

'That we shall, Joshua!' I spat through the headset.

'Okay, the controls are yours.'

My heart beat boldly. I gripped the controls and pulled them towards my chest, ready to show Josh my skill. *Hear my soul speak! The very instant that I saw you, Did my heart fly at your service.*

Josh and I chugged toward the sun, hot air sweeping through my mouth, singeing my lips. My stomach tucked into itself as we glided over the patchwork fields sprawled out across the plains. The occasional barn and house pudged up from the ground.

'How ya doing there?'

'I'm really great! How are you?'

'I'm doin' good, thanks.' Josh smiled, looking forward.

'How's that camp of yours going? You have your play yet?'

'No, not yet. It's gonna be next Friday. I keep forgetting my lines when I walk around the cauldron, so I have to keep practising.'

'Practice makes perfect, McDonald. You got the right idea.'

'We can practise them if you want, Josh.'

'Oh, I don't think we're gonna have that kind of time today, but if you wanna bring your lines next week, I'd be happy to try.'

Josh adjusted his microphone a bit, gripped the controls, and looked out far into the plains.

'Now, let's fly past the silo in that yellow field, then we can turn around and work on landings for today.'

Dad had warned me that landings were significantly more difficult than taking off.

Josh scanned the horizon, leaning back in his seat.

We reached the silo and turned north. The airport emerged from the fields with two spindly runways stretching out to the east and west. Josh adjusted his headset and gripped the throttle. He would lead until I picked up enough to land on my own.

'Alright, let's take the RPMs down to 2000. Pitch at 110 kias.'

Our two-seater vessel began to drop, hot air pushing up through the ceiling. My stomach reached for our former altitude, sweat crept up my neck. I smiled through gritted teeth and got back my breath for the descent. The plane glided down and we rolled down the runway to a stop.

'Looking a little pale there. You okay?'

I gulped the air, 'I'm so good, Josh.' *If music be the food of love, play on!*

We taxied, turned the plane south, and took off back into the warm heaving air. After a couple minutes in the sky, it was time for round two.

'Alright, let's do this one together.' Josh nodded to me and grinned.

'So, get us facing north and then pull the throttle.'

I did as he said, trying to ignore the sour spit sneaking under my tongue, tightening my throat.

'Okay, now when I say 'up', I want you to pull up as hard as you can.'

My forehead went cool, my stomach sticking close to my ribcage.

'Up.'

I pulled the nose up while the rest of the plane pushed down, holding my breath as the sky darted around the windscreen. The wheels smashed to the ground, bouncing up and crashing back down. My belly clenched. I turned to Josh, relieved we were on the sweet sweet ground, as everything from my insides catapulted out of my mouth and on to him.

'Oh God. Oh God. Oh no, I'm so sorry.'

He grabbed his sweater from the back and began sponging the puke off his body.

'Oh, it's alright! You're fine. You're fine!' He lightly chuckled and shook his head.

I immediately began spewing apologies, shame spilling out of my every pore.

I shall live in thy shame!

We parked the plane and decided it was best to call it an afternoon. 'Don't worry! It'll come out in the wash. Feel better, Kiddo. Get psyched up for next week, okay?'

I watched Josh go back into the airport for the last time and trudged over to Dad at the car.

'Don't fret, love.' Dad patted my shoulder as we pulled out in our trusty Saturn onto the dirt road heading home. We rolled down the windows, and I slumped my head out the side, breathing in the cool air, dirt and all. Dad got out the mix tape we'd made the summer before, heavy with weepy tracks from Simon and Garfunkel and various skinny men from the 70s. Dad gazed ahead. 'The course of true love never did run smooth.' I should have been embarrassed at the notion of Dad acknowledging my love for Josh, but instead my eyes stayed on the cooling sky. 'Nay,' I said. 'Nay.'

Invisible Bill

Rob Sharp

The following is an excerpt from a novel, exploring the relationship between two men, Bill and Saul, childhood friends who are reunited later in life and plan a crime.

He pulls the warm duvet aside and blinks at the light. Delicious bars of white stripe his torso. Rallying all the energy he can muster, he sits up and heads for the bathroom to brush his teeth.

His memories of the previous day seem barely credible. Funny how one's mood can turn overnight. Wilfully in denial of any uncertainty, Bill's optimism – the feeling that the world is working, for one moment, just for him – hardens inside.

He walks briskly downstairs, catching through a window the sprinkler system kicking in on the front lawn. Specks of dew swirl in constellations beneath the spray. Falling just short of congratulating himself, he collides with the smell of coffee rising up from the floor below.

Bart is already at breakfast, sitting centrally in a room full of sunshine. While it is skillful of him to flick through two comics simultaneously, the arrogance of the act suggests he wants to irritate his father, not read carefully. The boy uses his right hand to turn the two books' pages alternately, and in his other hand, he holds a half-eaten piece of toast, its missing crescent turned towards him like a hungry mouth.

Bill knows when tackling subjects of intense sensitivity that he should pick his moments carefully. Slather anxiety in paternal selflessness.

'Fucking around as usual,' he says.

'You're here,' says Bart, eyes wide. He glances up, like a bear caught with its paw in a honeypot.

'Don't you have school?' says Bill. 'Or did you oversleep?'

Bill has little control over his impulses and this doesn't square with how guilty it makes him feel. Turning, he stares at the garden, inhales. He got into topiary last summer, and now a stray cat scratches its back against the foot of one of his sculptures.

211

Eros? He suppresses the urge to go outside and shoo it away.

'Have you been taking your anti-depressants?'

Bart stays still. Just the crunch of his teeth through toast. Bill opens his arms, begging for mercy.

'You ask for those – those *pills* – you ask to go to a therapist, I pay for it, with the pittance I have for an income.' He gestures to the comics. 'Get the Jolly Green Giant to be your analyst. I hear he's an expert on Lacan.'

'Get off my case. You're always on my case.'

'Your *case*. If I was Columbo I'd be bored. You should be at school.'

Bart pulls a dog-eared letter from between a comic's sheets, hands it to him, folds his arms.

'Oh, *great,*' says Bill. 'This is all I need.' He takes in the letter's crest – a chimerical hybrid of owl and lion – and scans down the page. 'What is this? You had a lighter in school? Trying to set fire to another boy? Is this fucking Cape Town? You can't even finish your Maths test for Christ's sake. These people are supposed to be looking after you.' He slaps the back of his hand against the paper, which trembles. 'I cannot believe these idiots. *Bart unfortunately jeopardises our abilities to fulfil the Secretary of State's new criteria for classroom standards.*'

'He was a dickhead,' says Bart.

Bill shrugs, puffs his cheeks. 'You don't think everyone on Planet Earth goes to work for some dickhead every day of their life? The Pope has some boss in the Vatican with bad breath, wandering hands and a craving for power.'

'I didn't set him on fire. I tried to burn his rucksack. It wouldn't burn.'

'Oh that's great. So you're flunking Arson too. Your mother is going to go *insane.*'

Bart shakes his head and growls. When Bart speaks, he cannot extricate the emotion from his voice. Every utterance seems like defensive anger, or excitable pride, or fragile reproach. When he retaliates he parrots someone else's words, or is simply combative – but never with an emphasis on truth over feeling.

Bill looks him over. Bart has inherited Stella's skin, so his complexion isn't a worry. His unruly curls of hair, uncut, could be tidied. There is little Bill can do about the prominent nose they

212

both share. But, unlike the perfect freshness of Bart's features – the whiteness of the sclera of his eye, the silver down on his cheeks – his neck is slightly too long. He looks like a mannequin pulled together in a rush.

'You care the most about what Mum thinks, don't you?' says Bart. 'I think you're…' He stumbles, draws back to repeat himself. His words are monotone, delivered by rote. 'You're projecting your own anxieties of fatherhood onto me. You're afraid of me expressing my own will, because you see my will as… as an extension of yours. And so in a way, it's like a part of you revolting against you. It's your worst nightmare. Waking up and finding a part of you out of your control.'

'Oh great,' says Bill. 'What, does that therapist write your essays for you too? This is what I'm paying for. For some guy from Guildford to turn my son against me.'

'Whatever.'

'Whatever… that's very insightful.'

Over the next few seconds Bill can feel his beastly feelings nuzzling each other like dogs at the back of his mind as he hears his son on the stairs, bounding up them two at a time. Outside, the wind picks up, the fuchsia around the French doors slapping derisively against the glass. He makes an espresso, topped with a brown sludge like the wake behind a boat in a polluted river. He grimaces as he necks the shot in one. So strange how the day's promise can evaporate.

*

The doorbell rings.

'Hey there, sad sack.'

It's Saul. Sunglasses slipped down his nose, jacketless, with braces, drainpipe trousers and no socks with loafers. Behind him, a black cab, its door left open, a driver reading a newspaper and smoking a cigarette. Bill eyes the driver. The man looks back with little interest and continues to read.

Saul moves quickly, stepping from side to side and running his fingers through his silver comb of hair. His incessant movements are his provocation to the world, daring it to square up. Usually Bill feels that he is hanging on to Saul's attention by a tiny thread.

Today, he can't live up to his need for entertainment. He forces himself to be upbeat, but the weight of his words hangs heavy.

'Good to see you, Saul,' Bill says. 'I feel terrible.'

'You coming with me?'

'My life is a disaster.'

'Come on, we'll go for a drive. Where's Bart?'

'He's upstairs, hopefully not killing himself.'

Bill pulls on a clean pair of shoes, grabs his jacket from behind the door, waits a second, notes a distant slamming door, and follows Saul down the crazy paving to the car.

Before he can ask where they are going the cab's acceleration erupts, the vehicle's rickety interior clicking, and the countryside rolls by. They run past his neighbours' houses, people pushed out of London by rising house prices and now hermetically sealed into their generous gardens and integrated garages. Bill could only wish to have a detached, pebble-dashed home – he matches the mortgage payments on his two-bedroom terrace with a reliance on beta-blockers and still craves a pine-floored conservatory, better insulation and regular holiday.

Through the open window, the air feels hotter. Bill considers rain. In the distance, just visible through the windscreen, storm clouds assemble. But for the moment, the sun remains. Saul beams, his legs apart.

'I've got a plan,' he says.

'You know what,' says Bill. 'I'm really not in the mood. Is it going to be like the time you got me to impersonate a policeman to freak out that cold caller?'

'Listen to me.'

'He tried to sell me life insurance.'

'This is better. I've got a good plan. It'll be fun. Why are you always complaining?'

'Is it *good* in the sense that it's *effective*? Or that it has some sense of ethics? Because I have to tell you Saul, I for one still cherish some sense of a religious upbringing issuing edicts inside my rotten, pathetic, shriveled excuse for a soul.'

Is this true? Bill likes to play along with Saul, but worries about how willing he is to blame external forces for his failings. He laughs about it, but it isn't a joke, because Saul is always locking in on a new fall guy. Bill's instincts are at once self-serving and metaphysically benign and this confuses him. He can't fathom how to reconcile these two opposites.

'Oh I get it,' says Saul. 'You think I'm some kind of sociopath. You think I just calculate my interests in some utilitarian way, whereby I tell myself I can continue to function, and make money, as long as the happiness I experience is greater than the sum total of the pain I cause others. So it's all OK if the maths adds up. And any sense of intrinsic moral worth doesn't mean shit to me.'

'That is what I think,' says Bill.

'Well, you're *right*, of course,' says Saul, pulling out a stick of chewing gum and throwing it into his mouth. He checks his reflection in the cab's window. 'But you'll find that most western democracies are founded on this principal, my friend. Follow your natural instincts. Don't fight it. We're animals, we behave the way we do for a reason. You force us into unrealistic scenarios and before you know it three million people are headed for Siberia. OK, most play the system, and it's ugly, and they think they won't screw too many people over because it reflects badly on them. Who am I to blame them? And remember, well, I'm *not in* that system, Bill. And secondly at least I've got the guts to admit what I'm doing.'

Bill pauses and wonders why this stinks and then remembers Saul talking like this at college. It is incredible to him that the record hasn't changed in twenty years. It had been entertaining when they'd met at 18, during that first term. *Jesus.* He remembers the smell of Saul's room, the mustiness of the curtains because he never opened the window. When he recalls that time his guts swirl. Why? They'd spent hours in Saul's rooms getting drunk and devising their perfect future lives. Refusing invitations to parties and ignoring the other students had made them laugh, at least for a while.

'I'm not joking either, Saul,' he says. 'I'm just sick of having to justify these little scams to myself. It's great that we're free but I want to be able to look in the mirror without hating myself.'

'Man, I can't look at you in the mirror and not hate you.'

'You know what I mean. We've got to grow up, OK? I can't tell my son one thing and do another. I'm not a hypocrite.'

'Sure,' says Saul. They dawdle at some lights and the cab driver cuts into the outside lane. 'Me neither.'

Like most people, Bill wants to think of himself as an honest citizen, even though the empirical evidence for this is scant. Instances of his improper behaviour jump into his mind. The previous week, while on the Tube, a woman with a pram had needed help and Bill had pretended he was checking his phone. He'd now claimed three laptops against his tax. He pulls his weight in situations where it doesn't count. But if there is an honest-to-good moment when he is set to genuinely profit – and it is unclear what the repercussions of this might be for other people – could he be sure what he'd choose to do?

'I understand that we're going to do something with this al...'

'Algorithim? It's a fake,' says Saul.

'A fake?'

'The details I showed you were completely fabricated,' says Saul. 'It was just to hook you in. In all honesty I was pretty surprised you bought it. No, we'll be focusing on something else. It's better.'

He hands Bill a newspaper. Bill's hands are clammy and he observes his increased heart rate with alarm. His guts bubble and twist and he hopes he will not vomit inside the car. The newspaper shows an old woman, lying in a hospital bed. She is smiling into the camera and seems strangely familiar.

'Recognise her?'

They pull into a supermarket car park and Saul instructs the driver to slowly circulate around endless rows of VW estates, Range Rovers and BMWs being filled with shopping for the weekend. A cloud of cigarette smoke rolls through the open window. Bill sees someone who reminds him of a friend he once knew. It begins to rain, and streams of people run for cover in the time it takes for Saul to wind up the window, turn to him, and centre him in his penetrating gaze, his eyes sharp, nearly crazed.

'Who is this old woman?' asks Bill, but he suspects he already knows the answer.

'She's our mark,' says Saul.

*

Oaks Pleasant sits in a stretch of Green Belt reached by taxi in twenty minutes from Croydon Station. Although a new luxury apartment complex is being built overlooking the fifteenth hole – with its double dogleg and par four, not somewhere one can afford to feel *spied upon* – the course scores consistently well in *Golf Pro's* annual ranking of the country's finest courses. While his closest friends worship that list, Bill has Oaks's success down as lucky at best.

For one, its greens are a little overwatered. Bill pulls at his visor so that his hat's narrow towelling strip bites a band into the skin above his eyebrows and squints into the sun, which shivers as it falls inexorably towards the crenellated tree line ahead. Beneath it, the slightest wisp of a white flag flutters above the horizon when the wind catches. Bill knows he'll be lucky to reach the pin with his three wood, so switches to his driver, crouches, snatches a clump of grass, and sees its blades parachute away, one by one, from his fingertips.

'Mmm.'

If the greens are weighed down with water, there'll be little run on from his strike. He removes the cover from the driver and waggles it around, testing the integrity of its graphite shaft and that powerful, keen flexibility that courses through his arms into the metal itself. It's not just an extension of his body. It's him as he wants to be.

He counts his clubs, amazed for once that he hasn't forgotten any. He is too uncertain in his abilities to think this usual but still feels lucky. He wipes his forehead with his handkerchief.

It is his first time at Oaks Pleasant since the Oxshott Chemicals Texas Hold 'Em of '07. Back then he'd ruined what had otherwise been a successful round by becoming embroiled in a testy final hole with Jack Leverkühn, a Californian psychiatrist who Bill had thought was mocking him for his height but who later claimed to be pointing out the flag.

Today, peace reigns. He had met the old woman for early drinks as planned. His joke about the two Irishmen had gone down well – even Bill thought it was slightly racist – and from then on his confidence had grown.

'So what do you do?' she'd said, twisting the umbrella in her sparkling water.

'All sorts,' he'd replied. 'Development, accounts, a bit of media.'

217

'Doesn't sound like a proper job.'

'It isn't.'

But she was smiling. Since then, when he'd pulled his clubs on to his trolley like a pro, bumped into at least three people who he'd known, one of whom owed him money, he'd felt a fresh vitality in his limbs that belied the nerves he was feeling deep beneath his mask.

Now, each movement he executes is still purposeful and worthy of envy. He relaxes into his stride to the back of the tee, pulls out his glove, and stretches it over his hand as if preparing for a cavity search.

He imagines the three people watching him on this lush patch of grass considering his movements in pained awe, and he prowls to his trolley, sifting through tees and balls with ruthless disdain. He chooses an unblemished ball and places it down, ignoring the murmurs behind him, pauses, picks up the club, and tightens his fists around it. His palms sweat against the rubber of the club's grip, and he twists his hands, wipes them dry against the seat of his trousers and clasps again, bent half double with his perfect posture. He shuffles the club head, teasing it into a momentary dance, and then settles the iron heel against the neat, felted surface of the tee, just broken by a tiny wooden stalk topped by his perfectly flawed moon, Titleist 4, soon to be sent into orbit.

He considers the exquisite improbable parabola of his ball flying off to the horizon — struck, sun, spark, speck — and pulls his club back. He remembers to keep the head of the driver as close to the ground as he can for as long as possible, before bending his arms, though the club feels too big, somehow, too heavy in his delicate wrists. He banishes the thought in the long sweep up to the top, and at the apex he bends back his grip, the tautness of his muscles restricting his movement into one singular, inevitable motion, a golfing Vitruvian Man, and he knows to keep looking down while the club head stays violently aloft, its potential energy potently paused before its swooping descent. He freezes it there, just for a second, as it changes direction, like a ball thrown into the air held still for a moment before its fated return to Earth.

Now, in this inexorable fall before the club finally makes contact, Bill tries to extinguish any distraction that could cause him to miss or fail to connect properly. He begins the downswing like he is ringing a bell, pulling the club down vertically, and he allows the natural weight of the object to increase its momentum, and for the club to pendulously run its course towards its destination. The ball's flight seems headed for perfection, in the way one convinces oneself that a plane lifting off from a runway is inevitable and cannot crash, though this is untrue. And a thousand delicately adjusted instruments will not jam, Bill manages to figure at this instant, their spinning cogs enmeshing as they always have, and his shot will be *the* strike, the Platonic universal of strikes, the shot they heard around the world. His mind goes blank. He is nothing, the universe, the energy of the Big Bang from a void leading to action then reaction forever.

He hears the swipe, the sound of metal swinging through space, the whoosh of a dubbed Jackie Chan kung fu punch. The ball teeters on the lip of the tee and thinks for a moment before toppling, its fall an insulting thud leaving a dent like a nail just two inches away in the turf. It spins a desultory course into the rough, barely three metres away, and even that has help from gravity down the hill where the tee meets the path beside it.

'Fore,' cries the old woman behind him.

Selected Poems

Ralf Webb

The first poem is taken from a longer sequence, under the title 'September Fifth'. 'Yard #1' is taken from a short series of poems, under the title 'Polaroids of American Yards'. Thanks are due to Ambit Magazine, where 'Lemonade' and 'Foreigners' first appeared, in different forms.

1   Foreigners

The last day I saw you, you were a foreigner
in a foreign house. Steadfastly refusing the hospice

you insisted on living away, in a suburban asylum
for commuters to London. Leading up to the event

I missed you, riding rickety buses through woody lanes,
sitting in old pubs with gardens so overgrown that vines crept

into the glasses as you drank from them. You came home,
eventually. Shipped in a discreet van, by some zero-contract

Charon, and delivered to the local undertakers. Bankrupt,
famished, I didn't dare visit you in another foreign room.

Cocktail Hour

The round wickerwork table on the trimmed lawn
is littered with *Death in the Afternoons*,
lime twists, and crystal glasses of ice water.
Smoke is spun by conversationalists;
a cigarette holder, a Sobranie. A red-kissed filter tip
extinguished in a nacre ashtray. Petty miseries seep
across the garden: imperfect Riviera weather, *sour*
Spanish strawberries. Then, a parched whisper
from the Lord of the Manor: *the elderflowers*
will flourish in this sun, absolutely flourish.
Ice cubes chime and rattle. A varnished, gun-black
fingernail decapitates several ants
as they drink from pools of spilt water.
We won't have to worry — he goes on— *about the plums, either.*

Fishing

Floods came and went –
with spring breaching winter
the river rose and receded.
Strung up half submerged,
scaly tail barely visible
in the mud-brown waters,
dazzling in the eddying light,
an enormous trout swung,
speared at the throat
by a tree branch.
Eyes pecked and meat poached,
its rib bones blazed white.
Where the silt met water,
the water met scales still silver;
the branch alone bore bone.
The space between was washed
with pink and yellows.
Last year's leaves slowly spun
beneath, and in the air
the threat of greenness hung.

Lemonade

it
sprouts
and
swells:

a dead
june-bug
lying
upturned

in
a half
oyster
shell

atop
the
lazy
susan

the
young
summer
girls

flower-
crowns
in their
hair

playing
on
the lawn
scowling

at
the
cheap
lemonade

from Polaroids of American Yards

YARD # 1: MAGNOLIA AVE, FT. WORTH

This yard   has a broken   christmas decoration:
a foot-tall reindeer   with its head   caved in
brown weeds   growing all around it.   I think
it's Rudolph   because there are remnants   of red
on the nose.   A child's toys   are scattered:
a neon-yellow buggy,   dog-chewed figurines.
The porch is blue   and warped   in the centre.
I look at the eyes of a doll perched against a half-
dead sunflower. I look   for snakes   but see none.

Harry's

It's Alpine Texas and we're drinking at Harry's bar.
He's a German man with a fast crazy laugh and a fat belly,
fled to Lone Star and set up this shack by the road.
Won't stop talking about ten-gallon hats and six shooters.

Harry controls the music: *American Girl*, *Wagon Wheel*,
Big River. He tells us there's a storm coming in, so I look
at the sky above the Texaco that half-burnt down yesterday.
I can see for miles but I can't see a thing.

Eulogies are scrawled on Harry's bathroom walls: Oxycontin,
motorcycle crashes, bar brawls. A pitch-dark Sharpie
has written R.I.P RICKY COBOS, and surrounded it with stars.
Everyone drinks hard at Harry's, everyone except for Harry.

Short Chicago Blues

but I learnt
about humility
in *this* world:
hurt is a blue dog
lapping shade
and languid
at white noon

August in Arkansas

I could spend all day on this bridge
because I can see two men in the distance
casting lines into the water.

Smoke rises from them,
one wears blue shorts
and the other a trucker cap.

You're taking photographs of me,
and I pretend not to notice.
Maybe the locals are laughing at us.

It's only an old industrial bridge
lined with flowers and defunct lanterns,
the red-iron trusses arching over.

Its railings are hot on my palms
and the air is thick with mosquitos.
I've never had a shirt see so much sweat.

I've never had so little distance
between myself and another. Darling,
it's August in Arkansas,

let's go swim in the Mississippi river.
Okay, I'll be Huck, you say,
and you can be Tom Sawyer.

About the Authors

The authors can be contacted through Ward Wood Publishing

Denise Bigio worked for many years as the editor of a documentary film magazine in Los Angeles. Born in the UK, she studied at King's College, London, where she was awarded the Gilbert and Levinson Prize for English Literature. She now lives in London.

Liz Brown spent her teenage years in Nottingham followed by a four-year degree in French at the University of Kent at Canterbury. Although she was interested in languages, her main reason for choosing this course was the opportunity to spend a year in France, gap years being discouraged in the mid-1970s. After graduating she trained as an accountant and has spent the last twenty-eight years working for mainly European banks in the City of London. She began writing prose fiction in her spare time after buying a second home in Brighton. It is no coincidence that her story is set partly on the South Downs between Brighton and Lewes. Over the last seven years she has completed a part-time undergraduate degree with the Open University split between creative writing/English literature and history, including art history. Her sabbatical year studying for a Masters degree in creative writing at Royal Holloway has allowed her to develop a narrative that draws on her interests in history, art and languages.

Harley Carnell lives and writes in London. Among his influences are David Foster Wallace, Virginia Woolf and Thomas Pynchon. His fiction has been published in the journal *Confrontation*.

Eva Chan was born in colonial Hong Kong and has witnessed the changes in her childhood home since the turnover in 1997; Hong Kong is now somewhere she can no longer call home. After graduating from the University of Hong Kong with a degree in English Literature, she worked for a Japanese airline. During those four years, Japan has become her home away from home and she has travelled extensively from Russia to the Arctic Circle; these experiences have become her writing inspirations. She has

228

finally decided to pursue writing seriously by coming to London. She is still travelling in this globalized world, finding her home and writing voice.
Contact: ecevach@gmail.com

Sheila Chapman is the daughter of Indian and Scottish immigrants. Their amazing histories and inclination to tell tales sparked her interest in writing about families, journeys and the search for belonging. Sheila is a lawyer and, following eight years in Manhattan and a brief sojourn in Marrakesh, now lives and works in London with her husband and three young children.

Melissa Elliotte received her BA in European Studies from Vanderbilt University and her MA in French from Middlebury College. Through her work in international education, she has lived throughout Europe and now London. She is also a singer-songwriter so feel free to stop by *The Dog and Fox* in Wimbledon for a listen or visit www.melissaelliotte.com/music.

Haroon Hassan is a research analyst at an investment bank. He has been dabbling with creative fiction since he was a teenager and is now making a concerted effort to finish more stories while working on a novel set in 1970s Zambia while war reached a crescendo in neighbouring Rhodesia.

Peter Higgins was born in Dewsbury, West Yorkshire. He now lives and works in London. His short stories have appeared in magazines: *Open Pen*, *Pen Pusher* and *Litro*, and in anthologies: *Tales of the Decongested Volume 2* and *Lovers' Lies*. Two of his plays have been performed in the Leicester Square Theatre, as part of the world-famous Sitcom Trials, where they won the second prize, twice.

Jennifer Howells lives in Sussex. She is a qualified primary school teacher and has recently returned from working in the Netherlands for four years. She is currently supply teaching while working on her first novel.

Julie Lydall is a teacher, author and performer. Her short story

'One Night Wonder' was published in 2001 in the Women's Press anthology *Long Journey Home*. In 2008 her poem 'Not Too Bad, Mum' was one of the winners selected by Carol Ann Duffy for *Mslexia* magazine: 'the hardest kind of poem to write, of loss and bereavement, done perfectly.' She has performed her work at a variety of venues, from Foyles bookshop on Charing Cross Road to the Lyric Theatre, Hammersmith to the City Hall in Oslo. Julie is currently writing her first novel, about expatriate life in Norway. This work breaks away from the familiar 'Nordic Noir' of Scandinavia and exposes quite another breed of crime. It is rooted in the realities of displacement and of cultural and sexual difference. What happens to your identity when you move your life to a country known for scenery, snow and scoring no points in the Eurovision Song Contest?
Contact: julielydall@gmail.com

Eley McAinsh worked for over 25 years making programmes for BBC Radio 4, including seven years as Editor of 'Sunday', a short spell with 'Woman's Hour', and more recently, 15 years as Senior Producer of the long-running and popular independent production, 'Something Understood'. She left broadcasting briefly to work on communications for Oxfam's Africa Desk, and was also, for ten years until 2012, the director of a small, progressive research project in contemporary spirituality. Having written extensively in the course of her professional life, the MA in 'Place, Environment, Writing' has been a wonderful opportunity to revisit her long-standing desire to develop her own writing in a more personal and creative direction.

Bonnie (Kate) McDonald grew up in Colorado among self-described hippies, urban cowboys and other groups inclusive of adult ponytailed men. She has earned her MA in Life Writing and is completing a collection of short stories provisionally titled *Tribe*, documenting her quest to find where she belongs. You can find her camping in coffee shops across London as well as at bonnie.kathleen.mcdonald@gmail.com

Harriet Mercer is finishing her memoir, *Dodging Gargoyles*, which retraces the journeys of her mind during a rare and life threatening illness. Central to the narrative are weeks spent in Charing Cross Hospital that were dominated by sleeplessness and demons resurrected by wakefulness. Candles of humour flicker against the walls of these caverns, illuminating the passage out of darkness and to her solo walk of the Camino de Santiago. *Dodging Gargoyles* provided Harriet with the protagonist for her recent completion of Royal Holloway's Life Writing MA, in which she achieved Distinction.

David Merron was born in London's East End. After grammar school and National Service, he married then went out to join a young kibbutz in Israel. During some fifteen years as a member, he wrote short stories and an anecdotal book on kibbutz life. Back in England, he worked as a construction projects manager, and continued to write; short stories and novels, and a childhood evacuation memoir, now being published. He has a Masters degree from UCL, and is on an MA Creative Writing course while working on two further novels. He is married with three children and lives in North London.

Jamie Michaels is an unruly Hebrew born on the unforgiving prairies of Manitoba. He spent his youth sprinting through the streets of Winnipeg naked while howling at the moon. He has recently completed a novel *Tales from the Fart Warehouse,* exploring the human condition, as well as a graphic novel, *Canoe Boys,* the true story of three degenerate university dropouts canoeing from Canada to Mexico.

Annabel L. Mountford was born in 1990. She grew up in eighteen houses, five counties, two countries and with one ambition – to write stories. She currently lives in Salisbury with her partner and imaginary friends. She enjoys reading, origami, wine, long walks and smoking. Her favourite colour is green.

Zahra Mulroy A native Londoner, Zahra wrote her first story at age seven. Since then, she has been published in e-zines and has written and recited poems for open mic nights and weddings of close friends. *Fall* is her first novel, which she wrote over the course of the MA. She currently works on the online editorial team of a national newspaper and is concentrating on her second novel.

Rob Sharp is a freelance journalist and Teaching Fellow at the University of Sussex. His non-fiction writing has been published in *The Independent*, *The White Review*, *Night and Day*, and *Guernica*. Invisible Bill is his first novel.
www.robsharp.com

Ed Sibley is a writer of fiction from the mean streets of Brighton. He currently lives in London where he is the strongest of his flatmates. No joke, this week he did forty push-ups. For more information about his work, or to request a copy of the shaky camera-phone video of the aforementioned push-ups he can be reached at epsibley@gmail.com

Ariadne van de Ven was born in Holland and, after studying English in Utrecht, managed to become a Londoner in 1987. She has been taking her camera on holiday to Kolkata since 2002, wandering around the city's streets and frequently getting lost. *The Eyes of the Street Look Back* is the exploration of her own ignorance and of her encounters with the people of Kolkata. This 'anti-travel book' will be a project in words and black-and-white photographs.

Ralf Webb was born in 1991, and grew up near Bath, Somerset. In 2013, he graduated from Durham University with a Bachelors in Philosophy. He then took the Poetry strand of the Creative Writing MA at Royal Holloway. Currently, he is reviews editor and assistant poetry editor at *Ambit Magazine*, and works as a freelance copywriter.

Molly Wyer is from the Central Coast of California. She completed her BA in literature in the States, but her first love has always been writing fiction. Another great love is travel, from her first international trip (which. was, in fact, to Mexico) as a baby to this, her latest adventure in Europe.

Alphabetical Listing of Authors

Copyright Holders